CONTENTS

AUTHOR'S NOTE   IX

INTRODUCTION   XIII

1   FIRST THINGS FIRST   1
   • Resort or Sea Experience?
   • "I'm Not a Cruise-Type Person"
   • The Truth About Seasickness
   • Big Versus Small Cruise Lines
   • Ships: Is Bigger Better?
   • Destinations: Tropical, Arctic, or Something in Between?
      *Caribbean • Alaska • North America • Europe and Asia • Reposition-
      ing, Panama Canal, Transatlantic, Maiden Voyages, and Others*
   • Style: Formal or Relaxed?
   • Inexpensive Cruises: Do You Get What You Pay For?
   • Three Days, Seven Days, or Round the World in Eighty Days?
   • Health Issues
   • Security Issues
   • Passports and Visas

2   WHICH CRUISE IS BEST FOR ME?   25
   • Of All the Lines and Ships, Which Cater to Adults Older
     than Fifty?
   • I'm on a Tight Budget but Want It All—Suggest Something
   • I Want the Best
   • I Want to Avoid Kids
   • I'm Traveling with Grandkids—Does Any Ship Really Appeal to
     All Generations?
   • Seasickness Would Ruin My Vacation—Can I Avoid It?
   • I'm Traveling Alone—but Want to Cruise with Kindred Spirits
   • Theme Cruises—What's That About?

- Impress Me with the Food
- No Games for Me — I Want to Be One with the Sea
- Forget the Sea — I Want a Resort that Just Happens to Float
- Forget the Sea and Things to Do — I Want to Dance, Drink, and Let Loose
- I Just Want to Relax and Read a Book — Get Me Away from the Crowd
- Forget a Book, Make My Blood Pump — Adventure Cruising
- I'll Take Romance — Marriage and Honeymoon Trips
- I'm Gay — Where Do I Fit In?

3   SHOPPING FOR A SHIP   39
- Travel Agents: A Cruiser's Best Friend
- The Internet
- Sailing with the Big Boys — Mega-cruise Lines
- Brochures: Your Primary Contact with the Cruise Line
- Airfare or "Only Birds Fly Free"
- Advantages to Booking a Flight Through the Cruise Line
- Disadvantages to Booking a Flight Through the Cruise Line
- Itineraries or "If It's Tuesday, This Must Be Cancún"
- Traveling Solo: The Widow's Waltz
- Taking the Family — Reunions and Group Rates
- Access for the Disabled

4

MONEY: WADING THROUGH THE MUCK
TO FIND A BARGAIN   60
- Negotiating a Cruise Deal
- Paying for the Cruise
- Ways to Shave Money Off the Cost of a Cruise
- Ways to Add Money to the Cost of a Cruise
- Tips — Who, When, and Where

5

BOOKING   85
- Insurance: A Necessary Evil
  *Trip Cancellation · Trip Interruption · Trip Delay Protection ·
  Baggage Protection · Medical Coverage · Emergency Evacuation ·
  Emergency Assistance*
- Cabins: A Room with a View?
- Dining
- Understanding the Fine Print
- Making Your Reservation
- Confusing Things Explained
- The Quick List

CRUISE VACATIONS
FOR MATURE TRAVELERS

ALSO BY KERRY SMITH

Walt Disney World for Mature Travelers

CRUISE VACATIONS
FOR MATURE
TRAVELERS

Kerry Smith

ST. MARTIN'S GRIFFIN
NEW YORK

WWW.STMARTINS.COM

ISBN 0-312-26725-8

FIRST EDITION: MARCH 2001

10   9   8   7   6   5   4   3   2   1

6 PREPARING TO SET SAIL   109
- Travel Documents
- What to Pack, What to Pack . . .
- Money—Green, Foreign, or Plastic?
- Airport Departures and Arrivals
- Checking in at the Pier

7 ONCE ON BOARD   122
- What Do I Have to Pay For?
- Your Cabin
- Safety Drill
- Meals
- A Snapshot of Daily Cruise Life
- Getting Around
- Shore Excursions
- Private Islands
- Entertainment
- Services
- Shopping
- Religion
- Keeping in Touch
- Photos
- Tipping
- Who's Who
- Problems
- Disembarking

8 CRUISE LINE AND SHIP PROFILES   151
- What the Profiles Tell You . . .
- Large Mainstream Cruise Lines
  Carnival · Celebrity · Disney · Holland America · Norwegian (NCL) · Princess · Royal Caribbean
- Small Mainstream Cruise Lines
  American Hawaii · Cape Canaveral · Commodore · Costa · Crown · Crystal · Cunard · Delta Queen Steamboat Company · Mediterranean Shipping · Radisson Seven Seas · Regal · Royal Olympic · Seabourn · Silversea

• Small Specialty Cruise Lines
    Alaska's Glacier Bay Tours and Cruises • American Canadian
    Caribbean • American Safari • Clipper • Club Med • Cruise West •
    First European • Lindblad Expeditions • Sea Cloud • Star Clippers •
    Windjammer • Windstar • World Explorer
• Cruise Lines Not Serving the North American Market

9 PORTS OF CALL   208
• Home Ports to the Caribbean
    Miami • Fort Lauderdale • Port Canaveral • Tampa • New Orleans
• Home Ports to Alaska
    Vancouver • Anchorage and Seward
• Ports of Call—the Caribbean and Mexico
    Antigua • Aruba • Bahamas • Barbados • British Virgin Islands • Cay-
    mans • Cozumel/Playa del Carmen • Curaçao • Grenada • Guadeloupe
    • Jamaica • Martinique • Puerto Rico • St. Barthélemy • St. Kitts • St.
    Lucia • St. Martin/Sint Maarten • U.S. Virgin Islands

AFTERWORD   230

INDEX   231

AUTHOR'S NOTE

Cruise Vacations for Mature Travelers is for post-fifty adults—people with a hefty dose of wisdom under their belts who have unique interests, the desire for a great vacation, and the ability to choose a cruise line, ship, and itinerary intelligently. They understand that a successful sea cruise relies on more than a price, itinerary, or shipboard amenities. It's a combination of all three—adapted to a traveler's personal taste.

Currently, cruise lines tend to take the over-fifty traveler for granted. Older adults will cruise no matter what, they reason, but to really make big bucks, they've got to attract young families with children, a market niche that remains to be tapped. The lines advertise to older adults but with less enthusiasm. Older adults, however, make up a huge percentage of their revenue. On Carnival alone, a cruise line that markets its party atmosphere to generally young crowds, adults over age fifty-five still made up almost one-third of last year's passengers.

To attract the roughly 89 percent of Americans who have not cruised yet, the trend is to build bigger and better ships that offer a little something for all ages, meaning more lounges, more activities, and improved amenities—two to three times more than on ships launched just a decade ago. Royal Caribbean's *Legend of the Seas*, for example, has a complete eighteen-hole miniature golf course with sand traps and water hazards. While "cool," you can't miniature golf throughout a seven-day vacation. The basics—food, service, and style—still count.

Cruise Vacations for Mature Travelers is organized a bit differently than other cruise guides. A naval dictionary, for example, is not required. It's written for people who want to vacation at sea—not live there. I also tried to shun clichés used in the travel writing business and, as best I could, avoided phrases such as "the crystal-clear aquamarine water" and "a beach shaded by palm trees and kissed by tropical breezes."

Experienced sea people also clearly differentiate between a river cruise (Delta Queen, for example) and a sea cruise (Holland America, for example). None of that matters here. People who enter a travel agency have a style of vacation in mind, and many times a firm idea that they will find it on the water. The difference between a river cruise and a sea cruise may be interesting to them, and the difference will impact their eventual choice, but they're still considering the river or sea question as two variations on a single theme—not two different types of travel. As a result, Delta Queen and Holland America are listed side by side in these ratings.

You also won't find a sales pitch for cruising. While cruising provides a great vacation for almost everyone, a small number of people should stick to Mother Earth. Should those terra firma lovers be considering a cruise to please a loved one, however, this guide also suggests ways to make the most of it.

Most importantly, however, the guide describes the fun older adults can have on a cruise ship—and exactly which cruise lines pony up the perks for people over fifty. Traveling alone? No problem. Some ships actually provide dancing and touring escorts—"dance hosts"—as part of the service. Many provide family-type activities, but some do a better job scheduling things that mature adults like. How can I avoid kids? Which ship can please both older adults *and* grandchildren? Other concerns—luxury choices, seasickness, saving money, wheelchair accessibility, medical facilities, tipping, etc.—are also covered.

Finally, *Cruise Vacations for Mature Travelers* rates ships and cruise lines for each type of cruiser, from the tux-and-caviar crowd to the drunk-by-noon party people (see Chapter 2). The cruise line descriptions not only include things that make a line stand out, but also names competitors that offer a similar experience and enables you to choose one over the other. Want a luxury cruise but without formal service, for example? Chapter 8 lists the luxury options, then explains which ones jettison coat-and-tie dinners.

A note about length: The hardest part of writing this guide was deciding what not to include. Short is better, but that demands a few hard decisions. As a result, if you want to find the number of palm trees that grow within 500 feet of the dock in St. Croix, or the thread count of the linen on Carnival's *Ecstasy*, or a frank discussion on the quality of caviar served by Cunard, look elsewhere. But if you want to know how a ship "feels" followed by specifics on food, service, and accommodations, pull up a deck chair and read on. You'll get enough information to make intelligent decisions without ruining the sense of adventure.

For this book, "mature traveler" refers to adults who know what they want, both from a vacation and from life. Some overworked forty-year-olds want to prop their feet up and unwind for seven full days while the active retirees water-ski. Both groups will find advice and options here.

With all that said, I'm open to criticism and feedback. If you disagree with any evaluations or wish to see additional information in future additions, let me know—please.

Mail comments to:

Kerry Smith

Cruise Vacations for Mature Travelers
P.O. Box 622616
Oviedo, FL 32762
http://www.maturetravelers.com

Happy sails to you—with apologies to Roy Rogers and Dale Evans.

Things change—especially in the travel industry.

As *Cruise Vacations for Mature Travelers* went to press, two cruise lines—*Premier Cruises* and *Cape Canaveral Cruise Line*—lost the use of their ships, at least temporarily, due to ongoing financial problems. In both cases, the lines may disappear altogether, be purchased or renamed, separated piecemeal and absorbed by existing cruise lines, or even survive in some new form.

Every effort was made to ensure accuracy here, but with a crystal ball on the fritz, expect some changes and reconfirm all details before traveling.

INTRODUCTION

Why does anyone need a cruise guide?

Of all vacations, cruising is the easiest to book, self-explanatory once under way, and one of the most relaxing escapes in the world. To hit the high seas, there are only three things you absolutely must do: (1) pay for it, (2) show up on time, and (3) have the necessary documentation. Once on the ship, a hundred smiling cruise line employees will answer any questions you have, guide you, massage you, and serve you.

So why *does* anyone need a cruise guide?

First, a dose of truth: The "perfect cruise" does not exist, contrary to 99 percent of the cruise line information out there. As with any vacation, if you expect perfection you're asking to be disappointed. A cruise line, and specifically a cruise ship, must house you, feed you, entertain you, and, quite simply, make you happy. That's a tall order. Even the best cruise line has one or two things that, while great, could be better. And even the worst cruise has some things that are very nice.

While booking a cruise is easy, choosing the proper ship and itinerary is not. Cruising is big business and cruise line marketing departments find novel ways to woo travel agents through commission overrides (i.e., paying them more money) for selling their "product." That's not to say that travel agents can be "bought," only that the prospective cruiser with no concept of ships or destinations must rely on a travel agent's advice. With almost a hundred potential ships and almost as many itineraries, the agent will first pull out brochures for these "preferred" suppliers, meaning the ones that offer the agent more money. If one of those lines strikes your fancy and the booking process takes the travel agent twenty minutes rather than twenty hours, so much the better for them.

On a pragmatic level, a travel agent cannot spend four hours on one booking. Besides, some clients who have no idea where they want to go expect someone to take them by the hand and suggest things. If those preferred brochures spark an interest and, at the same time, net the agent up to 50 percent more money, everyone goes home happy. But it doesn't make sense to go on a ship because the cruise line pays a travel agent more money. You should sail on a ship that you prefer.

To attract customers, cruise lines market themselves to specific types of people. Carnival has "the fun ships"; Cunard has classic cruising; Disney has the famous mouse. Still, even with a clear brand image, each cruise line wants to attract older adults—there's just so many of them. Ask an NCL representative if mature travelers will enjoy his cruise—he'll assure you that they will. So will Princess. So will Seabourn.

To understand the problem, compare the individual cruise lines to different stores in a megamall, then assume that, in the future, you must do all your shopping at one and only one store, similar to the choice you must make when selecting a single cruise ship to service all your needs. In the mall, you love to buy clothes at Saks Fifth Avenue, but you buy sheets and towels from Sears, electronics from Circuit City, and cinnamon buns from that little shop with the willpower eroding smell.

Now choose one. Some people will, to everyone's surprise, choose the cinnamon bun store. A few more will choose Circuit City, caring little about clothes or white goods. Most people will choose either Sears or Saks Fifth Avenue because, overall, they offer more diversity and a known quality. But if you choose Sears, you're stuck with what's there. You may have a great selection of tools, a fair choice of clothes and white goods, and a workable array of electronics. It's not perfect but, in general, you're happy. You can point to specific details and say the selection or quality is better at Saks, but what you have, *overall*, is best for you. That's the cruise you want—the one where most elements are excellent and the others at least acceptable.

Now imagine that a traveling companion sees things differently. Tough, huh? Before hitting the high seas, you should do a little homework.

CRUISE VACATIONS

FOR MATURE TRAVELERS

1

FIRST THINGS FIRST

Before you pick up a brochure, study a port of call, or ring up Aunt Min to tell her you're going on a cruise, decide what you expect from the experience. It sounds basic and a bit like psychoanalysis, but cruising has changed in the past fifty years and no longer resembles pre-World War II sea travel. What you *expect* from the vacation and what you *get* may be worlds apart.

RESORT OR SEA EXPERIENCE?

Do you want to visit a resort or be one with the sea? On some ships—the ones most people choose—cruisers notice that there's an ocean outside the window on their walk from dinner to the 8:00 P.M. show; but otherwise, the ocean is unimportant. On other cruises, however, vacationers can steer the ship or swab the deck. Still other ships offer a combination of both worlds.

Many first-time cruisers expect traditional nautical decor such as wooden decks, brass handrails, and a spot where you feel ocean breezes, smell salt air, and watch the sun dip below the far horizon. While tradition can still be found, don't expect it on the mammoth newer ships. Atriums now extend from bottom to top decks; color schemes run from rich greens and browns to electric magentas and pinks. Casinos speak in neon, spas massage flesh, cigar bars fill up, and shops push Rolexes. The ocean is still out there. *Somewhere.* The cruise experience, however, is a palate of colors, social activities, and ports of call.

"I'M NOT A CRUISE-TYPE PERSON"

Most of today's cruise ships are, in reality, those resorts that just happen to float, and that's what most people want. For some, it's a camp for big kids, and they fill their days with scheduled activities. It bears a striking resemblance to other family vacations, but without the stress of planning and paying as you go.

Compare a cruise vacation to a self-guided road trip where travelers pick a destination, map out a route, decide when to arrive, and guess how long it will take to get there. They pencil in time for breaks and, when finished, tell their spouse to be ready to leave by 6:30 A.M. The couple must constantly reach agreement on when to eat, what to do, and how to handle the car's *ping-ping* sound as they endure hours of monotonous drive time.

On a cruise, someone else worries about the details. Passengers scan a smorgasbord of activities, pick those they like and ignore those they don't. If they wish, they do nothing. At dinner, they show up and pick an entrée, an appetizer, a dessert, and two or more other courses. If still hungry, they order a second entrée. They get off in St. Thomas—if they want. Or not. If they forgot to pack an iron, they turn to the room steward and ask for one. It's now *his* problem. Servants constantly ask if everything is okay, turn the bed down at night, place a chocolate on the pillow, and make sure you're happy on an emotional, do-you-feel-good level. Passengers feel as if they've moved up in the social order, tasting a lifestyle shared only by a select few, the Donald Trumps or the Leona Helmsleys.

A cruise disappoints few people. But—and there's always a "but" in life—cruising might not be the best vacation choice under the following conditions:

• **"I want to understand a country's culture."** While a number of cruises have educational themes and most offer pre-port destination lectures conducted by area experts, a cruise is usually not the best way to experience a country's culture. In the Mediterranean, for example, ships stop in different ports for less than a day, and may hit six different countries in one week. Passengers barely have time to see the tourist attractions, much less get a feel for how the people live. For that, travelers must stay inside a country, talk to cabdrivers, and eat in small, family-owned restaurants. Lost is the conversation with the hotel clerk, the one-day car rental into the countryside, and the sights, sounds, and smells of the open-air market. On a ship, the countries are an optional activity, the cruise the actual vacation.

- **"I don't like crowds."** Even full cruises don't feel crowded most of the time thanks to staggered mealtimes and diverse activities. Cruise passengers are, however, traveling with many other people, and cruising, by definition, is a social vacation. Any activity open to all passengers can create elbow-to-elbow conditions. Those who would kill for a little privacy should not be deterred, but remember that few places on a ship, outside a private cabin, offer complete seclusion. Expect some human contact.
- **"I'm afraid I'll get seasick,"** Sometimes a valid reason, sometimes not—see p. 4.

While the previous reasons may cause you to choose a different type of vacation, almost everyone would enjoy a cruise at least once or twice. But some people use the following nonlegit reasons as an excuse to avoid cruising:

- **"I'd get antsy on a ship. I'd feel enclosed."** That's a bit like standing in the middle of a football field and complaining that the stadiums are closing in. When viewing the ocean from the comfort of the main deck, humans feel almost powerless against the vastness of the earth and her oceans. From within the ship, guests not only enjoy massive theaters, dining rooms, and decks, but they can easily move from one to the other. On the largest ships, you'll barely see everything in seven days.
- **"It's too expensive,"** Almost never. You pay for a cruise, in full, at least six weeks before departure, meaning the vacation budget is tapped long before eating that first gourmet meal. Consequently, it *feels* more expensive to people writing a $3,000 check and seeing no immediate return for their outlay. But compare the costs.

Assume a driving trip costs $100 per night for a hotel room (a bargain rate most places). Further assume that it costs $100 a day for food (again, a bargain rate for two people), $75 per day for gas, admissions, cover charges, and tolls. That comes to $275 per day for a couple, $1925 for one week. To cruise for the same price, the trip would have to cost $962.50 per person.

Can a cruise cost that little? Easily for a middle-of-the-road line, especially for adults flexible on travel times and itineraries. It could net you a great cabin on an economy cruise line, or a moderate cabin on a luxury cruise line, and it comes without the stress and frustration of planning your days. If traveling with grandchildren, it comes with an additional priceless perk—*free* babysitting.

• **"I hate dressing for dinner."** Most mainstream lines ask passengers to dress for dinner once or twice, but even then, the rules are lax. Very few people wear a tux for formal cruise dinners; most wear a dark suit, a few wear a light suit, and a sprinkling of individualists wear only a jacket and button-down shirt. Women, of course, have greater leeway in fashion. Outside those formal dinners, almost anything goes, though most people go "resort casual," meaning something a notch above T-shirts and jeans. Only a handful of luxury liners would make you feel out of place, and even some luxury liners shun coats and ties, touting a "casual elegance" theme.

• **"I'll be bored."** On the one hand, ships schedule so many activities that cruisers can rise at dawn and not stop moving until they drop a tired patootie into bed somewhere around 3:00 A.M. On the other hand, if someone chooses not to participate in any of the activities and does indeed get bored, is it a vacation? Many times, the I'll-be-bored people are Type-A executives who don't know how to relax. They read market reports, not novels. They walk fast because they're late, not because it's good for their health. They see ocean waves and wonder how their company's stock is doing. Mature travelers, by definition, enjoy the sights, sounds, and smells of a cruise.

Immature travelers may, however, be bored.

• **"I'm afraid I'll get seasick."** This can be a legitimate reason to avoid cruising, though it's usually a sorry excuse. See the next section.

THE TRUTH ABOUT SEASICKNESS

Fear of seasickness keeps many people from cruising. Why, they reason, should I spend thousands of dollars on a vacation I might not enjoy? It's a rare sea that affects a modern ship, however, and even if it does, medical solutions are effective and readily available.

On today's large ships, the ship doesn't even seem to move most of the time. Compare that to fishing boats, the number one reason most people fear an ocean voyage. The typical story: A couple, while at the seashore, book a day trip on a fishing boat, the first time they've actually gone out to sea. They board at 8:00 A.M. Five hours later, they arrive at the dock, swearing never to return, their faces green, their stomachs empty. But that fishing trip has nothing to do with cruising.

Cruise ships built since the 1950s have stabilizers—massive fins below the waterline that, using computers, sense the roll of the waves and compensate to minimize rocking. While the sea does the jitterbug, the ship dances a waltz. While no stabilizer is perfect— i.e., the ship still moves in the worst storms—a rocky voyage is rare.

If worried about seasickness, be honest with yourself. How susceptible are you to motion sickness? Carsickness? One passenger I met gave up a career in ballet because she could not turn her head rapidly without feeling nauseous. Still, she willingly cruised the Caribbean. If you do not ordinarily get carsick, don't worry about a cruise. If you cannot look left without your brain gurgling, consider a river cruise—or a train.

Generally, the *fear* of seasickness is worse than the actual malady. Consider the following seasickness remedies:

• Either Dramamine or Bonine are over the-counter medications that fight seasickness, though they might make you sleepy. (Avoid alcohol.) Older adults may be affected more than young adults and kids thanks to slower metabolisms, so you may want to start with a half dose to see how it goes. Both medications can be purchased before departure at a local drugstore or on board the ship. On some cruises, one or both are handed out freely.

• A Transderm Scōp patch works in a similar way to Dramamine and Bonine, but the patch's medicine, absorbed through the skin, gives a more consistent dosage and lasts longer. Because it can cause side effects, it is available by prescription only. Talk to your doctor.

• The Sea-Band, a bracelet, supposedly eases nausea by putting pressure on strategic nerves (pressure points). Many drugstores carry them, as do travel stores, mail order catalogs, and ship's stores. Some people swear by them. Since they don't introduce medicine into the body, they're a good choice for people worried about drug interactions.

• Seasickness can be virtually wiped out by choosing the proper itinerary and ship. The Caribbean, for example, is usually smooth, while the North Atlantic can get rocky. In general, cruises on smaller bodies of water (Caribbean, Mediterranean, or Gulf of Mexico) rock and roll less than those on large bodies of water (Pacific, Atlantic, Indian Ocean, or South China Sea). In addition, big ships move less than their smaller counterparts. Putting the two together, a megaship sailing in the Caribbean rarely moves enough to cause anyone to get seasick, even during a storm. (For a guaranteed seasickness-free cruise, however, choose a river trip, such as one with the Delta Queen Steamboat Company.)

• The location of the cabin also affects the amount of rocking. On any size ship, the best cabins for avoiding seasickness are not necessarily the most expensive. Ships rock in two directions. The front of the ship cuts waves, moving up and down as the ship plows forward. As the front goes up, the back goes down and vice versa, rocking like a child's teeter-totter with the ship's center remaining relatively still—the reason cabins in the center fill faster.

The same principle works if the boat rocks side to side, called "roll." Picture a metronome rocking back and forth. The bottom of the metronome moves an inch or so; the top rocks five or six inches. On a ship, it works the same way. Cabins toward the bottom move a slight amount; cabins near the top roll more. Adding the two ship movements together, it follows that a central cabin on a lower deck will move much less than any other cabins on the ship.

• The traditional method of fighting seasickness is, to many, still the best. If you feel nauseous, head to an outer deck and concentrate on the far horizon. Eat some dry crackers to settle the stomach. Above all, avoid tasks that cause you to look down, such as writing postcards or reading.

BIG VERSUS SMALL CRUISE LINES

Very little can be determined by the size of a cruise line, though certain economies of scale result from owning many ships. The large cruise lines — Royal Caribbean, Carnival, Holland America, NCL, Princess, Star, Celebrity, and Costa — can negotiate lower prices from suppliers, meaning passengers get more for their money or the cruise line earns a higher profit. Carnival alone will have twenty ships in the water soon. Just as a mom-and-pop motel can be better than the nearby national chain, however, some small lines offer specialized service that the big guys cannot match. Because the most luxurious cruises are also the most expensive, for example, and unaffordable to most people, true gourmet cruising usually takes place on smaller lines.

In many cases, the big cruise lines actually own each other. Carnival Corp., for example, owns or has an ownership interest in Carnival, Holland America, Windstar, Costa, NCL, Cunard, and Seabourn. As ownership changes and vessels bounce from one company to another, score cards become somewhat meaningless. In other words, read their individual descriptions in Chapter 8 and don't be deterred by a David and Goliath analogy.

SHIPS: IS BIGGER BETTER?

Cruise line brochures, travel agents, and passengers operate on the "bigger is better" principle when selecting a ship, and most of the time, they're right. For limited ship motion, bigger *is* better. For sheer number of onboard activities, it is, too. And for newness and technical glitz, big beats small almost every time.

Consider a smaller ship, however, for:

- **Avoiding children.** Families want plenty of activities, meaning a big ship, to keep everyone happy.
- **Romance.** If hoping to meet that special someone, a small ship lowers the pool of potential partners, but may also offer a higher quality selection. Big ships, based simply on the number of people, still offer plenty of shopping opportunities though.

- **Intimate cruises.** With a limited number of small lounges on a small ship, it's easier to socialize and make friends.
- **Out-of-the-way ports of call.** Smaller ships can navigate into shallower ports and visit cities unmarred by thousands of previous tourists; many adults book passage on a small ship just to avoid the standard tourist traps. In fact, many smaller ships offer interesting ports of call to make up for their lack of onboard entertainment.
- **Traditional cruising.** Just as some folks take a train for the experience as much as the transportation, a smaller ship looks, smells, and feels like a classic ocean vessel. The motion of the sea is part of the adventure.
- **Five-star luxury.** Luxury costs money, and product demand from financially secure people cannot fill a megaship week after week. Plus, personal service and intimacy—the hallmark of a luxury cruise—can't be found in a crowd.

Unfortunately, like all aging things, some older ships are well kept and others are not. "Old" should not be confused with "small," but it is many times true—and that distinction feeds travel agent recommendations for bigger ships. While a well-kept older ship is a joy to behold, a not-so-well-kept older ship is no joy to be on. Imagine a Caribbean cruise without working air-conditioning in July. Scary. Plumbing can be dicey, carpets worn, and decor reminiscent of the 1960s. Booking passage on a new ship is the easy way to avoid poor maintenance problems.

DESTINATIONS: TROPICAL, ARCTIC, OR SOMETHING IN BETWEEN?

On a cruise ship, only tropical itineraries are truly warm. Ocean breezes can be blustery during the day and downright chilly at night. But other geographic differences are subtle.

Caribbean

In the Caribbean, the most popular warm weather destination, cruise ship amenities are paramount. Ports of call, while distinctly different culturally, look suspiciously alike geographically. If planning to tour interesting areas, consider a western Caribbean route (Mexico, Caymans, and Jamaica) or a southern Caribbean route (islands between Puerto Rico and Aruba). Late spring and the fall are usually less expensive. Avoid any time of the year when kids are out of school.

Alaska

Many ships cruising the Caribbean in winter head to Alaska in the summer where the season generally lasts from early May until late September. High season runs from June to August. For warmth, consider full summer, but for thinner crowds, go in May or September. Shoppers may want to consider the early fall—the end of the tourist season—when retailers discount prices to move merchandise. May and September cruises usually cost less, too.

North America

Besides Alaska, a handful of smaller ships visit small and large towns along the northeastern seaboard in late spring, summer, and fall. In middle and northwest American rivers, the Delta Queen Steamboat Company operates four ships that sail year-round, with theme cruises that reflect the seasons of the year. In Hawaii, American Hawaii offers an overview of the bigger islands year round.

Europe and Asia

Europe and Asia follow the same weather rules as North America. Summer is the time to go—unless you want to save money and don't mind cooler weather. For Mediterranean countries, expect an April to October sailing season, with value prices in spring and fall. For northerly destinations, such as Great Britain, look for a shorter window of opportunity between May and September.

Repositioning, Panama Canal, Transatlantic, Maiden Voyages, and Others

A *repositioning cruise*, by definition, repositions the ship from one place to another. Many lines move ships to Alaska during the summer, for example, and to the Caribbean in the winter. A cruise that starts in Alaska and ends in Miami, or vice versa, "repositions" the ship for another season. With sailing dates in the heart of a slow season, repositioning cruises generally come at a bargain rate but with additional perks—such as a visit to the Caribbean, Alaska, and even a trip through the Panama Canal.

Some *Panama Canal* sailings are scheduled year-round. The Canal, quite simply, transports a ship from the Atlantic Ocean to the Pacific Ocean, or vice versa, by going through the canal. To cross Panama, ships move forward into a lock that is either filled or emptied of water, depending on whether the ship needs to go up or down to reach the next ocean's level. Quite simply, it's a series of steps made of water. It's amazing, technologically intriguing, and Panama itself may soon be a major tourist draw. The U.S. reverted canal ownership back to Panama in 2000, and the country plans to develop its tourism industry further to entice visitors to spend a bit more time, and money, in their country.

A *transatlantic cruise* crosses . . . well, the Atlantic. Only one ship, the *QE 2 (Queen Elizabeth 2)* currently offers transatlantic cruises on a semi-regular basis; other ships cross the Atlantic sporadically or as part of a round-the-world cruise. The *QE 2*, owned by Cunard Lines, also offers an option to fly in one direction. Generally, a transatlantic cruise has a different shipboard ambience compared to other cruises, mainly because it has a goal to achieve and no ports of call along the way. Many passengers are either experienced cruisers or people who absolutely refuse to fly anywhere.

Some cruise lines operate ships in Europe for the summer months, but reposition to the Caribbean for winter, scheduling at least two transatlantic crossings per year. These transatlantic repositioning cruises sometimes offer bargain rates to boot.

An *inaugural cruise*, sometimes called a maiden voyage, is not really a distinct type of cruise; rather, it's the first voyage for a new ship. Cruise lovers and fans of a particular cruise line can get down-and-dirty excited when a new ship first enters the market, and demand for a virgin ship runs high, akin to driving home a new car. Besides, celebrities and cruise line executives usually travel along. On the downside, a cruise is a complicated interaction between different elements—a full-fledged hotel, restaurant, spa, tour company, and more. Something can go wrong and usually does. Problems with plumbing or electrical wiring or computer systems inevitably arise. Mature travelers expect delays, inconsistencies, and a service staff slightly uneasy with their role and product. Immature travelers may have problems, however.

Yet another warning: More than one person has booked a cruise scheduled for two to three months after an inaugural cruise, figuring that the ship will still be new, but the staff will, by then, have its act together. Due to construction delays, however, they suddenly discover themselves on an inaugural cruise. If you wish to avoid an inaugural cruise, consider a different ship or delay travel for at least six months.

STYLE: FORMAL OR RELAXED?

Mature travelers considering a first cruise may imagine evening gowns, tuxedos, sunsets, and champagne. However, this elegance actually scares some potential cruisers who don't think of themselves as "formal people." The husband doesn't own a tux, they rarely drink alcohol, and they haven't danced since Cousin Sid's wedding in '89. They watch television reruns of *The Love Boat* and worry that they'll feel out of place.

Won't happen.

If anything, the average cruise is more relaxed than noncruises realize. There are exceptions, and select ships appeal to those who routinely dress for dinner, but most lines now cater to the nonformal crowd. Even on scheduled formal dinners, few men show up in a tuxedo; most wear a dark suit, though some don't even go that far. While a woman may wear an evening gown and feel perfectly at home, expect no small number to wear a cocktail dress or pantsuit. Don't buy a new wardrobe. Almost everyone has the basics in their closet.

Many times—but not always—formality follows class lines and vacation costs. Budget cruises may plan one or two formal dinners, but otherwise demand little of guests who wear T-shirts most of the time. On a middle-of-the-road line, a few men wear a tux to formal dinners and the standard daily wear—described as "resort casual"—is a notch higher than on a budget cruise. Expensive cruises, on average, demand more formality in exchange for greater luxury. On a few, men wear a coat and tie to dinner every night.

Still, even with a top cruise, someone somewhere wears ratty attire a few times and gets away with it.

INEXPENSIVE CRUISES: DO YOU GET WHAT YOU PAY FOR?

There's no free lunch. It's a cliché, but true. There are, however, bargains. If looking for champagne accommodations on a beer budget, consider a less desirable cabin on a better ship, an off-season departure, a suite on a budget cruise line, and read Chapter 4.

In general, however—even if snaring a bargain—there are differences between budget and luxury cruise lines. Ships that, *on average*, charge less must cut costs somewhere. Wal-Mart and Saks Fifth Avenue both sell a wide range of products, many of them similar, a few of them identical. But Wal-Mart, to keep prices low, does not have ornate woodwork, and fluorescent lights bathe the entire store in a warehouse like white glow. A decision to shop at Wal-Mart rather than Saks depends on (1) a shopper's needs, (2) the amount of money they can afford to spend, and (3) their personal sense of place. Shopping for a cruise line depends on the same three variables.

To make it more confusing, cruise lines don't fit easily into budget/moderate/luxury categories. A single ship is a hotel, restaurant, lounge, exercise room, spa, store, and casino. A moderately priced ship may have a mediocre spa, excellent food, and average accommodations, so a simple "moderate" rating does not adequately explain the package. Still, as a cruise line lowers prices overall, quality must go. As lines grow less expensive, expect one of the following items to be limited:

- **Accommodations.** Budget lines don't build new ships—they buy them used from other lines. Large lines, striving to create a consistent product to attract repeat cruisers, don't want to put old ships in their brochures next to their new megaships—so they sell them to the budget lines.

If booking on an older ship, there are pluses. Cabins tend to be bigger and ship decor more traditional. With prices for a deluxe outside cabin comparable to inside cabins on other lines, a limited vacation budget goes further. Also, a number of ships undergo multimillion-dollar refurbishments when ownership changes, making them at least look new. On the other hand, "traditional" should not mean "water stains in the sink" or "plumbing that doesn't work." Besides mechanical glitches that need fixing, ships must periodically replace furniture, carpeting, drapes, and bedspreads. A ship charging top-dollar can redecorate often; a budget ship cannot. "Traditional" should also not mean the same thing as "we've used the same bedspreads since 1976."

• **Personnel.** Budget cruises employ fewer people, represented under the individual descriptions as the passenger/crew ratio. Almost one crew member per paying passenger—a ratio of 1.1—can be found when booking top-notch accommodations. On a budget sailing, expect passenger/crew ratios closer to 3:1 (three passengers per crew member). On a few ships, the rate approaches 5:1. The ratio doesn't explain whether a room steward serves three cabins or thirty-three cabins, but a high ratio implies that service suffers somewhere. For people who expect little more than a quick room cleaning, fresh linen, and standard food service in the dining room, a high ratio is not a problem. But if a guest needs special attention during the voyage—advice on a shore excursion or help removing stains from a favorite blouse—they can expect to wait longer on a budget cruise. Personnel could also be newer or less experienced than workers found on more expensive vessels.

• **Food.** A good chef costs more money than a mediocre chef does, but with food a major cruise draw on all lines, even budget cruises usually hire competent chefs, and food quality is at least fair across the board. Food selection, however, will be more circumscribed on a budget cruise with gourmet choices scarce. Lobster and prime rib may be served one night because, thanks to a picture in the brochure, passengers expect it; on other nights, though, look for modest selections with a lot of chicken served under French-sounding sauces. Lavish buffets may stock limited amounts of peel-your-own shrimp while generously offering turkey, hot dogs, and hamburgers.

For true gourmets, budget lines don't satisfy, but neither do many mainstream carriers. The fact is, a cruise dinner is nothing more than a banquet on big ships. Hundreds of people choose from perhaps six entrées at one time. Given that reality, the food is surprisingly good. As anyone in the catering business knows, serving 400 identical meals is not difficult, but making them appear fresh and individually prepared is. If happy with gourmet food and only gourmet food, sail on one of the smaller luxury lines.

Note that many things are not different between expensive and budget cruises. If in the Caribbean, all ships cross the same aquamarine water. Barbados is the same island no matter how you get there, as is St. Thomas and Bermuda. All weather is warm and the same balmy tropical breezes fan each deck.

On a budget cruise, you still escape the real world—you just don't escape as far.

THREE DAYS, SEVEN DAYS, OR ROUND THE WORLD IN EIGHTY DAYS?

First, "round the world" usually takes more than eighty days. Plan for a hundred, more or less. Second, people who can afford a round-the-world vacation have probably cruised before. It not, they should.

• **Short cruises.** For many people, their first cruise is a three- or four-day trip—just long enough to get their feet wet, no pun intended. For the rest, a seven-day cruise is standard. Retired travelers have the blessing of flexibility and can consider a ten-day or fourteen-day trip, though most don't opt for a longer cruise their first time out.

A three- or four-day cruise specifically appeals to people who (1) live near a port, are flexible, and want a quick get away; (2) want to start out small their first time out; (3) cannot leave work for an entire week (and need to take it easy); or (4) cannot afford seven days at sea. The downside to short cruising is the price of airfare, a hidden cost included in the cruise package. The per diem rate (cost per day—total cost divided by number of days) of a short cruise with air is higher than that of a long cruise. Assume that a cruise line charges $100 per day to feed and carry a passenger, and a one time fee of $200 to fly them to the port of departure. On a seven-day trip, the cost is actually about $129.00 per day ($100 times seven plus the $200 airfare divided by the seven days). On a three-day cruise, the cost is $167.00 per day ($100 times three plus the $200 airfare divided by the three days). Note that the example does not apply to passengers who can drive to the port.

Another disadvantage: Travelers who enjoy different ports of call cannot take many short cruises because most ships visit the same places. In Florida, almost all short cruises go to Nassau and/or Freeport in the Bahamas; a select few stop in Key West. In California, ships visit Mexico and Catalina Island. Even at top speed, ships just don't go very far in three or four days.

If considering a short cruise and wishing to avoid children, plan for a four-day trip that travels over weekdays. Most lines schedule their three-day cruises to coincide with a weekend, attracting younger adults who need to take only one day off work, as well as their offspring who won't miss much school. A four-day cruise generally runs from Sunday to Thursday or Monday to Friday.

• **Seven-day cruises.** The seven-day cruise is standard. For those not yet retired, it's a one-week vacation, easily scheduled, easily enjoyed. Travelers can pick from many different ships and itineraries, making it an attractive repeat vacation. Because it fits well with most nonretired work schedules, it also tends to draw a younger crowd overall, and more kids who go when their parents can get off work.

• **Longer cruises.** To avoid children, shoot for anything longer than a week. It has obvious advantages such as more ports and less pressure to fill days with activities. Working parents also find it less convenient. Ten-day, two-week, and longer cruises tend to be offered by upscale lines, due mainly to their cost, though most mainstream lines have at least a limited number of longer cruises.

• **A round-the-world cruise.** A round-the-world cruise is the vacation of a lifetime. Passengers see the world without jet lag, without rushing, and without stress. With few exceptions, those enjoying the world by sea are older, well-to-do, and adventurous.

While a number of European and Asian cruise lines schedule round-the-world trips, lines familiar to North Americans and with at least occasional world-circling excursions include top-of-the-line Seabourn and Cunard. Under mainstream lines, Holland America and Princess also offer an occasional round-the-world vacation. Because most passengers cannot afford the $29,000 to $300,000 price tag of a complete round-the-world cruise, many companies also sell segments. If you want to visit Australia, for example, you can pick up the ship in Los Angeles, enjoy island ports of call as you cross the Pacific, then disembark in Sydney. For more information, talk to your travel agent.

HEALTH ISSUES

More than one potential cruiser with a health condition has decided not to cruise because: "What happens if I get sick at sea — 1000 miles from the nearest hospital?"

Unless a ship is primarily used for other functions, such as a barge, and as long as it has at least fifty passengers on board, it will probably have some kind of medical facilities and staff. Most have at least one doctor with an emergency room capable of minor medical procedures; some have more. There is no accepted standard for medical facilities on a ship, however, and it's best not to make assumptions. Think of shipboard facilities as a good medical clinic in a small country town. They're more than adequate and can treat most problems, but if a malady requires a specialist, you'll be referred to a hospital in the big city. Here, that "big city" is the next port of call. Onboard doctors either correct simple problems or stabilize patients until the ship arrives at a larger facility.

For some mature travelers, the prospect of surgery or medical procedures in small foreign countries strikes fear in their hearts; some even forgo travel because of it. But good hospitals exist almost everywhere, and cruise passengers generally get referred to "the best hospital in (fill in city name)." In addition, cruise lines usually have a system in place to help passengers stuck in a port of call due to a medical emergency. An English-speaking liaison, for example, may visit you in the hospital, help with paperwork and, if necessary, translation. Other resources — a cruise line representative, insurance contact, or even personal credit card company — can arrange for a return home.

Most cruise ship medical emergencies involve new problems, such as heart attacks, but some passengers have existing illnesses that flare up. If you have a known medical condition that could require emergency service, tell your travel agent and ask extensive questions to make sure the ship can handle any recurring problems. In my opinion, health should rarely keep a person from traveling because traveling is one of the reasons for living. Still, be realistic. A cruise ship simply cannot do everything.

Most cruise lines require that a health form be filled out if someone has an existing medical problem; they also reserve the right to deny passage if, in the line's opinion, the medical condition could cause a problem while at sea. Generally Princess and Holland America have good reputations concerning their health-care facilities, as does the *QE 2*. Note that even with these large lines, actual staffing and facilities can vary from ship to ship.

Other health issues:

- **Ship doctors do not specialize.** That means they know a lot of things about the body, but may not be experts on your specific problem. If worried, ask your family doctor to make a copy of pertinent medical information and, should something occur on board, give it to the ship's doctor.
- **Doctors do not work for the cruise line.** Most cruise lines hire an outside firm to staff and work the infirmary, though exceptions exist. For all practical matters, you're going to an independent doctor, just as you do on land. There is also no guarantee that the doctor was trained in the U.S. Most large cruise lines report that their doctors are licensed in either the U.S., Canada, United Kingdom, or Scandinavian countries. If you have a special concern, have your travel agent check and get the answer in writing before finalizing vacation plans.
- **Insurance rules vary.** Call your own insurance plan before leaving home to find out if they cover cruise ship medical fees or procedures performed in foreign countries. Many policies, including Medicare, pay nothing. Zip. Nada. Since an evacuation from the ship can cost as much as $20,000, this is the best argument for buying travel health insurance (see Chapter 5).

A few insurance policies do cover onboard or foreign country medical treatments, but the rules vary from insurer to insurer. For example, passengers usually pay for medical service even if they're insured—on a ship, that means as they leave the infirmary—and then seek reimbursement after their return home. If this happens to you, keep the receipt and write down all information including doctors' and nurses' names. Keep copies for your records.

- **Prescription drugs.** Most ships stock prescription drugs, but if they're out, it's tough to order more when 300 miles from the shoreline. Stock up before leaving home, and make sure your supply will last as long as the trip. If taking a long cruise, talk to your doctor about refills and ask for guidance on taking medication when passing through time zones. You may have to adjust the timing of doses to keep your body on its natural rhythm.
- **Sanitation.** The U.S. Centers for Disease Control (*http://www.cdc.gov*) inspects ships every six months if they depart from a U.S. port and issues a public report on the findings. A perfect score, rarely achieved, is one hundred; anything eighty-five or lower is considered unacceptable. The CDC maintains a Web site— *http://www2.cdc.gov/nceh/vsp/vspmain.asp*—which posts each ship's most recent inspection report. For those without Internet access, the most recent report is also available by mail at:

> Vessel Sanitation Program
> National Center for Environmental Health
> 1015 North America Way, Room 107
> Miami, FL 33132

- **First aid.** Consider putting together a small first aid kit and taking it along. Band-Aids, sunburn lotion, and other supplies are usually available on the ship, but shops may be closed when you need them. Should you wish a simple medical procedure—blood pressure check or even just a thermometer to see if you're feverish—a visit to the doctor can be expensive. Be prepared.
- **Assistance.** If any medical condition requires something extra, such as oxygen, confirm in writing before departure that the ship can—and will—supply it or accommodate your supply. Rather than accept a simple "yes" answer, push for specifics on how they typically handle the problem.
- **Disease.** Sickness occurs worldwide, but few countries visited by cruise ships have notable problems. If traveling to an exotic destination, however, the Centers for Disease Control posts prevalent diseases, by country, at *http://www.cdc.gov/travel/blusheet.htm*.
- **Death at sea.** It happens, of course. Generally, a body can be refrigerated until the ship returns to the port of disembarkation. Arrangements can also be made to disembark at the next port of

call and have the body flown home. Expect paperwork and hassles, but the ship's crew will do everything they can to help.

Healthy Cruising Checklist

1. Be realistic. Check with your doctor to make sure you can safely cruise. Ask for a copy of pertinent medical records.
2. Be smart. Explain any health problems to the cruise line and confirm, in writing, that they can handle problems. Take a phone list of doctors that have treated you recently.
3. Bring extra medicine including first aid supplies. Be prepared to treat yourself for minor medical problems.
4. When booking, ask the cruise line about onboard facilities, the medical staff, and what equipment they use.
5. Check the ship's sanitation rating at *http://www2.cdc.gov/nceh/vsp/ vspmain.asp*.

SECURITY ISSUES

A cruise ship is, by definition, a closed environment. Petty thieves who find tourists easy prey do not frequent the dining room. It costs too much to get on board and there's no place to run. Big crimes, such as a ship hijacking, are also almost unheard of. After the infamous *Achille Lauro* episode in 1985, the industry bolstered its security, and now, boarding a ship requires a checkpoint similar to those passed through to board an airplane. In general, no one should avoid a cruise ship vacation based on a fear of crime. With that said, intelligent precautions should still be taken.

• **Oversight.** Ships spend most of their time in international waters. That means U.S. laws do not apply in the same way they do in Las Vegas, Orlando, or New York. The rules are different. If a cruise line case is even heard in a U.S. court, for example, it's generally a federal case rather than a state case. In addition, the cruise lines do not have the same obligation to report crimes to authorities if they occur outside U.S. waters.

Read the "cruise contract" carefully, including details and small print in the back of brochures. By paying money and signing the contract, you may obligate yourself to play by rules the cruise line has established, though it's generally a take-it-or-leave-it arrangement. If not acceptable, consider a ship that travels in the U.S. only. That way, at least, grievances work through the U.S. court system.

• **Sexual assault.** Any kind of sexual assault, including rape, is shocking. But it happens. When it happens on a cruise vacation, however, it seems somehow worse, perhaps because the very idea of a cruise is to escape the realities of life and rise to a level slightly above the mundane.

In July of 1999, at the request of a U.S. court, Carnival Cruise Lines revealed the number of sexual assaults that had occurred on their ships over the previous five-year period. (A crew member claimed that she'd been sexually assaulted by another crew member while still in U.S. waters.) Carnival's count: 108, according to *The Miami Herald*. The report created bad press for Carnival and also some other lines, such as Royal Caribbean, who unwillingly joined the scuffle.

In truth, the figure is misleading but not inaccurate. Carnival correctly claims that a reported sexual assault could be, and in some cases was, as mild as an unwelcome kiss—most of the 108 incidents did not involve rape. Also, the cruise line—the world's largest—carried 1.8 million people in just the previous twelve months, meaning there was a problem with about one in every 60,000 passengers. Further watering down the danger, many of the allegations, including the case already cited, came from a crew member and were directed at another crew member. In the overall scheme of things, it's a benign figure, perhaps one sexual assault per 100,000 passengers. Still, it happens on rare occasion.

Common sense is the best weapon. It's always wise to keep cabin doors closed when alone inside your room, and open when entertaining new friends. When visiting a port, err on the side of caution. Don't travel alone or in "shady" parts of town. Understand any problem areas of town before disembarking. Single women should remember that the crew is trained to be polite and outgoing when serving the public, but that does not mean they're nice all the time. Some are good actors, and that polite, good-looking guy in the dining room may not be so nice behind closed doors.

• **Theft.** Again, wear the badge of common sense. The newer cruise ships offer limited access to rooms, and on some of the absolute newest, a computer keeps a record of who has entered each room. Still, anything of value, especially jewelry, should not be taken along on any vacation, cruise or otherwise. A traveler I know takes great pride in her cubic zirconium collection of jewelry. She's replaced virtually every real piece she owns with a fake piece that looks almost like the original. If she loses one or all of her fake pieces, she's prepared to absorb the loss.

• **Fire.** The International Maritime Organization has a Safety of Life at Sea (SOLAS) program that, over time, mandates new fire protection and lifesaving standards for all cruise ships. The conversion of older ships costs a lot of money; as a result, many new ships are now coming on line and older ships retiring. To the cruise passenger, however, it means less danger from fires. While a fire can still occur on board, the new rules make it easier to contain the problem. A fire in the kitchen would, for example, create culinary problems but it shouldn't threaten lives. As always, passengers should take precautions. Throwing a cigarette or match over the side of the ship, for example, is dangerous since it could blow backward and enter decks below.

• **Sandbars, other ships, and icebergs.** The *Titanic* not withstanding, people don't die from cruise ship disasters. Even in the worst case imaginable, a ship sinking, current requirements for lifeboat accessibility minimize risk. In the past ten years, a handful of ships have lodged on a sandbar or faced some other type of problem. No one has died; no one has been injured. It's just not something to worry about. In the unlikely event your cruise is so affected, go with the flow, ask for your money back, and demand at least a 50 percent discount on your next cruise. Then look forward to it.

PASSPORTS AND VISAS

When traveling to a foreign country, U.S. travelers must prove they are U.S. citizens (with a passport or other approved documentation), and if visiting a handful of countries, ask permission to enter before arrival (a visa). Your travel agent should explain details specific to your trip before departure, but if she doesn't, ask.

No documentation is required for a cruise that starts and stops within the U.S. Currently, however, that includes the Delta Queen

Steamboat Company that plies the waters of the Mississippi and other rivers, American Hawaii that visits islands in the fiftieth state, and a handful of other summer cruises that explore the East Coast. For Caribbean itineraries or passage into Canada—along with selected other world sites—U.S. and Canadian citizens need at least an original birth certificate and an official picture ID such as a driver's license. A passport is acceptable, of course, and for other world destinations, it is mandatory.

One word of warning: When most mature travelers were born, the hospital issued an attractive, flowery, official-looking birth certificate with signatures and baby footprints and little angels in the corner. Frame it and hang it. It won't do any good on a cruise. "Original" birth certificate means one issued by the state (with a raised seal), though not necessarily at the time of birth.

TO GET A BIRTH CERTIFICATE: Either (a) dig it out of the folder Mom gave you when you turned forty, or (b) contact the state in which you were born and request another one. Every state in the U.S. has a department that keeps track of births. It might be called the "Department of Records," or perhaps the "Department of Vital Statistics," but all can issue a new certificate for a nominal fee, perhaps $10. If a birth certificate cannot be found and a new one must be ordered, however, start the process long before sailing. It can take six weeks or more—a pain in the neck for people now living in a different state. For last-minute people, it may be possible to get a birth certificate in just a few days, though it generally costs more money.

TO GET A PASSPORT: U.S. citizens who want to travel to foreign countries need a passport. Cruise itineraries to Europe and other parts of the world require one. To get a passport, travelers still need the aforementioned birth certificate, as well as two pictures (two inches by two inches, available at many travel agencies or camera centers), an application form, and $60 to pay the application fee. The passport is good for ten years. If buying a passport for a child fifteen or younger, the cost is only $40, but these passports expire in five years. Add $35 if you need quick service. For more information, check with your travel agent—many keep applications on file—or contact the U.S. Passport Office at 202-955-0232. The U.S. State Department also has extensive information on passports and the process on its Web site—*http://travel.state.gov/passport_services.html*—including a printable application. Any travel agent worth their salt can give you directions to the nearest government office or post office that accepts passport applications, as will the State Department's Web site.

TO GET A PASSPORT WITHOUT A BIRTH CERTIFICATE: A handful of births never made it into the legal record books, and some government records have been lost to fires or floods. As a result, a few adults may have difficulty finding their birth certificates. If that sounds like you, the State Department has a complicated—but not impossible—set of guidelines to overcome the problem. For answers, visit the Web site listed above or call the local office of the Immigration and Naturalization Service and request a Certificate of Citizenship. Their telephone number should be in the Government section of the local phone book.

TO GET A VISA: U.S. citizens do not need a visa to travel to foreign countries served by most cruise ships. For some exotic destinations, however, they do. A visa, quite simply, starts as a traveler's request to enter a foreign country. When (if) the foreign country decides to grant permission through a local office or embassy, it issues a visa, a stamp inside the passport itself, that essentially says, "He's okay. He can come onto our soil." Requirements vary from country to country and from time to time. Besides the visa, a handful of countries may also have additional entrance requirements such as a vaccination.

The easiest way to get a visa is through a visa service. Travel agents usually recommend someone they work with, but the Internet has also spawned a cottage industry of on-line companies. Should there be a problem, the visa service can do the laborious work and guarantee that the visa arrives on time. Cost for the service varies depending on the number of visas needed and the amount of time the service has to secure them.

Two booklets—*Foreign Entry Requirements* and *Passports—Applying for Them the EASY WAY*—give detailed information on how and where to apply for U.S. passports and visas. Both are available from the Consumer Information Center, Pueblo, CO 81009. They may also be accessed through the Internet at: *http://www.pueblo.gsa.gov/travel.htm*. Cost: $0.50 each by mail, free at the Web site.

TO TRAVEL WITH A GRANDCHILD: In addition to the same documentation required of everyone else—birth certificate/passport and/or visa—a child may need a notarized letter, signed by both parents (if not traveling with you), stating that the child has permission to travel outside the country. Mexico requires this, for example, even if a cruise ship spends only a few hours in Cancún.

AND NOW A WARNING: Securing the necessary documentation to travel is your responsibility. While a travel agent should outline trip requirements and offer instructions on how to obtain the necessary papers, travelers are on their own. If you show up inadequately prepared, ships will sail without you, money will not be refunded, and the travel agent will say, "I told you so." For any questions on passports, contact the U.S. Passport Office at 202-955-0232; for visa questions, call the State Department at 202-663-1225.

2

WHICH CRUISE
IS BEST FOR ME?

Few people book a cruise for the food—or the itinerary, or the theme, or any other single trait. One couple may want to avoid children but be willing to put up with a few when they discover that a ship's other amenities and itinerary fit them to a T. It's a compromise. The hunt does not focus on the best ship. Rather it focuses on the best ship for you.

This chapter gets you started. It may even be the final word for people with a specific and all-important goal in mind, such as a classic ship with traditional British service (Cunard's *QE 2*). Most people, however, will see themselves in two or three questions, seek out ships that appear in each, and make some compromises. Once your options have been narrowed down, a description of each cruise line can be found in Chapter 8.

OF ALL THE LINES AND SHIPS, WHICH
CATER TO ADULTS OLDER THAN FIFTY?

Almost all cruise lines cater to adults older than fifty, but to some lines, the mature traveler is their bread and butter. Most luxury lines, for example, attract older adults who can afford and appreciate them. Cruises that last over seven days also have an abundance of older travelers because younger adults can't take that much time off work. Certain destinations also appeal to the mature crowd, with Europe and Asia—anyplace far beyond U.S. waters—the biggest draw. In other words, pick any luxury ship sailing a ten-plus-day itinerary in the South Pacific for guaranteed satisfaction. Even in local waters, however, certain cruise lines host a preponderance of post-fifty people.

The Delta Queen Steamboat Co., a river cruise in North American waters, hosts older adults almost exclusively. Its Americana theme doesn't have the same attraction to kids or even younger adults who tend to avoid history-based vacations.

At sea, the luxury lines also appeal primarily to older adults, notably when they sail any itinerary that lasts over seven days. Only one semi-luxury line, however—Celebrity—uses large ships. For older adults seeking adult-friendliness yet with amenities that reflect those on the large cruise lines, it's the best choice. The second runner-up is Cunard's ships. While all their ships offer luxury cruising in an upscale atmosphere, the largest of the line—the QE 2—includes a wider age range, as it is the only ship that regularly crosses the Atlantic.

Smaller luxury lines filled by predominantly older adults include Seabourn, Silversea, and Crystal. Because they use smaller ships, their luxury accommodations can be more personal. As the most expensive fleets afloat, they also appeal only to those adults who can afford them. Another line, Radisson Seven Seas Cruises, also attracts primarily adults, but the average age dips a bit lower—around the low forties—and the passengers tend to be businesspeople attracted to the Radisson name, and many companies schedule meetings while afloat.

If interested in a sailing ship, two cruise lines fit neatly in the "small luxury" category too—Windstar or Sea Cloud. Windstar spends more time in waters close to the U.S.

In the mass-market cruise categories, Holland America is the undisputed leader in older adult cruising and just a notch below Celebrity, although it now offers an extensive children's program. The company and its newest ship have clearly aimed themselves at a more family demographic, but many travel agents still book older adults onto the line, and Holland America keeps offering the kinds of activities that they enjoy. While the other mass-market lines don't appeal to only older adults, the very size of their ships allows them to offer enough activities to keep all ages happy. Arguably, Princess, Royal Caribbean, and Norwegian Cruise Line are good choices. Carnival appeals to adults who appreciate Las Vegas–style entertainment options.

Other lines with a strong older adult following include American Hawaii (if touring the fiftieth state), and the smaller soft adventure lines that travel in Alaska and elsewhere, including Cruise West, Lindblad Expeditions, and, for something a bit less expensive, World Explorer Cruises.

I'M ON A TIGHT BUDGET BUT WANT IT ALL — SUGGEST SOMETHING

Travel off-season, book early (or last minute if a line offers deals), consider an inside cabin, and read Chapter 4. Great deals can be found. Overall, however, the budget lines offer consistently low-priced trips. On some lines, the cruise could cost only marginally more than staying at home.

Carnival Cruise Line, while not the absolute cheapest, has inexpensive cruises on huge ships with hundreds of activities. It's glitzy, but exciting in a theme park kind of way—and most ships are new, unlike some other bargain lines. The combination of a full cruise experience and reasonable prices has made the line the largest in the industry.

Otherwise, Commodore Cruise Line may be the best of the budget lot. Sailing out of New Orleans, the ship reports a high rate of returning passengers and, while featuring an older vessel, gives travelers a lot of vacation for the dollar. Other budget lines that offer standard cruise activities at bargain basement prices include Cape Canaveral Cruise Line, a very cheap three-day cruise deal; Regal Cruises, a seven-day vacation western Caribbean trip sailing out of Tampa; and Mediterranean Shipping Cruises, a budget line with an Italian flavor.

I WANT THE BEST

"Best" is a relative term, but more often than not refers to a luxury cruise line (most upscale) and the most expensive trips. "Money is no object" people won't be disappointed with Crystal if also looking for the biggest ship in the "best" category. Using smaller ships but offering no less luxury, Seabourn and Silversea continue to compete head-to-head for the upscale cruiser's business — and neither disappoints. Both feature a staff that anticipates every need and delivers service quietly and efficiently. Radisson Seven Seas, a bit less upscale but just as luxurious, also offers a won't-be-disappointed vacation.

For those seeking British standards of service on a large luxury ship, Cunard (*QE 2*) is the only choice, providing you book into one of the ship's top two categories. The last line with "classes of service," the *QE 2* gives the best cabins, service, and food to those guests who pay the most.

Meanwhile, over in the mass-market cruise line category, Celebrity comes closest to "best" if you're not willing to book on a smaller ship and uninterested in the *QE 2*'s itinerary or style. From a "best" perspective, Celebrity also offers a lot of luxury for the dollar — not cheap but also a good value.

If looking for a soft adventure cruise with a casual atmosphere that gets close to nature — but still the best of the lot — consider Lindblad Expeditions or, for a smaller, private yacht feel and less exercise, go with American Yacht Safaris.

In the sailboat category, Windstar offers a full sailing experience complemented with luxurious cabins stocked with everything that makes a journey comfortable. For a true private yacht vacation — meaning a very small ship — also consider Sea Cloud and cruise in (refurbished) ships once owned and operated by the rich and famous.

I WANT TO AVOID KIDS

Many adult-friendly cruise lines discourage children from traveling, have minimum age requirements, and offer no entertainment for the preteen set. Harried parents generally seek out a good kids' program to take the little nippers off their hands for a few precious minutes, so ships with nothing to offer—the ones that make parents entertain their own offspring—naturally host mainly adults.

With that said, most mainstream lines are so big that they can offer programs for each age group, and most child activities take place in out-of-the-way ship locations. On many, the only time you see kids is around the pool, during all-ship activities, or at dinner. If you prefer the large mainstream lines (most people do) and want to cut down on the number of youngsters, use the following suggestions:

• Sail for more than seven days. Parents generally take vacations in one-week increments.

• Choose a luxury line.

• Choose an adult-friendly destination. Families travel worldwide, but Alaska, for example, draws more older adults than the Caribbean. In general, trips far beyond U.S. waters attract fewer children. Europe also appeals to U.S. fifty-plusers, though you may still meet a lot of kids if cruising with a European-based line—they just speak a different language. Best bet: choose a larger U.S. cruise line that operates only one or two ships in European waters.

• Book a second seating dinner. Parents tend to eat early, either to get the kids to bed or to get it over with. As a result, they choose the first seating.

• In U.S. markets, sail when parents won't pull their kids out of school for a week. The two-week period surrounding Labor Day is usually good (except for three-day Labor Day cruises) since children begin a new school year. The same is true around Memorial Day when students take final exams. Also consider the first three weeks after Thanksgiving and the first three weeks after New Year's.

• Avoid holidays. Like the plague. While the entire summer is a kid-thick time to cruise, the weeks surrounding Easter and Christmas draw even more youngsters.

• For specific ship suggestions, reread the first question concerning ships that appeal to adults over fifty, but note that Cunard (*QE 2*) and Crystal offer children's programs on a limited basis during heavy family vacation times.

- Silversea and Seabourn truly don't appeal to kids. Also, American Canadian Caribbean Line and Club Med don't allow children younger than ten and twelve, respectively, to cruise.

I'M TRAVELING WITH GRANDKIDS—
DOES ANY SHIP REALLY APPEAL TO
ALL GENERATIONS?

A lot of ships appeal to all generations, but the question is: "How much?" Of all vacation options, a cruise is the A-number-one choice for grandtravel. Most older adults travel with grandchildren to become closer and, on the side, show them what the world has to offer. A cruise does that while, simultaneously, eliminating the messy stuff—the argument over why they can't order lobster (They won't like it. They won't eat it.), the when-are-we-going-to-get-there whining, and the every-five-minutes "I'm bored" announcements. During the day, a good kids' program relieves you of responsibility, secure in the knowledge that they're having a good time.

Most mainstream ships offer some kind of kids' program—they must if they want to attract the family market—but some do a better job than others. To gauge any kids' program, check to see if they break it into age groups, with at least one for toddlers (under five), kids (five to nine), tweens (ten to thirteen), and teenagers (fourteen to seventeen). Many ships also offer cribs if traveling with an infant. Request one at the time of booking.

If taking an "I don't matter—this is all for the grandkids" attitude, pick the Disney Cruise Line. It not only has the Disney characters and the best children's program afloat, it's also a quality product. Disney has an adults-only beach on their private island and a no-kids restaurant on board; however, Disney does not have the full slate of mature entertainment found on other cruise lines.

If taking a "Can't we *all* have a good time?" attitude, a large ship on a mainstream cruise line is, hands down, the best bet. Holland America, for example, holds a strong appeal to post-fifty adults, but in a push to attract the family market, also has a good kids' program. In Alaska, they even offer shore excursion programs just for kids. American Hawaii does the same.

Other mainstream lines with a good children's program include:

- **Carnival:** Kids love Carnival's style and overall festive atmosphere. It may be too much for some adults, but most appreciate the line for what it is—and what it charges.
- **Royal Caribbean:** Their biggest ships offer everything from miniature golf to extensive video arcades with plenty left over for adults. Post-toddlers love it.

To make life easier when traveling with grandchildren, buy a pair of walkie-talkies before leaving home and stock enough batteries to last through the cruise. If you can avoid just one three-times-around-the-ship hike to find young John Jr, the cost is paltry. Also, to help kids find the cabin, put some distinguishing mark—perhaps one of their drawings—on the outside door upon first arrival and have them memorize the cabin number.

SEASICKNESS WOULD RUIN MY VACATION—CAN I AVOID IT?

Complete information can be found in Chapter 1, but generally, new ships have stabilizers that fight the rocking of the sea. Avoid older ships, pick big ones (less affected by the motion), and cruise in calmer waters (Caribbean and other small seas). Also, choose a cabin located on a lower deck toward the center of the ship. If overly worried, take a river cruise.

I'M TRAVELING ALONE—BUT WANT TO CRUISE WITH KINDRED SPIRITS

But for the extra cost, a cruise is the perfect single's vacation. People dine in groups of six to ten, meaning passengers get to know their dinner partners. Most ships even host a singles get-together the first night out. Some experts estimate that one in four cruise passengers is single. Statistically speaking, that's a lot of people.

For more information, read "Traveling Solo: The Widow's Waltz" in Chapter 3.

THEME CRUISES — WHAT'S THAT ABOUT?

A theme cruise adds two more dimensions to a cruise vacation. It guarantees that a sizable number of other passengers will share one of your hobbies, and it guarantees that a number of onboard activities will be interesting to you. The theme can either be a hallmark of the cruise line itself, such as American Hawaii's focus on the islands, or a single cruise on a mass-market ship, such as a Big Band Cruise on NCL.

Disney Cruise Line is another company dedicated to a single theme — Disney. Other lines fall uneasily into this category of a cruise-line-wide theme, based mainly on the nationality of the crew and the type of food served. Rather than a theme, however, these "lean" toward a specific interest. For example, consider Costa for Italian cruising or its less expensive counterpart, Mediterranean Shipping Cruises. Programs and other activities do not all have an Italian flavor, but with an Italian crew and propensity to serve pasta, the theme cannot be missed. For a Greek flavor, consider Royal Olympic; for French, choose First European.

On the other hand, mass-market ships schedule theme cruises that are a break from their standard week-by-week offerings. They usually select topics of high mass-market appeal, ones sure to net the customers that they may not otherwise see. The most common theme cruises include ones highlighting jazz, big band sounds, music of the fifties, sports heroes, and food (such as a chocoholic cruise).

The concept of theme cruising began with Commodore and Norwegian Cruise Line, and they still offer the best programs, though most mainstream lines offer at least a few throughout the year — notably in slow seasons to increase bookings. Delta Queen Steamboat Co. has its own highly refined theme cruises that relate in some way to American history. Crystal Cruises is known for its gourmet and wine themes.

IMPRESS ME WITH THE FOOD

It is very rare to travel on a gourmet line and, during the course of the cruise, not find something worth criticizing. On the flip side, even a budget cruise tends to offer at least one or two entrées that uniquely please the palate. With that said, however, top-dollar cruise lines serve the best food, not just in terms of cuisine, but also style—a feeling that it's not simply banquet fare prepared hours earlier and kept heated.

In the you-won't-be-disappointed category, consider Celebrity, Crystal, Cunard, Radisson Seven Seas, Seabourn, Sea Cloud, Silversea, and Windstar. Without exception, these lines' chefs take pride in their work and offer up attractive and, more important, good food. In the almost-but-not-quite-as-good category, look to Club Med or Star Clippers.

The megaships can serve 2,000 or more people per meal, and chefs strive to make each meal appear individually prepared. They meet with differing amounts of success, though no large line serves bad food. Even the budget lines, while unimaginative, tend to serve solid fare that's reasonably tasty even if not exciting. Still, two mainstream lines stand out from the crowd in quality of onboard cuisine—Princess and Holland America. If going mainstream and interested in food, put them at the top of your list.

If seeking a soft adventure cruise with great food (not gourmet), look to Clipper Cruise Line or Lindblad Expeditions.

NO GAMES FOR ME—I WANT TO BE ONE WITH THE SEA

For the true sea experience, nothing beats the sailing class ships, though under those sails, some actually rely more on motors than wind. Nevertheless, consider Clipper Cruise Line, Star Clippers, or Windjammer. For top-shelf oneness with the sea, go with Windstar or Sea Cloud.

FORGET THE SEA—I WANT A RESORT THAT JUST HAPPENS TO FLOAT

The best resorts are the biggest resorts—the mega and mega-plus ships. (But make sure they are megaships. A few lines—even industry mammoth Carnival—still own one or two older ships that don't have quite as much space; hence, they have less to offer.) For the resort experience—the one seen on television and talked about over coffee—consider Carnival, Disney (with grandkids), Norwegian Cruise Lines, Princess, or Royal Caribbean. For slightly smaller large ships (an oxymoron?), look to Celebrity (top dollar), Costa, Crown, or Holland America.

For an inexpensive to cheap resort cruise—meaning they offer everything but in a limited way and on older, somewhat smaller ships—go with Commodore or Regal.

FORGET THE SEA AND THINGS TO DO—I WANT TO DANCE, DRINK, AND LET LOOSE

You can let more "go" on Windjammer than any other line—perhaps even some things you wish to hang on to. Beyond Windjammer, Carnival is the undisputed leader in party cruising even though it offers the full slate of resort activities. Club Med, with only one ship, also has a party-hearty reputation.

Otherwise, the large ships, once again, have something for everyone. Even if only 10 percent of 1,800 passengers party until the wee hours, you still have 180 people going strong at midnight. For more than adequate kick-up-your-heels facilities and a staff that encourages it, look to Royal Caribbean, Princess, or Norwegian Cruise Line. In the inexpensive category, check out Commodore or Regal. Party people many times prefer an inexpensive cruise because they serve the same alcohol and play the same music as the more expensive lines, and after four rum punches, they can't tell the difference.

I JUST WANT TO RELAX AND READ A BOOK—GET ME AWAY FROM THE CROWD

Almost every cruise line says that passengers can "do as much or as little as they wish." While true, some lines push slightly harder to get people involved, as if passengers must enjoy ship-sponsored activities to have a truly good time. While some shy people do need a subtle push, most mature travelers have reached an age where they know what they want. They just want to be able to do it.

If looking for a vacation in every sense of the word—meaning relaxation—the lines that don't incite book-reading passengers into needless action include Delta Queen, Cunard, Radisson Seven Seas, Seabourn, Sea Cloud, Silversea, and Windstar.

FORGET A BOOK, MAKE MY BLOOD PUMP— ADVENTURE CRUISING

In travel lingo, you can book an adventure trip or a soft adventure trip. Adventure trips involve activity that requires at least some physical training—a white-water raft expedition, cross-country bike ride, or climb up the Matterhorn, for example. Soft adventure also requires physical exertion, but all reasonably fit people can participate. They may not be a good option for couch potatoes but are a great way to see the world for those who can hike short to medium distances, kayak, or snorkel. Most soft adventure cruises take place on small ships that visit out-of-the-way ports and, once there, arrange exploration via foot, bike, or other means though virtually all large ships also offer optional soft adventure shore excursions.

For an American audience, the majority of soft adventure cruises operate in Alaska. Alaska's Glacier Bay Tours and Cruises demands a bit more than other lines on two of their ships, while their other two ships offer easier itineraries. Soft-adventure cruise lines include American Canadian Caribbean Line, American Safaris (less demanding and luxurious), Cruise West, Lindblad Expeditions (top choice for quality and soft adventure), and World Explorer Cruises (relatively inexpensive).

I'LL TAKE ROMANCE — MARRIAGE AND HONEYMOON TRIPS

Cruising is romantic thanks to the sea, the sunset, the wine, and reruns of *The Love Boat*. If looking for a mate, however, see the single cruising question above. If your loved one is already "found" and sailing with you, look here.

HONEYMOONS. All the large cruise lines do special things for honeymooners. Perks may include a private cocktail party with other honeymooners, a table for two, complimentary champagne, an "official" certificate, flowers, and ship souvenirs. Make sure your travel agent explains your honeymoon status to the cruise line at the time of booking. As unromantic as it sounds, women changing their last name to that of a spouse should use their maiden name on all bookings, especially if flying internationally. Since passports, driver's licenses, and other documents still bear unmarried name at the time of booking, it makes travel easier. If using a married name is important to you, take a copy of the marriage certificate along.

Honeymoon cruises tend to have a lot of honeymooners. Most Caribbean cruises depart on a Saturday, and most weddings take place on a Saturday; consequently, the few Sunday departures attract all the "just married" couples. Larger ships can host fifty couples in the high wedding seasons. If you prefer not to be grouped with other "just marrieds," consider a smaller romantic ship such as *Sea Cloud*. In all cases, though, confirm that your cabin has a double bed or twin beds that, pushed together, convert to a queen.

MARRIAGES. In the movies, the captain marries a dewy-eyed couple on the bow of the ship. Good stuff. Watch it again. Doesn't happen in real life. On rare occasion, legal arrangements allow the captain to marry couples; in fewer cases does the captain actually do so. One ship in the Princess fleet, the *Grand Princess*, is an exception. With a wedding chapel aboard and a willing captain, marriages can be scheduled ahead of time. Should this option draw in enough guests, expect other large lines to follow suit.

In practice, couples have a cruise ship marriage in one of three ways. The first is to actually get married on the ship—but bring your own minister, rabbi, or other official. Since any wedding generally includes a small wedding party with parents and/or children and/or grandchildren, some people take a wedding official along, too. In this case, planning a cruise ship wedding has all the same frustrations and joys of planning a land wedding, though (usually) with fewer guests. It's ideal, however, for older couples marrying for the second time who want immediate family there but, otherwise, won't be wearing white, expecting presents, or planning the same type of reception they enjoyed in 1969.

The second way to get married is to have a morning ceremony on land the day of departure, a reception afterward on board the ship, and a cruise with those guests who choose (and pay) to stay. Most large cruise lines can help with arrangements or, alternately, will connect you with a local wedding specialist. Even smaller ships have been asked the "Can I get married on board?" question more than once and should be able to recommend a local wedding specialist for you. In some cases, the wedding companies have packages and work through travel agents (and pay them a commission) for making arrangements. In this case, your travel agent also becomes your wedding consultant. In all cases, confirm details in writing.

The third way to get married is in a port of call. In practice, this is difficult. Most islands have different rules on marriage and most have a mandatory waiting period. Even if the waiting period is only one day, however, it won't work for cruises that arrive at 10:00 A.M. and depart at midnight. Seven-day cruises to Bermuda from New York may work, however, since most ships spend up to three days on the island. In that example, horse-drawn carriages can meet you at the ship, transport you to a verdant yard that overlooks the countryside, and marry you with the sea to your back and the sun setting on the horizon.

RENEWAL OF VOWS. Renewals, not requiring any official paperwork, are a growing market niche for the cruise lines. Usually, the captain or other official simply has a couple—they're usually celebrating a major anniversary—recommit to each other. Sometimes kids and grandchildren attend; sometimes they do not. A party may be arranged on board following the ceremony.

I'M GAY—WHERE DO I FIT IN?

There are no gay cruise lines or ships, but there are gay travel agents and gay charter cruises. On a charter cruise, a tour company books an entire ship en masse and sells the cabins in-house. Wind-jammer, for example, often has an all-gay cruise reserved and sold by a gay tour company. Gay and lesbian tour companies that book cruises include:

RSVP CRUISES: 2800 University Ave. SE, Minneapolis, MN 55414. Phone: 800-328-RSVP. Internet: *www.rsvp.net*. Example: RSVP Cruises has booked Holland America's *Maasdam* for two trips in 2001.

PIED PIPER TRAVEL: 330 West 42nd Street, Suite 1804, New York, NY 10036. Phone: 800-TRIP-312. Internet: *http://home.att. net/~PIED-PIPER-TRAVEL*. Examples: 2001 scheduled cruises go to the Caribbean, Alaska, and Hawaii; and sail with Cunard (*QE 2* and *Caronia*), Princess (*Grand Princess* and *Ocean Princess*), Celebrity (*Galaxy, Horizon*, and *Millennium*), American Hawaii, and Norwegian Cruise Lines (*Norway*).

OLIVIA CRUISES AND RESORTS: 4400 Market Street, Oakland, CA 94608 Phone: 800-631-6277. Internet: *www.olivia-travel.com*. Olivia specializes in lesbian cruises. Examples: Lines used in 2000 included Commodore (*Enchanted Isle*), Windstar (*Wind Surf*), and Royal Olympic (*Stella Solaris*).

3

SHOPPING FOR A SHIP

TRAVEL AGENTS: A CRUISER'S BEST FRIEND

To cruise, you need a travel agent. For those who like to do everything themselves—down to and including calling airlines directly—this may be a new experience. Worry not. While many travel agents now charge a fee for airline bookings, most offer cruise advice free. (If they don't, call around first.)

Essentially, a travel agent represents travel companies that have agreed to pay her a commission if she sells their product. (Apologies to all male travel agents for using female pronouns.) That group she represents includes most airlines (except for a few small budget carriers and foreign lines), most cruise lines (except for very small ones), most hotels, most tour operators, and all the largest car rental companies. The standard commission paid to an agent is 10 percent of the cost before taxes. (In the real world, that 10 percent varies and is now much lower for airfares—see Chapter 4: Money: Wading Through the Muck to Find a Bargain.)

Because of the commission, travel agents love to book cruises. They're easy and they're lucrative. (With one payment, a travel agent gets 10 percent of the total vacation—food, airline tickets, and passage.) That means the travel agent is not doing you any favors by dispensing cruise advice. Ask questions. Make her work.

On the flip side, if you discuss a cruise for one hour and don't book through that agent, she has wasted working time on an activity that does not generate revenue. That's not to say you owe the agent your business just because she hollered "Next!" when you walked through the travel agency's door, of course, but keep in mind that the agent has two goals. The first is to find you the perfect cruise at the perfect price. The second is to collect your money. If forced to choose between those two goals, intelligent agents—I speak from experience here—select the latter.

If friends cannot recommend a travel agent, the hunt begins. To find the person who can best book your cruise, it helps to understand what kind of agents are willing to fight for your business.

A *full-service travel agent* works for an agency that has received accreditation—meaning approval to sell services—from airlines, cars, planes, trains, hotels, and most other vendors. She will work through a computer system that gives her the "world at her fingertips." The full-service agency she works for had to prove their reliability before receiving access to airline tickets and other expensive property, so this agent comes with at least a basic guarantee of financial reliability. An IATAN (International Association Travel Agent Network) number identifies her agency as a full-service firm. Most full-service agents are cruise experts, but some specialize in business travel. Full-agency status, by itself, does not guarantee a knowledgeable agent. Find out if they're qualified before booking.

There are also two kinds of *cruise-only travel agencies*. To blindly state the obvious: One type, we'll call it Cruise Agency A, books only cruises—not tours, airline tickets, cars, or hotels. Any service normally handled by a cruise line reservationist, such as pre-cruise tours or airline tickets, can be booked by this cruise-only agent. It may seem as if they can arrange other travel, but if they do, they must somehow work through a full-service agency, either as an outside agent (they're not paid a salary) or indirectly through a full-time travel agent. Within the travel industry, the joke is that to become a cruise-only agent, all you need is a phone line. The smallest "agency" may be a single person working out of her living room and making reservations through her home phone line. She may be fresh out of travel school and never been to sea; on the other hand, she may be a world traveler with eighty-three cruises under her belt—booking cruises is only a hobby. Even the best small-time cruise agent may not have access to the last-minute discounts faxed to the larger firms, however. Find out.

The second type of cruise-only agency, Cruise Agency B, is, in fact, a full-service travel agency in disguise. They have simply defined themselves as a cruise-only agency to serve the highly profitable cruising market niche. If the Sunday travel section posts full-page ads for a cruise-only agency, for example, they could be a full-service firm. These cruise-only agencies many times offer the best prices and/or the best advice simply because they sell the most cruises. They also tend to be aggressive in selling their services—there's a lot of competition—but may also offer the best deals, perhaps promising to "beat everyone else's price." Some—not all—shortchange customer service for sales, however, hiring people who can sell rather than people who really understand the business. Find out.

Membership in an industry association does not guarantee competence or knowledge, but it does tend to weed out the truly bad eggs. One independent travel association, NACOA (National Association of Cruise Only Agencies), does minor policing of the cruise-only ranks. For more information, contact NACOA at (305) 663-5626, or write to them at: 7600 Red Road, Suite 128, Miami, FL 33143.

Full-service agencies may be a member of ASTA (American Society of Travel Agents). These agencies adhere to a code of ethics and, like NACOA, the affiliation does not guarantee quality, but few questionable firms are members. Most agencies affiliated with either ASTA or NACOA post a sticker on their front door or somewhere inside.

While agencies may be certified, there's no test or licensing board to qualify people to become cruise counselors. Having access to a cruise line reservationist is the only requirement. One association, however—CLIA (Cruise Line International Association)—does have voluntary independent training programs for agents. Once trained, a travel agent may use the initials ACC (Accredited Cruise Counselor) or, with additional training, MCC (Master Cruise Counselor) after their name. Many great travel agents who understand the cruise market are not accredited ACC or MCC counselors. But if blindly calling around to find a competent agent, both designations identify an agent who takes her job seriously, and, in my experience, there are few losers in the bunch. Those in the business just for the money rarely invest in the program.

CLIA also certifies travel agencies as cruise experts, though the designation does not provide a guarantee that every travel agent employed within is a cruise expert. Best bet if searching for a cruise-competent agent: Go to a CLIA travel agency and ask for either an ACC or MCC accredited agent. To find a CLIA certified travel agent nearby, visit their Web site—*www.cruising.org*—or call them at (212) 921-0066. Most CLIA agencies display the CLIA logo on the agency's front door; many also use it in their local phone book ads.

THE INTERNET

To get a cruise line overview and compare lines, the Internet provides the perfect forum. While travel agencies stock brochures, they don't always have information on the smaller lines—but the Internet does. In addition, cruise line Web sites can offer far more information than that found in any single brochure, especially when the search has been narrowed and you're ready for specific information on a ship or itinerary. For those without Internet access, most libraries offer free connections and, once online, it's easy to use the addresses listed here to move from site to site.

A handful of cruise lines even allow guests to book directly through their Web site, though most do not. And of those who do accept direct bookings, they rarely offer better deals than you can get through a travel agent. One exception: Selected travel agencies that work online have become dumping grounds for cheap, last-minute cabin sales. For more information, go to Chapter 4.

Web site addresses, by cruise line, are listed in Chapter 8. Most lines also allow visitors to request a "real" brochure by mail, making the Internet a convenient way to request a range of information. Carnival itself offers a mega-site of all its companies—Carnival, Holland America, Windstar, Cunard, Seabourn, and Costa—at *www.leaderships.com*.

SAILING WITH THE BIG BOYS— MEGA-CRUISE LINES

Even non-cruisers know most of the big players in the cruise market, though you only need a brochure and old tugboat to call yourself a cruise line. The mega-lines, however, have many ships, a young fleet, and a reputation to uphold. Each also tries to cultivate a distinct brand image to separate it from the competition. Generally, relatives don't recognize ship names; they do, however, know cruise lines. A "cruise on the *Ecstasy*" may not mean much; a "Carnival cruise" does.

Members of the big boy club include Carnival Cruise Lines, Celebrity Cruises, Holland America Line, Norwegian Cruise Line (NCL), Princess Cruises, Royal Caribbean, and, in non-U.S. waters, Star Cruises. Up-and-coming stars include the Disney Cruise Line and Costa. The down-but-coming-back boys include Cunard and Premier.

While the big boys strive to differentiate themselves from each other, in a true contradiction, they're very much alike. Even as they serve up a resort-style vacation with activities for all generations, they hone their product to appeal to a specific type of passenger. Within the industry, for example, Holland America is generally known as a line for older adults, but they also have a good kids' program. They appreciate the "good for older travelers" designation if it brings in passengers, but fight it when it drives away families. The rest follow suit in some way—fine for everyone but perfect for a specific type of passenger.

Carnival Corp., parent company of Carnival Cruise Lines, is the Microsoft of the high seas, controlling a huge share of the industry through more than one cruise line. For that, it deserves special mention. In this and most guides, the name "Carnival" refers simply to Carnival Cruise Lines—the corporation's largest division— rather than the parent company. For those turned off by Carnival's (the line not the company) balance of affordability and glitzy style, however, Carnival Corp. has other mass-market lines that don't directly compete for the same type of cruiser. Holland America, in fact, is part of the family, as is the upscale sailing ships of Windstar Cruises. For big and formal cruising, go with company-owned Cunard Line; for upscale luxury on smaller ships, sail with corporate-owned Seabourn Cruise Line. Carnival Corp. even holds an interest in Costa Cruises and, in 2000, became a partial owner of NCL.

A final note on the big boys: Since most members fight for roughly the same audience, they have a vested interest in keeping prices competitive. People considering a Princess cruise, for example, may be simultaneously considering Royal Caribbean. As a result, they tend to even out service. Many clients base a final decision on a pile of brochures and a travel agent's advice; at that point, passengers tend to compare prices. To justify an extra $10 per person per day, for example, one line must offer at least one service that's dramatically better than the competition. "Excellent" food compared to "okay" food might justify a price difference, but "somewhat better" food usually does not. In other words, competition forces the big players to become more alike—or give potential clients some very good reasons to pay more for their service.

While they have distinct differences, Royal Caribbean, Princess, Holland America, Carnival, and NCL fight each other for the same passengers. As they continue to add ships and grow, expect their quality to become even more alike, even as they continue to refine their "style" to appeal to specific types of people.

The cruise industry today is a mass of consolidation. The big guys get bigger and the little guys hold their own by appealing to a clearly defined special interest passenger.

BROCHURES: YOUR PRIMARY CONTACT WITH THE CRUISE LINE

Cruise lines cannot interact directly with consumers. They rely on travel agents to take care of booking details, and they rely on brochures to convince passengers that they're the best on the market. While Internet Web sites have started to gain ground on the lowly brochure, most people still make a decision based on what they read in their printed material.

As the primary means of advertising, cruise line brochures come on quality paper with flashy photos and intriguing ad copy. Some lines produce several brochures, each highlighting a different ship, area of the world, or type of cruise. Other lines produce one large brochure that features every ship and itinerary in their fleet. Regardless of organization method, though, all look vaguely alike.

Brochures start with a commercial. They highlight pictures of food, probably lobster or steak. They showcase drinks with little umbrellas and couples gazing lovingly into each other's eyes or into the sunset across the rail of a ship. Tanned and lean twenty-somethings may be working out in the gym or enjoying a massage. One or two shots will even focus on mature couples, usually dressed to the nines and eating, drinking, or dancing on an outside deck. The ad copy not only pushes the cruise line, it also pushes cruising as "the best vacation value on the market today," since travelers-to-be may be in the early stages of vacation planning—not yet sure if they want to cruise, tour, or go it alone. Today, roughly 11 percent of Americans have cruised. That means that 89 percent have not— a huge market the cruise lines desperately want to tap.

After the first few pages, the brochure gives specific information on itineraries and ships. Depending on the line, a ship may be described alongside its itinerary, or the ship and itinerary may be in separate sections. Look for the following details:

• **Prices.** Not completely worthless, the listed brochure prices can best be described as "guidelines." They're good for comparing one cruise line to another. They're vaguely worthwhile for comparing one cabin category to another. They may even be almost accurate if planning a cruise over the winter holidays. Otherwise, the price actually paid should be less than that listed and only remotely related. (See Ways to Shave Money off the Cost of a Cruise.)

• **Port charges.** The current trend, expected to continue, is to include port charges in the total brochure cost quoted to a passenger. Port charges are basically the fees that ships pay to foreign governments for the right to use their ports. Part of a port charge goes to keeping the port accessible, clean, and working. Most goes to keep the local government functioning without raising residents' taxes. In the past, the port charge was listed separately from the total cruise price on the weak argument that "countries can raise the tax at any time and we reserve the right to increase the amount, even after a booking has been made." But that extra and somewhat hidden expense proved too tempting for many cruise lines. Because cruise passengers tend to compare cabin prices, one line could keep rates low and say that "Prices start at $799"—yet still *raise* rates by increasing the unadvertised-yet-additional port charge, even if no foreign government raised the actual port taxes lately. Once one line used this method to hoodwink customers, others felt they had to follow suit to keep their advertised prices competitive. With charges of fraud and deceptive advertising flying about in courts of law, policies began to change. Nevertheless, check the individual line's policy closely. If they do add port charges separately, it should be listed on the same page that details cabin prices.

• **Air transportation.** The stated price may or may not include airfare, but their system is explained somewhere in the brochure. For a complete outline on the advantages of using cruise line air, see the next section.

• **Ship diagrams.** These can be confusing at best. Like a set of building blocks, side-by-side colored diagrams show the ship's decks in the order in which they're stacked from top deck to bottom deck. If you use your imagination, you can guess whether a cabin is above or below the disco.

Cabins are usually color-coded, with each shade representing a different price category. Public areas—restaurants, casinos, spas, stores, and others—include tiny tables, chairs, and dance floors. While these detailed drawings reinforce the "we've got everything" sales pitch, they add unnecessary detail when you actually select a cabin. Take a magnifying glass along to the travel agency.

• **Bed configuration.** Unless considering a newer ship where "all twin beds convert to a queen," look for small diagrams within cabins specifying the type of beds available. If you demand a double bed, do a quick scan of the options. On older ships, expect most beds to be twin beds that are difficult or impossible to push together. In the least expensive cabins—each ship generally has only a few—expect "upper and lower berths," meaning bunk beds.

An "upper berth" in nonsuite cabins may accommodate up to four (rarely five) people in one cabin if you're traveling with grandchildren or another couple you feel very close to. (In a single cabin, take "close to" literally.) "Upper berth" means that a bed drops down from the wall for nighttime sleeping. During the day, the room steward returns the berth to its upright position, making the room feel less confining. Few cabins, however, can accommodate four people without feeling like a sardine can.

• **Pre- and post-cruise packages.** Many guests want to extend their vacation on the If-I'm-flying-all-the-way-to-Florida-I-might-as-well-see-Disney-World theory. The brochure will list a series of optional trips, called "add-ons," with prices. Add-ons may be taken either before the ship sails or after it returns. In general (meaning check the specifics), a pre- or post-cruise package includes hotel room, hotel taxes, admission to local parks or attractions, and some kind of transportation—in most cases, a rental car. Fine print will give the cruise line the right to change hotels or other package details after booking, but as a matter of course, that rarely happens.

Booking a hotel and seeing the sights can be done without cruise line help, of course, but there are advantages in using the cruise line's add-ons.

• Advantages: By booking a brochure add-on, your entire vacation comes under the cruise line's umbrella. You need only turn to the travel agent and say, "We'd like to add these three days in Orlando." She calls the cruise line; they do the rest. When travel documents arrive, vouchers will be included to cover the rental car, transfers, hotel, admissions, and anything else offered. At the hotel, simply hand over the hotel voucher. At parks or attractions, don't worry about standing in line to buy tickets.

Perhaps the strongest reason to book one of the cruise line's add-on packages comes into play only if something goes wrong. More than one vacationer made a hotel reservation three months in advance and, after arrival, listened to the front desk clerk say, "I'm sorry, but we're not showing a 'John Smith' in our computer." Should this happen on a cruise package, you have recourse. A quick call to the cruise line starts a series of phone calls, perhaps from cruise rep to hotel rep and on up the ladder of responsibility. Someone, somewhere, will find you a room—if not in the promised hotel then perhaps in something better. The same is true for other potential travel problems. Since the cruise line made your reservation, they accept responsibility if something goes wrong.

• Disadvantages: Passengers may not want to take a cruise line's package for, say, Disney World if they've been there before and know where they want to stay and what they want to do. The cruise line will offer only a few hotel options. Because their add-ons must appeal to all segments of the population, they tend to be middle-of-the-road accommodations or just one luxury choice. In the Orlando example, included tickets may not cover the sites you really wish to see. If portions go unused, money is wasted.

Also, that add-on may not be a bargain. Most tourist destinations have "seasons" but cruise add-ons may not. That "add-on" may be a financial bonanza if it's February in the Caribbean, but the same accommodations may be overpriced if visiting in May. In addition, cruise add-ons never honor discounts from AARP, AAA, or other programs that may be valid if booking the package on your own.

One more reason to avoid add-ons: Guests may wish to spend a day or two on their own or visiting nearby relatives. Most add-ons are take-it-or-leave-it.

As a rule of thumb, people visiting an area for the first time tend to take a cruise line's package. People visiting for the second time already know the lay of the land, and some—but not all—feel confined by an add-on's limited options.

• **Legal information.** Called something like "The Fine Print," "General Information," or "What You Need to Know," one to three pages in the back of the brochure list the nitty-gritty things that really matter. Because it contains need-to-know facts, a full description can be found in Chapter 5.

Airfare or "Only Birds Fly Free"

One trend, falling out of vogue, is to say, "Free airfare from your home city." Many lines now list a cruise-only price in the brochure, and then add a few dollars to the "air add-on" to make the entire package more expensive. Get a feel for this by comparing costs. If Cruise Line A charges $100 more than Cruise Line B for airfare from Cincinnati to Miami and the cruise price quoted is identical, Cruise Line A either turns a higher profit, offers a better cruise, or negotiated poorly with the airlines.

ADVANTAGES TO BOOKING A FLIGHT THROUGH THE CRUISE LINE

Like the "add-ons" just discussed, the strongest argument for flying to a cruise on air booked by the cruise line are (a) simplicity and (b) peace of mind. It's simple because clients tell their travel agent to include the airfare, she tells the cruise line, and the cruise line issues the tickets—a morning flight the day of departure. Tickets arrive in the travel agent's office with all other cruise documents. If a snowstorm hits the day of departure and all flights are canceled, cruise-booked airline guests are covered. If a substantial number of people run late thanks to bad weather, the cruise line even holds the ship. If a handful of people run late, the cruise line may give them a hotel room and fly them to the first port of call. They key word is "cruise line." *You* don't have to worry.

One additional advantage to booking cruise line airspace is, on rare occasion, also a disadvantage: Most large cruise lines include luggage tags with the final documents. Guests fill out the tags, attach them to luggage, and check them in at their airport of departure. Cruise line personnel collect the luggage at the final airport and transfer it to the ship. Once checked, guests don't see their luggage until a few hours after they board. While that sounds like a strong advantage, on very rare occasions, luggage gets lost and guests have no way of knowing where it might have gone. It's not uncommon for an airline to say they delivered the luggage to the cruise line, and for a cruise line to say they never received it. The passenger—caught in the middle—doesn't know who to blame and may be ineligible for compensation from either one. To avoid this problem, a few cruise lines expect passengers to claim their own luggage before handing it to company bus drivers upon arrival in a port city. If you prefer, that's always your option. If you want to keep tabs on your luggage—and are willing to forgo the luxury of not toting bags around an airport—don't put the cruise line's tags on until after your luggage has been claimed, then hand them to the cruise line's greeters. If the luggage doesn't show up . . . well, at least you know who to blame.

DISADVANTAGES TO BOOKING A FLIGHT THROUGH THE CRUISE LINE

To oversimplify a complicated deal: (1) It's usually cheaper to let the cruise line book air tickets during peak travel times. (2) It's usually cheaper to book your own tickets in slower seasons or off-days. (3) Sometimes, the last two statements are false.

Airlines change fares constantly depending on a lot of variables including fuel costs and new competition in the market. Airfare prices in cruise line brochures are negotiated many months in advance. If air ticket prices go down, the brochure rates may be more expensive; if ticket prices go up, the brochure may offer a good deal. Since this varies by city, date, and market conditions, a travel agent offers the best advice.

Today's best travel deals are usually found through newer airlines, with Southwest the best example. On occasion, it's still possible to fly coast to coast for around $200 if you take the time to request e-mail updates from Southwest and travel in slower seasons. If Southwest or its low-fared airline friends serve a city near you—many times a small city that's close to a big city—the money you save could be used to arrive one day early and pay for a hotel room, guaranteeing an on-time arrival at the ship and a bonus day to enjoy the local sights.

A second disadvantage to cruise line flights: Many travelers hate commuter planes, those thirty-passenger turboprops that connect small cities to larger ones. But if booking air through a cruise line, travelers give up control over the size of the plane and the route it will take. Two weeks before sailing, you receive tickets and itinerary, only to discover a two-hour layover in Detroit, even though you're flying from Kansas City to Miami. Your plane? A turboprop once used by Sky King. (In fairness, most cruise line-booked flights are convenient and reasonably timed, but they rarely avoid smaller planes.)

IF YOU DO CHOOSE TO LET THE CRUISE LINE BOOK YOUR TICKETS: First, request anything you specifically want. If you ask to fly on only jets, you may be told that "the cruise line tries to accommodate special requests, but does not guarantee it." If you want to connect through "any airport except Atlanta," you'll hear the same thing, as you will if you request a Delta flight to rack up extra frequent flyer points. Still, most cruise lines try to honor special flight requests.

Assume the worst has happened: You booked air through the cruise line, and against your adamant wishes, it consists of three flight segments, all on turboprops. If the cruise line cannot do anything or it's too late to reissue tickets, ask your travel agent to call the airlines directly and, quite simply, beg. An airline representative may quote rules and regulations, but the bottom line is that they own the planes, they schedule the flights, and they can do whatever they want. They may want to charge you for the flight change in the range of $50; or they may try to charge you substantially more for booking a last-minute ticket rather than handling it as a change. The first charge you probably cannot avoid; the second charge you can argue about.

The best advice: For peace of mind, people who book air through the cruise line should plan to live with whatever they get. Most of the time, it will be extremely convenient. Ninety-nine percent of the time, it will be fine. If part of the unlucky 1 percent, make a fuss.

Some cruise lines will guarantee special airline requests, but may charge a fee for the service, roughly $30 to $50 per person. Check the cruise line brochure for details. In general, airline tickets are the last thing issued by a cruise line. When you reserve a cruise, the line "blocks off" airspace (tells the airline to hold seats). About one month before departure, the cruise line checks for flight changes that may have occurred since blocking off the seats, and if still acceptable, prints tickets. Once printed, the tickets are official—subject to the airline's cancellation and change rules, a fact clearly stated in the cruise line brochure. To save time and money, make any airfare requests at least two months ahead of time—and preferably when you make your cruise reservation.

One more note on cruise line-issued air tickets: Confirm your own seat assignments. If not done, you may get stuck between two sumo wrestlers. Many big cruise lines now pre-assign seats as a customer courtesy; and if they don't, a good travel agent takes care of this detail. If in going through your travel documents two weeks before departure you discover that you don't have seat assignments, however, call the airline or your travel agent. Rules vary from airline to airline, but most allow passengers to pre-assign seats three or four weeks before departure on a first come/first served basis.

IF YOU CHOOSE TO BOOK AIRLINE TICKETS ON YOUR OWN: Plan for the worst. Everything will probably run like clockwork, but have a backup plan. Budget carriers may operate only one flight per day out of a city, for example. If it's canceled or postponed, hours may pass before guests are assigned to another airline or the company substitutes a different plane. Depending on schedule, a three-hour delay could mean the difference between cruising and missing the ship. Should a carrier postpone or delay a flight, demand that they put you on the next departing flight, regardless of the airline. With competition from other frustrated passengers who also demand justice, the squeakiest wheels many times get the most grease. To avoid this problem, consider taking a flight the day before and relaxing until time to board.

Finally, if booking your own flights, take care of the details. A travel agent should arrange for seat assignments, boarding passes (if allowed), and special meals. If booking flights directly or through the Internet, however, these details are your responsibility.

ITINERARIES OR "IF IT'S TUESDAY, THIS MUST BE CANCÚN"

In general, Alaska travelers want to see Alaska, European travelers want to see Europe, and Asian travelers want to see Asia. In the Caribbean and a few other destinations, however, most people just want to cruise and, while out there, see something else. While a cruise ship continues to function while in port, expect fewer activities since most passengers disembark. Most times, casinos shut down in deference to local laws.

"I JUST WANT THE CRUISE." To avoid land, consider a repositioning cruise, a trans-ocean sailing (Pacific or Atlantic), or the Caribbean. In general, an eastern Caribbean itinerary leaves from a Florida port and stops in St. Thomas, the Bahamas, and possibly a third country or a cruise line's private island. It requires a lot of water-time to get to everything, however, and ships usually spend two to three full days at sea, making it the best choice for those who wish to avoid ports. Trans-ocean sailings do the same thing but with even fewer ports, while a repositioning cruise (one that "repositions" a ship from Alaska to the Caribbean, for example) also spends a lot of time at sea.

"THE SHIP IS MY HOTEL, THE PORTS ARE MY DESTI-NATION." Obviously, a cruise filled with daily port excursions answers this need, but be wary of trips that pack in too much. On cruise schedules, ports tend to be visited in the morning, with either a late afternoon or evening departure. With many things to see and perhaps only nine hours to see them, many passengers take on a racetrack mentality. The starting gun goes off when the ship announces that it's safe to disembark. From there, the passengers who see the most win the race. There's nothing wrong with that, but it turns an excursion into a marathon, especially if repeating the process every day.

More ports, interpreted by immature travelers as "more things to see," does not make a specific cruise more valuable. Most mature travelers seek a balance between ports and days at sea, and don't overdo either one.

TRAVELING SOLO: THE WIDOW'S WALTZ

Except for the paying-for-a-room part, cruising is the ideal vacation for single women. If looking for a mate, you may be successful. If looking for a good time and companionship, what are you waiting for? On many ships, more than 25 percent of the passengers are single. The communal dining atmosphere of a cruise lends itself to conversation, and a request to dine with other singles is usually honored.

On cruises as in life, most older singles tend to be women. A number of cruise lines recognize that and pepper the mix with dance hosts (or social hosts). These hosts, in exchange for a free or inexpensive cruise, agree to show up at all social functions and dances. They also take part in other activities where the male/female mix sparks the activity and there's likely to be an overabundance of the latter. Wishing not to taint their image with charges of less-than-honorable conduct, cruise lines have strict rules for hosts when it comes to romance, and they offer companionship only—at least while at sea.

The Working Vacation Inc., a cruise consulting firm, hires gentleman hosts (dance hosts) for some of the cruise lines. Their clients include Cunard (all cruises), Delta Queen Steamboat Co. (all cruises), Holland America (all ships but not all cruises), Radisson Seven Seas (occasionally), Seabourn (all cruises), Silversea (all ships but not all sailings), and World Explorer (Alaska only). For more information on The Working Vacation's partner cruises—or to find out how to apply for a job as a gentleman host—visit their Web site at *http://www.theworkingvacation.com*. Other cruise lines that use dance hosts include Commodore (*Enchanted Isle* during the summer months), Crown (selected sailings only), and Crystal (four or more on each cruise).

If traveling alone, two potential problems arise: the crew and the cost. First, the crew.

Men make up the lion's share of a ship's staff. Employed at sea, they meet few single women other than passengers and can dish out romance like Tom Jones in concert. If looking for love on the high seas, rest assured that a crew member wants to make sure you find it. Just don't leave your common sense at the dock. That's not to insult all crew members, but a handful of men on all lines willingly offer romance sugarcoated with lies and finalized with you'll-never-hear-from-me-agains. Know the score, understand yourself, and do what makes you happy. I do know of one case where a crew member met a travel agent, kept in touch, and their romance is in full bloom. Still, that's the exception—not the rule (also see Security in Chapter 1).

The cost of single travel may be another story. From a business angle, cruise rates are based on double occupancy, meaning two individuals' fares equal the total amount of money received per cabin. If one person takes an entire cabin, that cuts cruise line income by half—unless they charge that single passenger more. And they do. The single cost could go as high as double for a holiday sailing or suite or, rarely, be nonexistent if the ship sails partially empty (see Chapter 4 for details on pricing).

• **Romance.** If your cruise vacation has a goal, such as finding a mate, pick a large ship. Size, quite simply, provides a bigger pool of potential partners. To up the chances of finding a similar-aged spouse, consider Holland America, Princess, or Royal Caribbean. Crystal and the *QE 2* generally host a number of single women over fifty. (Good for men; perhaps not so good for women.)

- **Theme cruise.** By choosing a theme cruise—big band, for example—there's a good chance that other single travelers will share at least one of your hobbies. The same is true with a soft adventure cruise—a small ship in Alaska, for example.
- **Wild oats.** The adults tend to be younger, but Windjammer must be mentioned. Many passengers seeking romance and a bit more find it on Windjammer. With fewer older adults and a smaller ship, there are no guarantees, but . . .
- **Find a friend.** Of course, finding a friend to travel with may be the best and simplest solution to traveling alone. Check first in familiar haunts, such as where you worship, where you bowl, where you volunteer, where you work, or within a special interest group. There are also a handful of resources for women seeking travel partners. While women-only travel groups don't usually offer many cruises—they're too easy to book alone—many have bulletin boards on the Internet for those seeking same-sex companionship. Consider:
  - **Elderhostel,** 75 Federal St., Boston, Mass. 02110. Phone: 877-426-8056. Web site: *www.elderhostel.org.*
  - **The Travel Companion Exchange,** P.O. Box 833, Amityville, NY 11701. Phone: 800-392-1256.
  - **The Women's Travel Club,** 21401 N.E. 38th Ave., Aventura, FL 33180. Phone: 800-480-4448. Web site: *www.womenstravelclub.com.*
  - **Women Traveling Together,** 1642 Fairhill Drive, Edgewater, MD 21037. Phone: 800-795-7135. Web site: *www.women-traveling.com.*

TAKING THE FAMILY—REUNIONS AND GROUP RATES

Cruising is the perfect family reunion vacation if you can afford to take all the kids, grandkids, and miscellaneous loved ones. Few vacations can be called "perfect," but on the large resort ships, the activities and group meals can keep everyone happy, except maybe for the fifteen-year-olds that aren't happy anywhere. Besides, spending your kid's inheritance doesn't seem so shameful if you take them along.

On a cruise, family togetherness usually revolves around meals, where all ages sit together and spend a guaranteed hour or two per meal conversing. Since everyone orders what he or she wants and no one fights over the check, the pressure is off. During the day, kids can go to the children's program, adults to an educational lecture, and teens to the swimming pool, all while poor cousin Fred loses his last dollar in the casino.

In addition, a family (or any group) can get sizable discounts and free cabins if enough people go along. See Chapter 4 for more information.

ACCESS FOR THE DISABLED

Traditional ocean vessels were not built for people with physical disabilities—they were built to float and keep errant water outside the ship. To do that, builders put lips (a one-inch-plus piece of metal sticking up from the floor that must be stepped over) in doorways so water could not enter, inadvertently blocking wheelchair access at the same time. With a finite amount of space on board, they also maximized the use of space, which generally means keeping hallways tight and bathrooms small. While other physical disabilities—poor eyesight, hearing loss, etc.—can be accommodated easily, wheelchair passengers face the greatest challenge.

On the newest ships, that's changing. While the Americans with Disabilities Act requires wheelchair access for most U.S. buildings, ships—registered in other countries and sailing in international waters—do not have to obey U.S. laws. Still, from a pure business point of view, it behooves the lines to be accessible; as a result, many now are. Princess, for example, adheres to the ADA accessibility requirements, even though it's not required. In general, ships built in the last five or so years tend to be completely accessible. Ships between five and ten years old are fairly accessible. Check all others closely before booking.

• **Wheelchairs.** Adults who can walk short distances should be okay on most cruises. The main problem, however, is transfering to land on a tender, a small boat, used when a ship cannot dock against a pier and passengers must be transported to land. The move from ship to tender, by way of a ramp with railings, generally requires a sense of balance and a bit of upper body strength. Moving the empty wheelchair from ship to tender to land may also prove difficult. If this sounds like a problem, confirm details with your travel agent before putting down a deposit—or plan to stay aboard when in port.

For those confined to a wheelchair, the first rule of thumb: Avoid older ships. Even pre-1990 ships fitted with wheelchair accessible rooms may have inaccessible public areas thanks to lips on doorways or thin hallways. Second rule of thumb: Get all guarantees in writing from both travel agent and cruise line representative. If you request one of the ship's four wheelchair accessible rooms and discover, once on board, that the ship reassigned you, those names, dates, and black-and-white receipts may be worth their weight in gold.

If traveling in a wheelchair, confirm the following before booking passage:

1. Is the cabin completely accessible? Do bathroom doors open out, closets have low hooks, furniture sit far enough apart to navigate on wheels, and entrances accommodate the width of a wheelchair?

2. Does the bathroom have a lip at the entrance? Does the shower have bars or enough room for a wheelchair? Are cabinets low enough to use?

3. Where is the ship's elevator in relation to your cabin? Does the elevator stop on all decks? Perhaps just as important: In the unlikely event of an emergency where elevators cannot be used, such as a fire, how would a wheelchair-bound passenger escape? Can lifeboats be reached without the use of an elevator? Are lifeboats wheelchair accessible?

4. Are all ship doorways wheelchair friendly or only a select few—just enough for the cruise line to call itself "accessible"?

5. Are any rooms or balconies or bathrooms accessed by way of a too-skinny hallway?

6. Does the cruise line offer wheelchair-accessible transfers from plane to ship?

7. How often will you need to board a tender to transfer from ship to port? What is the procedure? What are the

difficulties? Note too that accessibility laws in port cities may not match those in the U.S. On shore excursions, taxis, vans, helicopters, and other boats may not accommodate wheelchair guests.

8. Are pre- and post-cruise transfers, airlines, hotels, and rental cars accessible? Your travel agent should confirm that everybody along the way is prepared to do his or her part.

9. If you need special services, such as a collapsible wheelchair, does the cruise line provide it?

10. Traveling solo while in a wheelchair can, at times, present a challenge. If traveling alone, find out how much the crew will help with transfers. Generally, help is not a problem, but it may depend on the nuances of ship policy and the limitations of their liability insurance.

When booking, consider a larger cabin if it fits into the budget. Even accessible cabins tend to be small, making it more difficult to maneuver. Also, check with the maître d' upon arrival to make sure your table accommodates a wheelchair and sits outside the main walkway.

• **Hearing impaired.** Hearing-impaired guests rarely have trouble beyond that experienced on land. Public address system announcements may, however, be a problem. While this may actually be a benefit on those lines that announce something every two minutes—from bingo in the ballroom to little Suzy's second birthday—emergency instructions or time-to-go-ashore announcements may be missed. Before booking, find out if the ship can retrofit rooms with auxiliary devices, or if room stewards willingly take on the responsibility of keeping hearing-challenged guests updated on events. Passengers that rely on hearing aids should always pack extra batteries—they can be hard to find on many ships and in many ports. Many ships have accessibility kits that can adapt any cabin to accommodate the hearing impaired.

• **Sight impaired.** Many ships—but not all—allow guide dogs on board. Foreign countries have their own rules, however, and shore excursions may prove difficult if a country requires animal shots or incubation periods. Again, check the proposed itinerary and rules before booking.

For all disabilities, most cruise lines require an able-bodied traveling companion to go along, and they may also require a signed waiver that relieves them of responsibility. Read any waiver carefully and sign it only if comfortable with their demands. It probably will not be negotiable, however.

For more information on accessible travel on cruises and throughout the world, visit the Society for the Advancement of Travel for the Handicapped (SATH) Web site at **http://www.sath.org**, or write SATH at 347 Fifth Avenue, Suite 610, New York, NY 10016. Phone: 212-447-7284.

4

MONEY: WADING THROUGH THE MUCK TO FIND A BARGAIN

First, an assumption: You like to travel and, over time, plan to use a travel agent more than once. If you have no desire to find a permanent travel agent, speed read the first few paragraphs.

Unless you jumped directly to this chapter, you realize the value of a travel agent when things go wrong. For the 95 percent of cruise vacationers that require no more than advice, reservations, and final document presentation, it does not matter. But if you're one of the 5 percent that experiences some kind of problem—and before a problem occurs you don't know if you're part of the 5 percent or not—then you want a dedicated, full-service agent. If you've used a travel agent in the past and liked her, return.

NEGOTIATING A CRUISE DEAL

To find the least expensive cruise that fits your needs, take the following steps:

Step 1: Find a good travel agent. Start by questioning neighbors and friends. Ask them not only how helpful their travel agent is, but also ask how she handled problems if they arose (see Chapter 3).

If neither friends nor family can recommend an agent, you're on your own. With apologies to every good travel agent working in a small agency (I was one), large travel agencies usually offer better cruise deals than small ones. Agents work for a commission, and commission percentages (10 percent, 12 percent, etc.) go up based on total agency sales (and percentage of cruise sales sent to a given line). Hence, large agencies offer better cruise deals. In the end, an agency with forty agents sells a lot more than a mom-and-pop operation at 101 Main Street.

In most agencies, the first agent with a free second helps new clients that walk in the door. But if an agent has a "free second," she also tends to be the newest—or worse, the one whose past clients didn't like her well enough to return. For a stronger start, call agencies first. No matter who answers the phone, ask for the agent who has been on the most cruises. You'll probably get a name, say Kelly, followed by a "but I can help you." Thank her and ask how long Kelly has worked there, accepting any answer greater than two years. Thank her again and ask to be transferred to Kelly. If that seems rude, hang up and call back. Try not to have a lengthy conversation with the first agent—if you do, it becomes more difficult to then go with Kelly. It can be done, of course, and you're the one with the power, but it sends the not-so-subtle message that the first agent was not good enough to close the deal.

It's unrealistic to expect a travel agent to personally experience every ship and every cruise line. She should, however, know the answer to basic questions, such as, "What do I wear?" or "Do I need a birth certificate?" For a true test question, ask her about the "worst travel problem ever faced by one of your clients." An experienced agent without a good horror story is either new, forgetful, or lying. After the agent explains her "worst travel problem," ask how she handled it. Did she demand to talk to people higher up the supervisory ladder? Did she call the travel company owner or manager? Many agents work well when things go right; a golden few shine through when things go wrong.

If Kelly doesn't seem competent by this point, use the same technique at another large agency.

Step 2: Consider the agent you found, Kelly in the case above, your primary agent, the one who will *probably* book your cruise.

Remember that, if commissioned, Kelly stands to make a lot of money off this deal. If not commissioned, her agency will make a lot of money. You, in all good faith, plan to book through her. It's your nickel.

First, some background on how travel agencies work: Cruise lines—and all travel suppliers for that matter—understand that the travel agent sells many different travel products. As such, a travel agent's referral to any specific product, say an NCL cruise, carries a lot of weight. To increase the chances of a referral, cruise lines offer incentives to persuade an agent to recommend their product rather than the competition's ships. These incentives could be free travel or, the usual case, more money.

Cruise Line A may pay a travel agent the industry standard, 10 percent, on every cruise booked. Cruise Line B, however, may pay 14 percent. It comes as no surprise that the agent would rather sell Cruise Line B. Cruise Line B, grateful for the extra bookings, continues to pay that 14 percent, possibly pushing it up to 15 percent if total sales go high enough. Cruise Line A's commission rate stays at 10 percent, but that's okay. Cruise Line A has a similar arrangement with the travel agency down the street. In other words, all things considered, Kelly wants to give you the perfect cruise, but all things being equal, she'll recommend Cruise Line B over Cruise Line A. Travel agencies call the high-paying companies their "preferred suppliers."

How does a client know if a preferred cruise line is being pushed on them? In my experience, most travel agents want the 15 percent commission, but truly want the client to be happy. It's not just kindness; agents work for the long haul and want each client to return to book other travel and recommend them to all their friends. A steady roster of customers—a "following"—makes an agent invaluable to her employer.

But the truth is, many cruise lines have similar amenities. Princess and Royal Caribbean, for example, have many things in common including a general level of service, decor, and amenities. For the first-time cruiser who wants "what I saw on TV," either one fills the bill. If the agent makes 15 percent off Princess and 10 percent off Royal Caribbean—and if the cruise client has no preference—the travel agent will suggest Princess. And she'll make more money.

To understand the rules of the game, ask Kelly the following questions:

WHICH CRUISE LINES ARE PREFERRED SUPPLIERS?
Simple and direct, her ideal answer is that she has a "good working relationship" with (fill in the cruise line names), but she's booked clients on every cruise line. Most agencies have preferred suppliers. There's no sin in that. It is a sin to lie about it.

WHICH LINES HAVE YOU CRUISED WITH? Agents cannot go on every line, but as a matter of human nature, tend to refer clients to ones they've experienced, perhaps because they feel more comfortable talking about them. (Not coincidentally, they tend to cruise with preferred suppliers.)

Step 3: Narrow down the choices and don't be afraid to commit. If you seem like a dreamer rather than a doer, Kelly will probably hand you a small pile of brochures, suggest you "look through them," and "give me a call when you decide."

Barring that scenario, most agents walk clients through their options, narrow the choices down to one cruise line and one ship, and then suggest calling to see what's available, the first step leading to "holding something for you." Like a used car salesman—no offense intended—the travel agent sells a major product, and step by step, she leads clients up to the point of sale. That's their job. If they don't close the sale, they've wasted their time. Sensing this impending sales closing, some people want to escape, to walk out with that pile of brochures rather than directly contact a cruise line. If unsure when to cruise or on what line, those instincts are good. But if you have it narrowed down and, within reason, want to know how much the trip will cost, allow her to make the call. Many agents do not want your money on a first visit as much as they want to "hold something." That level of commitment raises the conversation to the level of a "serious sale," even if you walk out the door without putting down a deposit.

The travel agent makes the call or pulls up info on her computer screen. Because prices fluctuate from one ship sailing to another, the agent will, in your presence, ask about cabins available on a specific date, such as the September 3 sailing of the *Norway*. While on the phone, Kelly will point to cabins within a brochure's ship diagram. She'll say something like: "They have nothing left in category F through H, but we can get you a category E for only $1120 per person." Depending on the cruise line, she may quote a cabin number where, on the diagram before you, you can see where you will stay.

After discussing other open cabins, possible upgrades, and other deals, you'll probably find a cabin location you like at a reasonable price. The agent will then ask if you'd like to "hold" the cabin, assuring you that there's no obligation for doing so, but holding the cabin guarantees that it will still be available if you decide to accept the offer. That's true.

If the sailing date and price seem possible, allow her to hold the cabin. To complete the hold, she'll ask for exact names of passengers along with other details such as phone numbers, preferred dining times, and other questions that vary by line. (Now or at the time of deposit, make sure all names are spelled as they appear on a birth certificate or passport.)

Step 4: After a cabin is held, ask Kelly if there is any way to get a cheaper cruise. A good agent has already asked you if you're flexible, and if so, how much. While on the phone to the first cruise line, she should have already asked the cruise line rep about earlier or later sailing dates. She'll have discussed possible discounts already — traveling in the very slow season, booking a cheap cabin on a good ship, booking a good cabin on a cheap ship, etc. — and narrowed down your options. Once a cabin has been held, if not before, she should also talk about other cruise lines sailing the same itinerary at the same time, especially those that compete on roughly the same level of service. Now, she should call each of them for a price. Since extra calls take extra time, however, she may need a subtle push to continue working for your business.

When calling other lines, she can hold other cruise line's cabins if you wish. If she seems less enthusiastic, assume the first line she called is a preferred supplier and she'd rather sell you that space.

Step 5: Thank her for her time, take the brochures, and go home to "think it over."

If more than one cabin has been held in your name, pick the one you prefer. Once home, call at least three other travel agencies. Call one or two large agencies that advertise cruises heavily in the Sunday paper and have done so for a while. Many times—not always—they offer a better price. Tell them only that you're price shopping and give them the same date, ship, and cabin price category (not cabin number) already held in your name. If flexible and willing to travel with a different line, a different date, or a different itinerary, tell them that too—but always request a quote on the same ship being held by the first agent. For now, don't tell them you have a price quote already or, more importantly, what that price is. Then they'll know what they have to beat.

One of four things may happen. They may call back and (a) quote a price similar to the one quoted by the first agent, (b) quote a cheaper price but on a different cruise line or date, (c) quote a cheaper price or (d) quote a higher price.

If "a," it reconfirms that the first agent did a good job; if "d," she did a great job.

If "b," the agent can't even match the first quoted price or, thanks to her agency's preferred status with a different cruise line, can get a great deal but on a different line. This answer forces you to rethink where or when you'll be traveling. If you consider the newly recommended cruise reasonably priced and acceptable, call your first agent back and ask her to check availability on the newly recommended cruise line and get a price.

If "c," the second agency either has a better relationship with the cruise line, a special arrangement for that sailing, the agent cut her commission to offer a better deal, or some combination of the above. Travel agencies who net a 15 percent commission (or more) sell a lot of cruises. They also know that a potential customer who telephones is probably comparing prices, and they'll cut their commission even without knowing what price other travel agencies have quoted. Some agencies never cut commissions; many others do. When I worked as a commissioned travel agent, I quoted whatever I wanted. Most times, if the cruise line reservationist quoted a $1,000 per person cost and we made $150 (15 percent commission), I'd subtract $50 (5 percent) and without missing a beat, quote $950. I offered a competitive price while the agency still earned $100 per person. If booking two or more cabins at one time, I'd cut the price even more, figuring that the total amount of work will only be marginally more than the amount used for booking a single cabin—yet the total income substantially higher.

Most people don't realize that travel agencies can cut commissions and most travel agencies like it that way. If I quoted a lower rate and told a client that I'd cut my commission, the client would turn to the next agency and say, "So-and-so cut their commission by 5 percent. How much will you cut your commission?" It's not cost effective for travel agencies to get into a bidding war with the agency just down the street. If pushed for an explanation, the agent might say she "has some discount coupons in the back that we'll use for you," or the old standby, "I don't know why we're cheaper. I guess it's because we do such a large volume."

Step 6: If a competitor quotes a lower rate (choice "c" above), call your first agent, tell them about the lower price, and ask if they can match it. You can blame a concerned neighbor who "got a rate for me from her travel agent" if you don't want to admit that you went price shopping. Your original agent will ask if it's the same cabin category, the same sailing date, and the same ship. She will want to make sure the deal is identical — no hidden expenses to be added later. If she can't beat the competitor's price, she may lower her original quote a bit with a quiet apology of "that's the best I can do."

At this point, you can relax in the knowledge that you've received the lowest rate for your cruise, even if it came from a competing agency and a travel agent you're not sure you like. You've played agencies off each other without looking like a jerk and can now make an intelligent cruise decision.

One note of warning, however: If the savings quoted by one agency are dramatically less than another, make sure that the lower-quoting agent got all the details right. Ask directly: "Is this the total I would pay — no add-ons?" Port charges, airfare, and other "extras" may have been forgotten.

Step 7: Make your deposit. Most people automatically book with the low-quoting agency, even if it only saves them $10 per person. If, however, the prices are close — say $30 or less per person — *consider staying with your original travel agent and paying more.* Why? The original agent spent a lot of time helping you, but she's in a competitive business and that reason alone is no reason to be loyal. However, you know something about your first agent. You found her through either friends' recommendations or your own research.

At this point, she's trustworthy and likable. Think of a good travel agent as cruise insurance. Some (not all) big cruise-only agencies hire untrained agents, tell them how to close a cruise sale, and let them go. Agents receive rewards for booking guests, not building up agency business. You trust your bank, your supermarket, and your hairstylist. Finding a travel agent you trust (and like) is no less important.

ONE ADDENDUM TO THE BOOKING STRATEGY: Cruise lines usually hold cabins for seven to ten days (depending on cruise line and day of departure) before automatically canceling. A travel agent can usually request an extension, however, if you let her know you're still interested. Cruise lines do not, however, like to hold a reservation twice and, without telling you, more than one agent may try to hold a cabin. If a cruise line realizes what's happening—meaning two agents try to book under the same name—the line may deny the hold request from the second agent. If that second agent is the one you prefer to use, you may have to call the original agent and request that they transfer the reservation or cancel the "hold," hoping that the second agent can quickly go in and book the same room. Between phone calls, however, it could go to someone else. One trick may alleviate this: Keep the host cruise line's computer from recognizing the double booking by giving only a last name and first initials.

PAYING FOR THE CRUISE

While a cabin may be held in your name for seven or more days, it takes money to confirm it. Paying for the cruise is not difficult. Every brochure explains the cruise line's system, and every travel agent knows how to take your money. The actual amount of money required for a deposit varies, but could be a set dollar figure or a percentage of the total package. Crystal Cruises, for example, charges 10 percent of the total cruise package—an amount that can range from a $221 deposit per person for an inside room on a seven-day sailing up to $4,037 for the Crystal Penthouse on a twenty-three-day cruise.

Rule of thumb: the more expensive the cruise line, the higher the deposit. Most of the big players charge something like $100 per person for a three- or four-day sailing, $250 per person for a seven-day sailing, and $300 for anything ten days or longer.

Without a deposit on record (called in by the travel agent—not necessarily received yet) by the time a "hold" automatically cancels, a cabin goes back into inventory and you lose it unless you return, rebook, and miraculously find it still available. Once a deposit is received, however, few cruise lines automatically cancel a reservation if final payment is not received by the brochure-stated deadline—generally forty-five to sixty days before departure—but they will hound your travel agent for the money who, in turn, will hound you. The cruise line will not send airline tickets, cruise boarding passes, and other documents until final payment has been received, so it doesn't pay to delay the inevitable.

A few cruise lines now offer their own credit payment system that allows you to pay for a cruise over time. From a credit perspective, that's not wise, but if interested, ask your travel agent for more details.

Most cruise lines accept personal checks and major credit cards. They'll refund the full deposit amount for cancellation up to the point where full payment is due. (Read the brochure's fine print for your line's policy.) Also, ask your travel agent if she charges anything for a cancellation. A cancellation nets the travel agency nothing, and a reasonable fee can be expected unless you consistently bring travel business into the agency.

WAYS TO SHAVE MONEY OFF THE COST OF A CRUISE

Cruise lines must fill their ships, and they'd all like to have a guest in each cabin every cruise of the year—and paying the rate stated in the brochure. But it doesn't work that way. Certain seasons and destinations always have a higher demand than others do. The Caribbean beckons travelers in the winter as they escape foul weather. Alaska draws people in summer. Hordes of people love a Christmas cruise, but two weeks earlier, in the heart of the Christmas shopping season, many ships sail only partially full. Same ship, same itinerary, but much higher prices by choosing December 25 rather than December 11. Add cruise line competition into the mix—a battle heating up as new ships hit the water—and filling cabins proves to be an ongoing challenge for the cruise lines.

Many a high-paid marketer wants to find the magic formula to persuade a Christmas cruiser to sail a few weeks earlier, and over the years, the lines' marketing departments have come up with some tricks. It might be a theme cruise to draw big band lovers to a September departure. It might be a corporate meeting to wine and dine Fortune 500 bigwigs in early January. Most of the time, however, cruise lines simply cut the cost of a cabin to attract passengers.

A few years ago, cruise lines gave early reservations a marginal discount, and then, as the cruise departure date approached and they saw that the ship was not filling to expectations, they lowered the price. The savvy cruiser on a flexible schedule simply planned to depart in a slow season, waited until the last minute, and booked a cabin. Soon, however, everyone waited to book a cabin, and the cruise lines realized that they had lost control of their product. As a result, the system changed. Today, the early booker gets the cheap deal—usually. Unfortunately, the old problem still exists. If a ship has 500 cabins and, one month before sailing, has sold only 325 of them even with generous early booking discounts, it may not break even on costs.

QUICK ECONOMIC LESSON: Most ships have a break-even point for profits, and compared to the percentage of cabins, it's fairly high. In the 500-cabin example, the line may need 400 filled cabins to simply break even. That may seem high, but that makes the final 100 almost pure profit. While each cabin represents a marginally higher cost for food, most of a cruise line's costs are fixed—staff, fuel, loan payments, etc. That means that the 401st cabin sale—even at half price—represents almost pure profit.

Now assume that the ship has sold 425 cabins. Seventy-five remain empty, they've met their costs and, by twenty-five cabins, made a bit of a profit. It is to their advantage to sell those remaining seventy-five cabins, even at extremely low rates. But how to do that without offending those passengers who have already paid more? That is the challenge, and the lines have novel ways to deal with it.

NOTE: If comparing prices between two packages, break everything down into a per diem rate. ("Per diem" means "per day," and I don't know why we don't just say the "per day rate," but we don't.) Simply add up all costs per person—cruise, port charges, mystery things—and divide by the number of cruise days. For most mainstream cruise lines, the figure will be somewhere in the 100s per day, but can change substantially depending on ship and itinerary.

The following are ways to net a cheaper cruise deal, starting with the most obvious discounts and moving on to the less obvious ones:

• **Book early.** Six months or more before a sailing, cruise lines offer some of their lowest rates—on many ships, prices will never be lower. (Though that may change as more new ships enter service—especially if the economy enters a minor recession.)

How much will you save? When do you have to book? Most cruise lines have a discount rate published in their brochure. It could be a set figure or a sliding amount. The Delta Queen Steamboat Co., for example, offers a $250 travel allowance per person, or free airfare, if a cruise lasts six nights or longer and is booked six months in advance. Carnival's brochure, however, says, "Make reservations early and save up to $1,300 per stateroom" on the Carnival *Destiny*, though it's short on dates, applicable cabin categories, and seasons of the year. In other words, Carnival's savings vary.

Internally, some cruise lines—notably the ones with consistently high demand—hope the published early booking discount fills a ship six months in advance. Other lines, notably bigger ones, tinker with the amount of the early booking discount. If early reservations are weak, for example, the discount goes up. (A ship offering a $400 discount per person seven months out may, on just one seasonal sailing, offer an additional $100 discount if marketers predict that they'll have difficulty selling all the cabins.) Also, if the early booking discount ends six months out and a cruise has not sold enough cabins, it's common to hear a reservationist say, "Our early booking discount has been extended through (some new date)." If bookings seem slow for an entire season, the cruise line faxes news releases to travel agencies announcing the "early booking discount extension."

• **Off-season travel.** No secret, this is listed in the brochure rate structure. Some lines have two seasons; some have three. They may have names that vary from line to line, such as "value season" or "low season." Generally, a high season rate covers holidays such as

Christmas and New Year's, Easter, Fourth of July, and anytime the cruise line expects strong demand. An in-between rate, or base rate, covers times when people vacation. For a Caribbean cruise, that would be the winter months as well as traditional summer vacation months. In Alaska and Europe, it covers June through August.

Finally, the least expensive season—value season—covers times of low demand. In Alaska, May and September are cooler and less desirable. In the Caribbean, the lines' soft season includes late fall (not over Thanksgiving), early December, and late spring cruises. In Europe, spring and fall cost less.

When hoping for an off-season discount, consider dates in the brochure as the cruise line's best-guess estimate on which seasons will have the lowest demand and, hence, the lowest prices. As a rule of thumb too general to make (but made anyway), expect the best discounts to occur in the middle of a value season. For a cheaper cruise, people may be willing to travel one or two weeks earlier or later—but not six weeks. A value season cruise nestled snugly against a base season cruise will be the first to lose an off-season discount.

• **Call for a rate.** In practice, the seasons are not as clear-cut as they seem, and people rarely pay the brochure rate. A brochure rate may be $1,600, but when a travel agent calls to check availability, the cruise line reservationist may say, "I can let you have a category H (a price category) cabin for only $1,100." You don't know why the reservationist quoted a lower price; the travel agent does not know why. Some cruise line accountant or software program simply guessed that $1,100 is, at least for now, the necessary price to attract passengers. Alternately, the reservationist may say, "I can give you a category H cabin at the category K rate." That means that the $1,600 category H cabin will cost you only the $1,100 category K rate. Same savings—just a different way to word it. Without understanding where these lower prices come from, however, it puts passengers at an extreme disadvantage.

A cruise over Easter, for example, may be priced as high season. The following week may be base season, the week after value season. But since the cruise line can tinker with the prices for all three cruises, that value season cruise may cost almost the same as the base season cruise. You won't know that until you call though.

Since cruise line deals can change daily, the brochure price now becomes completely worthless.

• **Mature adult discounts.** These have a variety of names, but mature passengers (you) have all the characteristics necessary to fill off-season cabins—flexibility, a desire to travel, and money. Most times, they're not called a "mature travelers discount," but rather, they're given a special sale name and then marketed through older adult organizations. AARP members could, for example, "Save $200 per cabin on the S.S. *Anyship* throughout the month of October based on space availability." That "space availability" means that should the ship start to sell out, they'll drop the special like a hot potato. If the cruise line offers a generic discount, such as 5 percent off the brochure rate, ask for details—but many times, it's no better than other discounts offered on the same slow-booking cruise.

• **Third or fourth passengers cruise free.** This works well in seasons where families do not travel. Given the lack of privacy—not to mention space—with four people in one cabin, only parents or grandparents with children tend to use them. Two couples traveling together usually book separate cabins. Should you have some friends—very good friends—that you could share a cabin with, however, this deal can save a substantial amount of money. With two people traveling free, the total cost can be split four ways. Check the fine print before getting excited, however. They probably still levy port charges and other "extras." Airfare, for example, won't be included. Figure out the per diem rate described earlier to see if it's really a bargain.

• **"Two-for-one" cruise specials or "50 percent off second passenger."** The first person pays full brochure rate, the second travels free or at 50 percent discount off the brochure rate. Sounds great, but check if port charges and airfare are included in the deal. Remember also that the brochure rate is rarely charged in an actual price quote, and the first person's rate is higher than usual. Add port charges and airfare to the package and the deal may not be so great at all, sometimes no better than simply paying the going rate for the cruise. Another rule of thumb too general to make but made anyway: A two-for-one offer is probably a decent deal; a 50-percent-off-second-passenger offer is probably not.

• **Group discounts.** Deals vary if traveling with a group, but actual savings result from three factors: (a) who plans the trip, (b)

why they plan the trip, and (c) how many people go. A group booking works just like any other booking, and everyone nets some kind
of discount off the brochure rate, perhaps 10 to 30 percent. The
amount of the discount depends on overall passenger demand for
that particular sailing and the number of people you promise to
produce. A date with low booking expectations will garnish the
highest discount rate, as will a large group of people. Since few
people actually pay the published brochure rate, however, actual
savings vary.

The true advantage to a group booking comes from the free
cabins. Standards vary by line, but one person generally cruises
free with every fifteen paid passengers. If sixteen cabins are
booked (thirty-two people), one cabin (two people) cruises free.
How the group uses those free cabins affects the cost of the trip.

If your daughter-in-law plans the trip as a family reunion, for
example, those free cabins could either be given to the relative who
can least afford to go or split evenly, giving everyone a cheaper rate.
(Or your selfish daughter-in-law keeps it for herself and lies to you.)

Travel agencies may even book their own group sailings and sell
any free cabins to earn additional money. In this way, a large travel
agency can offer a "20 percent discount on the June 14 Alaska
cruise on Holland America." From Holland America's perspective,
this big agency now pushes their ship to people who otherwise
might have considered Princess. From the agency's perspective,
they can advertise cheaper prices and, with enough bookings, keep
100 percent of the money paid for their free cabins. From the
mature traveler's perspective, they can save 20 percent.

Many organizations such as AARP plan group sailings as a
service to members and to make money. Since these group organiz-
ers attract travelers from their own membership, it also guarantees
that passengers have something in common.

One other type of person tends to book group tours—people
who want to travel free. Since group tours book through travel
agents the same way individual cruises do, it's easy to arrange one—
a tour organizer needs only a busload of friends. And by selling the
minimum number of cabins, the organizer can cruise free. If interested in trying this, and to keep headaches to a minimum, let the
cruise line book airspace or, alternately, provide bus transportation
to the pier. (The cruise line may provide a bus if the group is big

enough and relatively close to the point of departure.) The tour planner takes on the headache of sales. She also takes on the headache of organization—what to do when Lou's Aunt Madie takes sick the day before sailing and, contrary to her best warnings, Lou did not take out insurance and must decide between losing money or ignoring Aunt Madie. Still, for many mature travelers, the perks of free travel more than compensate for the work involved with booking them.

- **Back-to-back cruises.** Take two cruises instead of one but stay on the same ship. A ship may depart Miami for the eastern Caribbean, for example, stopping in the Bahamas, St. Thomas, and their own private island before returning to Miami. The following week, the same ship could tour the western Caribbean, stopping in Mexico, Grand Cayman, and Jamaica, again returning to Miami. If you book both sailings at one time, many lines offer discounts.

- **Cabin upgrades.** Many lines offer, for a limited time, a "complimentary two-category (or three or four) cabin upgrade." Since the least expensive and most expensive cabins tend to sell out first, and since the cruise is already sailing at less-than-full capacity, the ship probably has available cabins in the middle categories. Whether or not it's a bargain depends on the rate they quote for the cabin and the guaranteed amount of the upgrade.

- **Category guarantee.** Sometimes passengers book a "category guarantee." When this happens, the agent will say something like: "I can guarantee a category H cabin or better at the category J price." In this example, clients get a two-category cabin upgrade and a *chance* to go even higher, though you will not be assigned an actual cabin until the day of departure. (Generally, however, your travel agent can call a day or two earlier and find out.) If considering this deal, look at the cabins within category H, the guaranteed minimum, and decide if they're acceptable. Look for cabins with a view obstructed by lifeboats or cabins on decks with an outside promenade. If any cabins are unacceptable, ask the travel agent to note them. She should say, "With the guaranteed upgrade, we can't promise anything, but I'll make sure your request is put into the record."

From the cruise line's perspective, the cabin guarantees give them flexibility. They can continue to sell whatever cabin categories they want, sure in the knowledge that they can stick you wherever they want. To be happy with the arrangement, however, never plan to get a cabin higher than the guarantee. It's not that a better one won't be offered, but it cuts the risk of disappointment. Perhaps 10 to 20 percent of passengers go no higher than their category guarantee while the rest receive a better cabin.

• **Last-minute discounts.** Faxes and e-mails pour into travel agencies, offering everything from free air to cabin upgrades to special packages if they book passengers on X cruise and X ship. For mature travelers with flexibility and a willingness to head out next week, these represent an opportunity. To take advantage of them, tell your travel agent the things you want in a cruise—perhaps a European cruise on a moderate to good cruise line for seven to ten days. Ask her to keep you "in mind" as those faxes come through, then call her back periodically to assure her you're still interested. Should a deal match your desires, she will certainly call.

• **Travel clubs.** Travel clubs charge a nominal fee to join and then offer great deals to members willing to travel at the last minute in unconventional ways or in times of low demand. Some cruise lines may also offer a large employer great last-minute deals. Thanks to the Internet, however, the cruise lines have found other avenues for dispensing cheap cruises and no longer need to use travel clubs as often. I predict, however, that as more people learn about the Internet deals currently being offered (see below), travel clubs will come back into vogue as a prime place for cruise lines to dump their excess cabins.

• **Repeat passengers.** Most cruise lines offer substantial discounts to customers who have sailed with them already, and many even have special names for them. Deals can range from standard discounts on any sailing, to selective specials mailed to your home. Some even offer substantial savings on a second cruise if it's booked aboard ship during your first voyage.

• **Complete flexibility.** If you see a great deal in the newspaper, call the advertiser and specifically request that price. You may have to go tomorrow, you may have to sleep in bunk beds, but you'll get a great deal.

• **"Book a (specific cruise) and get a free (whatever)."** This offer is pretty much ad copy. Figure out the per diem rate and include the "free whatever" in the calculations, assuming you actually want the "free whatever."

• **Back office systems.** Cruise lines cannot, six months in advance, sell a cabin for $1100 per person, and then publicly discount it later to $900 per person. Someone who books early, as the lines recommend, deserves the best deal. If a line does discount a cabin further—and if a travel agent calls and requests that lower price—the cruise line will probably lower the fare you must pay. Unfortunately, the travel agent—or you—has to know that the price has dropped. With hundreds of bookings to organize, even the best agent can miss this. Besides, a $400 per cabin price drop, if caught, can take $40 to $60 in travel agent commissions out of her pocket. While most agents work hard for their clients, there's a strong incentive to overlook price changes.

A travel agency's back office system—if they have one—keeps track of travel offers that come in, however, and compares new deals to the agency's existing reservations. If it finds a match, the system notifies the agent who then notifies the client—you. Should you go with an agency that does not automatically keep track of new deals that come in—many do not—check newspapers and Web sites for announced deals and call your travel agent if you find anything.

Yet one more note of warning: Many times, new and cheaper deals are subtly different than what you booked. Neither cruise line nor travel agent wants to lower prices, so the new deal may be "free airfare with a two-category cabin upgrade" rather than a simple price cut. It makes it hard to compare it to your deal, which may have been an early booking discount. To compare, figure out the per diem rate for both packages. Even if the new deal is cheaper, however, the cruise line may say it doesn't apply to your booking since you technically have a different package. You may even offer to cancel the first reservation and rebook (though that's silly) but continue to get static. If that's the case, insist that your travel agent call her local cruise line sales representative and explain the situation. If the travel agency has a good relationship with the sales rep, doors may open.

• **Live in Florida (or any port city).** A cruise deal is not always offered to travel agencies worldwide. If May bookings are down on a ship, a great deal may be faxed or e-mailed to every U.S. travel agency. But if only one May sailing is half empty, cruise lines may choose to selectively advertise a better rate. More often than not, those agencies selected are ones with clients who can drive to the port of embarkation. For Caribbean sailings, the lines target Florida agencies. For Alaska, they may target Seattle. For Bermuda trips, they may target New York, Philadelphia, or Boston. If they need only a slight increase in bookings, the cruise line may send the message only to their highest-producing agencies in Florida, or even just the highest-producing agencies in a single city such as Miami. If you're in a position to take advantage of these deals— meaning within driving distance of a port—contact a large reputable agency located nearby.

• **Internet.** For now, the Internet is a good place to nab a last-minute cruise deal, even though "last minute" may be a month or more away. It's ideal for adults who can travel on relatively short notice and gives the lines an outlet for advertising that does not get the local travel agencies involved.

Many cruise lines—but not all—accept bookings through their own Internet site, though only a few list last-minute bargains (see Chapter 3). Most sites offer to mail you a brochure. If you want specific info or are ready to book, however, they offer to "forward your request to your nearest travel agent."

The big guys don't want to offend agents by selling cruises behind their backs, but neither do they want to lose potential customers surfing the Internet. So they compromise. Those that accept bookings rarely undercut deals by a travel agent unless the line is so small that no single agency sends a significant number of bookings their way. A handful, however, tentatively plan to post last-minute deals on their site in the coming year or two. Should this tactic be successful, especially if done in the future by a major cruise line, expect other lines to follow suit out of sheer necessity. Even at a better price, however, there's one downside to direct Internet bookings: Should something go wrong, it's you against the cruise line. A travel agent has at least some leverage; you don't.

Most current Internet deals come through an on-line travel agency. The lines send favored agencies notice of their last-minute deals—generally agencies willing to sell cabins like a used car salesman. As more ships hit the seas, the amount of discounted cabins has grown, and something can usually be found year-round except for holiday periods. If booking through an Internet travel agency, make sure the supplier is reputable, a task easier said than done. Take the following steps:

1. Conduct a search for reliable vendors. I'd like to insert a list of the best ones here, but it could be wrong by the time you read it—and cost you a lot of money. Travel agency ownership changes, recessions hit, and with falling airline commissions, other problems plague the industry. Also, the Internet is volatile right now. New Web sites pop up each day, then consolidate with other sites. When searching, look for an agency that has a brick-and-mortar building somewhere—not a "dot-com company" only—and that has been in business for three years or more. If their Web site does not have a section that details the company's history, be careful.

2. Once narrowed down to two or three choices, check out the Internet agency's policies. While some allow you to book on-line and even choose a cabin assignment by directly tapping into the cruise line's computers, you should also be able to speak to a real human being if you wish. Even if everything seems ideal and you don't need human contact, give the agency a call before making a deposit. Ask key questions such as, "What's the worst problem you ever dealt with?" followed by, "How did you handle it?" Note names, dates, and other important information.

3. Before making a deposit, e-mail or call the chosen cruise line directly—most have a contact page on their Web site—and give them the name of your Internet travel agency. Ask if they've had any problems with that company in the past. If the answer is "no," jot down the full name of the person you talked to and note the date and time.

4. Pay by credit card. Should anything go wrong, most credit card companies—check your issuer's policies—allow charges to be denied to a vendor if complaints are registered in writing. Should the worst occur, especially for a cruise sailing within the next four weeks, you have an "out." On-line information security continues to be a hot topic, however. Your call.

5. Clearly understand what's required and when documents will arrive. Many times, a cruise line will not mail docu-

ments for a last-minute sailing. You may receive only an airline confirmation number by e-mail with documents to be "picked up at the pier." If driving, arrive early armed with the booking agency's phone number and a printed copy of any relevant Web pages, especially a confirmation page or e-mail confirmation for the cruise. To be safe, call the cruise line directly the day before arrival and confirm the reservation.

6. Make sure you have important personal documents such as passports or birth certificates.

Personal prediction: Right now, the Internet is the perfect way for cruise lines to sell last-minute deals. As the Internet gains in popularity and older adults learn the tricks of the trade, however, it will start to compete with those early-booking incentives and, more importantly, local travel agencies. Also, travel agencies will continue to develop their own sites and bristle at the deals offered by selected vendors. That will be bad for business. As a result, the Web will lose its ability to dump excess cabins to a select few people. When that happens, travel clubs — or password-protected Web sites that charge a small fee for membership — will become the primary site used by savvy travelers looking for last-minute bargains.

• **Single travelers.** Recent widows and widowers face unique problems. Most couples have specific duties when traveling, and the duties usually performed by a spouse — perhaps tipping or studying ports of call before arrival, for example — are new. A cruise solves a lot of first-time-out problems by incorporating everything into one package. As a social trip, it also provides opportunities to converse with other people. For widows, many lines have a dance host (or gentleman host) program (see Chapter 3: Traveling Solo: The Widow's Waltz).

Beyond the psychology of traveling alone, however, lies finances, and single people need to find a bargain. Most cruise lines charge a premium price for those sailing sans spouse or significant other — up to 200 percent over the regular passenger price. If a ship has 100 cabins and charges $1,000 per person, a ship filled with couples would bring in $200,000. A ship filled with singles at the same per person rate would bring in $100,000. Cruise lines would like the $200,000 thank you very much and sorry for the inconvenience of paying double everyone else's rate. While food costs would run marginally lower on an all-single-cabin sailing, the big expenses such as fuel and personnel would not change; therefore, the cruise lines have a financial interest in deterring single passengers. Some take the high road and offer reasonable single fares regardless of profit; others do not. The simple solution: talk a friend into going along.

If unfeasible, consider a "single share." Simply put, you pay the single rate, but you (probably) get a roommate. Not all cruise lines offer a single share program, but many do—far more than the number that offer a reasonable single rate in the first place. Should the line not be able to provide a roommate of the same sex, you may even get a room to yourself without paying the exorbitant amount usually charged to singles. Even if a cruise line does not advertise a single share rate, ask for one. The program may be unadvertised. Also, they may have a single cruise deal on sailings in slow seasons, perhaps rates as low as the double rate or, perhaps, 110 percent of the double rate.

All cruise line descriptions in Chapter 8 list a range of rates they charge for a single supplement as well as share programs and number of dance hosts that travel on a cruise.

WAYS TO ADD MONEY TO THE COST OF A CRUISE

You add money to a cruise's cost by paying for things not included in the cruise price. It could be fun things such as a photo, or un-fun things such as insurance. These individual topics receive more space elsewhere in the guide, but when planning a vacation, it's important to have an overall view of where your money might go.

Mandatory Extra Costs

• **Raise the price.** All contracts say that the cruise line may raise your rate, even after a price confirmation at time of booking and a deposit has been received. Some, such as Carnival, guarantee a price when deposit is received, but legally give themselves an out for things such as a "fuel surcharge." Generally, that gives the cruise line an out if fuel prices head skyward. Since fuel is part of the cruise fare the price can still go up. Cruise lines hate to raise rates, though—it creates too much bad publicity, and it's rarely done. In worst-case scenarios, a cruise line may create a cutoff date. Passengers who have paid in full by the cutoff date sail at the original rate; passengers only on deposit must pay the higher rate. Should you receive word that your cruise fare has gone up—again, an unlikely occurrence—feel free to say, "They can't do that." But they can.

• **Port charges/taxes.** For most cruise lines, port charges are now included in the base fare quoted by a travel agent. When receiving a cruise price quote, immediately ask about any other fees. There should not be any—but check before making a final booking decision, especially with a smaller cruise line or group tour controlled by the local planner. In the past, port charges were quoted separately from the cruise rate. After heavy criticism both verbally and legally when cruise prices remained stable and the separate port charges went skyward, the lines tucked port charges into the base fares. Also, look for unexpected expenses with code names such as "tourist fees" or a "fee for charges levied by the ports along the way." Any line that nickel-and-dimes you at booking will surely do the same thing at sea. (As will some others that don't nickel-and-dime you at booking.)

Optional Extra Items—but You'll Probably Want Some

• **Selected food.** Generally, all food is included in a cruise's base price, but the cheaper the cruise, the greater the chance that something will cost extra. Many ships offer pizza and/or ice cream somewhere near the pool; a few lines charge for it. Espresso is not alcoholic, but on some ships, you pay for it. If a cabin comes stocked with an honor bar that includes snacks, expect to see them restocked daily and expect to see them on your bill delivered the final night unless sailing with a luxury line.

• **Liquor.** On occasion, such as the captain's party, the ship serves complimentary cocktails. And, on a handful of luxury lines, complimentary wine accompanies all meals. Otherwise, liquor costs extra. Drink prices compete favorably with resort prices on land—generally on the very low side—since ships buy alcohol tax-free. Gratuities to bartenders cost additional, but most ships now automatically add 15 percent to every bar bill, in part to guarantee the servers make a decent wage and in part because most people prefer to charge drinks to their master account rather than carry cash.

- **Beauty and spa services.** A massage can cost $35 or more. Beauty services begin around $20, but can go higher depending on how beautiful you plan to become. Most of these people also expect a tip.
- **Phone calls.** Any contact with land requires a long-range connection and a fee that costs at least $7 and can go as high as $15 or more. It's cheaper to call from a port if you can arrange to call relatives and friends at a time when you know you'll be ashore.
- **Photos.** Photos start around $6, but can go much higher depending both on cruise line and size of the photo.
- **Special activities.** Any onboard activity that requires supplies—a painting class, a book for a lecture series, etc.—usually costs more. Prices vary.
- **Casinos.** You bets your money and you takes your chances.
- **In-room movies.** Essentially a pay-per-view service of first-run movies, these cost around $7 each.
- **Golf.** Most cruise lines offer golf shore excursions, and the cost varies depending on the course. A few ships also have a golf simulator on board that can cost up to $20 for fifteen minutes.
- **Baby-sitting.** Baby-sitting during the day—only they call it Kids Camp or some other term—is free. To drop grandkids off in the evening or have in-room sitters, expect to pay between $6 and $11 per hour depending on level of service and cruise line.
- **Shore excursions.** With very few exceptions, a cruise ship sells shore excursions, but the excursion itself is designed and operated by an independent company. A short bus tour around the port city may cost $25, while a plane or helicopter trip may cost over $200. A single golf package on the *QE 2*—six rounds of golf in different Mediterranean ports—runs the cost up to $1,560. Request information on shore excursions before departure to beat the booking rush the first day at sea.
- **Travel insurance.** For some travelers, this is a mandatory extra, but many people forgo the insurance anyway. The larger cruise lines offer their own insurance packages and travel agencies sell policies from independent companies. Brace yourself: It's all

confusing. Costs run from $5 to $15 for every $100 worth of travel with the difference usually based on the amount of coverage (read the fine print). For more information, see Chapter 5.

TIPS — WHO, WHEN, AND WHERE

The room steward, waiter, and busperson are generally tipped the final night of the cruise; all others are tipped as you go. Suggested amounts listed below assume a seven-day voyage, a moderately fine cruise line, and decent service. They also represent the absolute minimum unless something has gone wrong.

Room steward: $3 per day, or $21 per week, per person.

Waiter: $3 per day, or $21 per week, per person.

Busboy: $1.50 per day, or about $11.00 per week, per person.

Luggage handlers: $1 per bag. Generally, anytime someone helps with the bag, they should be tipped if it involves contact with you. Handlers on board some ships do not have to be tipped, but almost all accept money if offered.

Special requests: A minimum of $5 depending on request. If you wish to move to a different cabin simply because it's vacant and you like the view better, consider an immediate tip to whoever helps you, even if it's the room steward whom you'll be tipping on the last night.

Maître d': $10 depending on request. $20 if requesting a difficult switch, such as one from early to late dining.

Bartenders: $15 percent, but the amount is usually automatically added to the bar bill.

Shore excursion guides: Tip a shore excursion's tour conductor $5 per couple (depending on the guide's expertise and length of the tour) when the tour ends.

Bus drivers: Tip nothing if connecting cruise line to airport or around $2 if it's expected on a shore excursion. You'll know if it's expected — a tip jar will probably be located near the front.

Beauty salon: About 15 percent or $3 for a haircut.

Spa attendants: 15 percent for a massage or other personal service.

Room service: $3 per couple. On most cruise lines, the food is free, however.

For the average cruise, expect tips to run close to $60 per person for the entire voyage. With other tips thrown in, the cost can go up an extra $20 or $30. Realistically, the service will probably be good, you'll probably tip a bit more because "they deserve it," and you'll spend about $100 per person.

5

BOOKING

To actually book a cruise, you must confirm only a small amount of information. With most lines, you're asked (a) inside or outside cabin? (b) smoking or nonsmoking? (c) cash or charge? Most also ask whether you prefer early or late dining, but few guarantee it.

Other issues should be considered, however—a whole chapter's worth.

INSURANCE: A NECESSARY EVIL

This section provides an overview of insurance benefits, different types of policies, and options, but is by no means the final word. Most plans give you a brief synopsis with a promise that "a full description of coverage detailing the terms, conditions, and exclusions will be sent with your policy." When that "full description" arrives, it could be pages and pages long, a ponderous legal document that still does not seem clear. In addition, different types of travel insurance cover different problems. It could include separate policies for trip cancellation, trip interruption, trip delay protection, baggage protection, medical coverage, emergency evacuation, and emergency assistance. In most cases, however, two or more will be offered in an umbrella policy. Trip cancellation and trip interruption, for example, usually come as a single package.

The sad truth about any travel insurance coverage: It's overpriced and a big moneymaker for the insurer, travel agent, and/or cruise line. For most people, it's simply money thrown out the window. The flip side of that same truth: If something happens, insurance is a bargain—worth every penny. Decide how much risk you feel comfortable shouldering and choose wisely.

CRUISE LINE VERSUS PRIVATE INSURANCE: Many large lines offer their own insurance plan explained somewhere in the brochure. If they do not, travel agents offer insurance plans through other companies such as Travelers. The noncruise plans may also be used with a cruise purchase in place of the cruise line's optional policy, though you may be comparing apples to oranges as you try to decide which offers better coverage. A cruise line policy may include limited coverage for lost baggage, medical emergencies, and trip cancellation, while an independent plan may price all three separately. Also, the independent coverage may cover higher losses than the cruise line's policy—or lower losses. This is the "fine print" you hear so much about with contracts.

Cruise line coverage does offer convenience and, many times, a better deal. If it's quoted as a single dollar amount, it may also be a bargain on higher-priced cabins. American Hawaii, for example, charges $125 per person or a maximum of $275 per cabin if traveling with three or more people. The insurance price is the same whether you paid $3,000 per person for the Superior Suite (insurance cost: 4 percent of total cruise) or $1250 for upper and lower berths (insurance cost: 10 percent of total cruise). On Carnival, comparable insurance costs $99 per person regardless of cabin cost.

Confusing note: Most cruise lines do not own their insurance plan—they subcontract through a large existing carrier. Therefore, the company that issues the policy and pays the benefits has no responsibility to the cruise line. If something goes wrong, you may be expected to pay for plane tickets or medical care out of your own pocket; after the fact, you submit claims and wait for reimbursement.

When buying *private insurance,* a travel agent generally hands you a brochure with a cafeteria-style benefits package. You pick the things you want, the dollar amount you want to cover, and pay her directly. While the first risk-based decision is whether you want insurance at all, the second risk-based decision begs the question: How much? Most people cover the cost of the cruise, but that helps only if disaster strikes before leaving home. Problems that occur at sea could cost far more. Most private insurance plans run around

$5 to $8 for every $100 of travel. Assuming that $5 rate a cruise for two could cost $100 for $2000 worth of vacation, meaning the insurance company will pay up to $2000 in benefits. If you get sick on the cruise and must fly home, however, that $2000 may not cover the lost part of your vacation *and* two one-way tickets back to the U.S.—tickets that can be very expensive (and that assumes trip interruption is included.) Should you insure more than the cost of the trip? Again, there are not right-or-wrong decisions here.

One more note if purchasing private insurance: The cost of the insurance is nonrefundable. If you book a cruise eight months ahead of time and, at the same time, take out private insurance, you will still lose the cost of that insurance, even if you cancel one month later. The cruise line returns all your money since the reservation has not entered the penalty phase. The insurer, whose insurance you no longer need or want, does not.

For either personal or cruise line insurance, it's best to note when cruise cancellation penalties start to kick in and take out insurance shortly before that time—if the rules allow it. Different insurers, notably those offered by the cruise lines, have deadline dates for taking out the insurance and it may be an all-or-nothing product that must be taken out when the deposit is made. Check the fine print one more time.

The following (should) come under any blanket protection policy, but each type of coverage may be negotiated separately with the insurance offered by a travel agent. Check also for the *dollar amount* covered, consider all contingencies, and decide if it's enough.

Trip Cancellation

In a travel agent's office, most people say, "I'm going on this cruise come hell or high water." When they say it, they mean it. Unfortunately, we rarely consider all possibilities such as the death of an aging parent or even spouse. If you have an accident or have a sudden family emergency the day before sailing, you won't be able to go and you'll lose all your vacation money. The important point here: realistically decide what could go wrong before or during a cruise, and if it did, how much it would cost you. Base an "Ah, I don't need insurance" decision on that realistic appraisal.

When most adults consider travel insurance, they worry that the money used to pay for the trip will be lost if something happens, and that's what they want to insure through Trip Cancellation insurance. It covers cancellations due to medical problems that affect the traveler, spouse, or immediate family member prior to departure.

It is not, however, a carte blanche plan (though exceptions exist) that allows you to cancel for any reason. A woman who booked a cruise nine months early, walked into my travel agency one day before sailing, plopped into a chair, and said, "We're not going tomorrow. We separated two weeks ago, and I decided last night that I'm filing for divorce. There's no way I could spend seven days with that man. Thank God we took out insurance." Well, insurance companies, while not unfeeling about domestic squabbles and personal pain, believe that you choose to get a divorce. It is neither an act of God nor an accident. And it's not refundable.

To overgeneralize — meaning check the brochure carefully because it varies — cruise lines allow you to cancel seven-day cruises without penalty up to sixty days before departure. Any deposit you put down is refunded (in their own good time). From four to six weeks before departure, the penalty jumps to about $100 or more per guest. From thirty days out to a few days before sailing, you'll pay a penalty of about $200 per guest. In the final three days before departure, no refund is made. For longer cruises or ones on luxury lines, expect higher penalties, longer lead times, or both.

If your mom dies and you haven't taken out trip cancellation insurance, don't expect the cruise line to understand and refund money as a goodwill gesture. In the event one of life's tragic occurrences schedules a visit two days before sailing, no one — including the cruise line — will be unsympathetic. But cruising is a business, and the cruise line company assumes that (a) you read the brochure, (b) your travel agent explained the cancellation penalties, and (c) you made a conscious decision about risk when you decided to (or not to) take out insurance. Since *you* accepted the risk of an accident (by knowing the risks yet still not taking out insurance), then *you* must shoulder any financial responsibility if you cannot go.

Also, beware of a "preexisting conditions" clause. From the insurer's perspective, someone with a terminal condition, say cancer, may plan to cruise in five months on the assumption that the chemotherapy will work—but the passenger takes out Trip Cancellation insurance "just in case." Unfortunately, "preexisting conditions" are not usually covered in an insurance policy. Anyone with an ongoing health problem should confirm before getting insurance that related health events will be covered. In this case, either call the insurance company directly, get a guarantee, and—most important—note the date, time, and complete name of the person who confirms the coverage. If your travel agent calls for you, have her do the same.

As with all insurance, companies tend to deny claims if they see any remote justification to do so. If told something is "not covered—check the fine print," many people will utter a few choice words and get on with their lives. A few will fight the decision. (Insurance companies tend to deny benefits first and ask questions later.) A client of mine had breast cancer but still booked a cruise. Shortly before sailing, her doctor discovered cancer in another organ. She canceled the cruise for immediate chemotherapy but the company denied reimbursement under trip cancellation coverage because her cancer was a preexisting condition. However, we successfully fought it because the cancer had appeared in a different organ and, in this case, could be medically defined as a new cancer. It was not, strictly speaking, a preexisting condition. Another time, a client had a mental breakdown, and the insurer denied coverage. After a fight, the company produced the cash.

Trip Interruption

This coverage mirrors that of Trip Cancellation insurance, but it deals with emergencies that occur after you've set sail. Most times, a single policy covers both trip cancellation and interruption. If your ninety-three-year-old mother passes away on the second day of a seven-day trip, Trip Interruption will reimburse you for the unused portion of your cruise. It will also pay for your return flight home, a significant protection since last-minute, one-way air flights cost exorbitant amounts of money.

Trip Delay Protection

You may miss the ship due to forces beyond your control such as problems with the airline. This coverage may (check the fine print) cover the cost of a hotel room in the city of embarkation, as well as transportation to fly you to the first port of call where you can then connect with the ship. It usually does not cover a specific expense, such as a hotel room, but offers either a maximum amount per day, such as $100, or a maximum amount for the event, such as $500.

Baggage Protection

Up to a specified dollar amount, you'll receive money for lost bags, perhaps $1,000 to $1,500. If your bags do not make it somewhere from home to the cruise ship, it will also reimburse you for some living expenses until the luggage is found. For those flying, airlines already have an obligation to pay for lost baggage, but the amount paid varies dramatically based on where you're flying—international flights pay very little. Check your plane ticket for details.

Medical Coverage

Anyone with a health insurance policy knows that no two are alike. Still, this separate insurance probably replicates your existing medical coverage, up to a specified dollar amount, should you get sick or injured while cruising. This policy can be especially beneficial to those who rely on Medicare because, in a foreign country, Medicare does not cover them. For those on Medicare (and important to note for those who plan to enlist within the next decade), most medigap plans cover "80 percent of medically necessary emergency care in a foreign country after you pay a deductible." (For Medicare soon-to-be's, Medicare falls woefully short in many areas, but private companies offer different medigap plans. These work in tandem with Medicare to bring coverage up to standards generally offered by private insurers. When selecting a medigap plan, you have different coverage options. More coverage, of course, costs more money.)

Other personal insurance policies—but not all—have some sort of coverage for "emergency services in a foreign country." Since foreign hospitals or doctors do not have contractual arrangements with U.S.-based insurance companies, you usually must pay your own expenses, save receipts, and fill out requests for insurance company reimbursement. Sometimes, companies have rules on how soon they must be notified in case of any emergency. Check your policy before leaving home.

Emergency Evacuation

Should a serious medical condition arise, you would need to leave the ship for a nearby hospital or, possibly, flown home. Emergency Evacuation covers transportation costs associated with a medical emergency. Costs are usually listed as a maximum dollar amount, such as $30,000 or $100,000.

Emergency Assistance

In essence, this is a phone number you can call either from home or when visiting foreign countries. On the other end of the phone line sits a friendly person who knows how to solve problems for Americans in foreign lands. Problems can include missing the ship, losing your passport, or even emergency medical attention.

When considering insurance, make sure you actually get insurance. Holland America, for example, offers a Cancellation Protection Plan (CPP). While they clearly explain that this is not insurance, it nevertheless acts in many ways as Trip Cancellation insurance. The differences, however, are subtle. First, its cancellation coverage works up to twenty-four hours before departure. Should you get sick while on the cruise or hours before setting sail, you receive no reimbursement. It also does not cover the other types of insurance explained above. On the plus side, Holland America's CPP allows you to cancel "for any reason" up to that twenty-four-hour cutoff. This is where that divorce example mentioned before may work. Or you might simply change your mind. Since Holland America's cancellation penalties are a bit stricter than the norm, you might consider this insurance, or you may prefer their CPP Platinum Plan that adds more benefits and does include some other types of insurance.

Two items may not be covered by insurance: jewelry and travel agency bankruptcy. Expensive jewelry should not be taken on a trip anyway, but if you do, check your homeowner's insurance policy to see how it's handled. In cases of travel agent bankruptcy, a check may have made it into an agency's account, but the agency may not have sent a check to the cruise line. Legally, the cruise line is not responsible. This is rare but not unheard of, and it adds one more reason to the why-I-need-a-good-travel-agent list.

IF THE HITHERTO INCONCEIVABLE EMERGENCY OCCURS AND YOU DIDN'T TAKE OUT TRIP CANCELLATION INSURANCE: All cruise lines have some kind of local representative who covers an area. Small cruise lines may share one independent rep with other tour companies and travel products. Large cruise lines, however, have a single representative who covers specific geographic turf. This rep visits most travel agencies on a regular basis, and a large part of their job is keeping these agencies happy. If good at their job, however, a cruise line rep also does not give much away. However, on rare occasions, a good travel agent can talk this rep into getting your money back even if you're past the point of refundability. More often, they can talk the rep into giving you credit for a future cruise, possibly in the off-season. At times, the rep may give you a refund minus some sort of cancellation penalty that applied earlier.

This agent-representative dickering is limited and depends on the circumstances:

• Reps tend to help agents who rarely need help. Most reps have a set number of favors they're willing to grant without feeling used. A good agent may also have trouble if the agency, as a whole, complains a lot.

• Money talks. If the agency has historically been a strong seller for the cruise line — and if most agents are competent — you stand a better chance of success. The cruise line wants to keep them happy and selling.

• Holiday cruisers receive fewer favors than those sailing in the off-season. If an off-season cruise already had empty cabins, one less reservation represents lost income only if the passengers (you) never travel. If you're willing to sail on another slow booking date, the cruise line comes out financially even. But if you miss a Christmas cruise booked to the gills, the cruise line would simply lose money and scheduling a future cruise will not make up for the loss.

• How good a client are you? If you've never dealt with the agency before, agents will be less inclined to spend hours writing letters and making phone calls on your behalf, especially since their efforts, if successful, mean they will make no money whatsoever off the deal. If, however, you've booked many flights, tours, and hotel rooms through a single agent or agency, they'll go to bat for you, knowing that they must serve you well now in order to guarantee your future business. A good client may find that the agency's owner personally gets on the phone and talks directly to the vice president of something-or-other. Suddenly, doors open.

If you decide to throw yourself on the mercy of your travel agent and the cruise line, there is little you can do directly. Kindness works better than anger. If you did not take insurance and the agent does not volunteer to call her cruise line rep on your behalf, you may ask her to make the call. Remember that the agent does not own the product or have your money in-house. Without the cruise line rep's okay, she cannot get your money back. If negotiating, plan on getting back something less than a full refund and be willing to negotiate—but (kindly) request a full refund at first. If you get little results, ask to speak to the cruise line representative directly. If the rep does not offer you any money or credit, ask for her supervisor's name. And then her supervisor's supervisor's name. And so on.

CABINS: A ROOM WITH A VIEW?

For the average Joe with a sub-Rockefeller-sized vacation budget who cannot afford a luxury suite, the biggest choice when booking a cruise is whether to get an inside or outside cabin. Money, of course, influences that decision. To overgeneralize, expect to pay at least $150 more, per person, for a view of the ocean. If you can afford a suite without gasping, buy it.

Is an outside cabin worth it? If you're at all claustrophobic, it is. Even large inside cabins have a boxed-in feel once the door shuts. However, beds in inside cabins are just as big as beds in outside cabins, towels as soft, service as efficient. Note that once you go to bed, you'll sleep in complete darkness with, perhaps, only a shard of hall light eking in under the door. That same shard of light will eke in whether it is 2:00 in the morning or 1:00 in the afternoon. For nonclaustrophobics who love to sleep late, it may be a little slice of heaven.

Other things to consider: How much time will you spend in your cabin and what outside-the-window sights will you miss? Most Alaskan cruisers go for the sightseeing as much as the cruise amenities. An outside cabin with a view of the coastline makes the additional cost worthwhile. (But make sure you book an outside cabin on the coastal side of the ship.) Some older ships and many newer ships also have private balconies, creating a private spot for drinks or romance. If that appeals to you, an inside cabin doesn't cut it. Also, people spend more time in their cabin on long cruises. If an inside cabin works well on a three-day cruise, it still may not be preferable on a twenty-day trip.

Other what-cabin-do-I-pick concerns are pragmatic or social, such as, "Where does the ship rock the least?" or "What will people think if they find out I sleep in a broom closet?" Cabins are never big, but some are extremely not big. Anything around 180 square feet is average for the industry.

When considering your cabin location relative to other onboard activities, look at the ship diagram and locate the major activity areas. Decide which activities you expect to do more than once per day. Eating, of course, comes to mind. Since you eat at least three times per day (probably more), a cabin with easy access to dining rooms makes sense.

Special note to mature adults traveling with children: find the children's facilities on the ship and try to book an easily accessible cabin, a consideration as important as the dining room's location. Since the kids' program may meet in the morning, the afternoon, and the evening—and since you'll have to drop your grandchild off and pick him up—you could find yourself traipsing across the ship six times per day. That gets old by Tuesday.

The Specifics

FOR THOSE WHO CARE WHAT PEOPLE THINK: Every ship has high-status cabins. Many are called a President's Suite, Superior Veranda Suite, Grand Suite, or something similar. Without exception, these have excellent views of the ocean, larger bathrooms, and look like small apartments with separate areas for sleeping and entertaining. Some newer ships also have smaller suites. These mini-suites have a sitting area set apart from the bed, but the actual division between the two may be nonexistent or, at the least, a curtain. (Meaning not really a suite at all.) In bygone days, ships had separate classes, from the ruling aristocracy that slept and dined on a ship's top decks to the poor folks down in steerage who hocked the family cow for a trip to the New World. Today, the tradition continues, and the most expensive suites can still be found on top decks.

On many cruise lines, notably the luxury ones, the larger suites also come with personal amenities above and beyond those given to people in standard cabins. Crystal Cruises, for example, offers suite guests staying on deck ten a personal butler who will not only make dinner reservations and unpack bags, but will also plan a private party inside the penthouse. Most cruise lines offer upgrades such as robes, umbrellas, and other amenities.

FOR THOSE WHO CARE ABOUT MONEY: Think small, low, and (on older ships) bunk beds, though on newer ships it generally just means low. Almost all new vessels have standardized the room sizes and, outside the suites near the top of the ship, all cabins are identical. An inside cabin on the lowest passenger deck (crew cabins may be below the waterline but guest cabins never are) may be identical to ones five decks higher and selling for a few hundred dollars more per person. Beyond deck level and cabin size, all guests enjoy the same cruise package—quality of food, choice of mealtimes, etc. (For the lone exception, see the description of the *QE 2*, p. 174.) Some ships, even new ones, do still offer bunk beds in small cabins. Due to their affordability and scarcity, however, they must be booked early.

FOR THOSE WHO CARE ABOUT WALKING: Book a cabin close to an elevator. This comes with one addendum, however: Expect crowds. Meals, shows, and island disembarking start at the same time for at least half the people on the ship. During these times, elevators may not only be slow when arriving, but they could stop on every floor en route to your destination. While there's no way to completely avoid trouble, consider a cabin near, or one floor below, the dining room. That should avoid trouble at least three times per day. You might also consider taking the stairs during busy times.

FOR THOSE WHO CARE ABOUT NOISE: Using 3-D thinking, look at the brochure and mentally put one deck on top of another. Think twice about a cabin located above or below a disco or club open until the wee hours. Even minor noise seems to amplify if you're trying to sleep. There may also be noise and vibration from the engine that affects lower cabins toward the rear of the ship. In any case, if unexpected noise appears once on board, immediately ask for a cabin transfer.

Other Concerns

THIRD AND FOURTH PASSENGERS: Many newer ships add upper berths to standard cabins. During the day, these berths disappear into the wall. At night, however, a sardine may have more room when they come down. It's tight if traveling with grand-children and close to impossible if sharing expenses with another couple. If money is tight, go for it, plan to spend most of your time on deck, and when things get crowded, laugh about it.

PRIVATE BALCONIES: New ships tend to have balconies. If attracted to the romance of a glass of champagne and eggs benedict while wearing nothing but a smile, however, make sure (before booking) that the balconies also have solid dividers that separate them from other cabins' balconies. Many do; many do not.

MOVEMENT: Cabins on the lowest decks toward the center of the ship move least. Cabins toward the front or back of the ship on a lower deck, or in the middle of the ship on upper decks, move a bit more. Cabins on higher decks close to the front or back of the ship move the most. (Fore and aft for those already seaworthy.)

DOUBLE BEDS: Most new ships have twin beds that convert into double- or queen-size beds. Older ships tend to have twins that may not convert. ("Convert" is a pretty way to say that they can push them together for you.) If you must have a double bed on an older ship, book early—they go fast.

OBSTRUCTED VIEWS: Some outside cabins are outside only in the academic sense: They have a window and light comes in. A lifeboat, however, may hide the ocean. Brochures should explain this, but not all do. Ask. Also, check the diagram to see if an open passenger deck separates the window from the sea, meaning jog-gers can look inside as you dress. Passengers should look out port-holes, never into portholes.

ONE MORE MINOR DETAIL: Most people either want to spend money or save money. Consequently, the first cabins to sell out tend to be at both ends of the cost spectrum—the high-end suites and the bunk bed and lower cabins. If you select a date and ship about five months before intended departure, your travel agent will probably say, "Categories A, B, Y, and Z are sold out, but I can get you Category M for this much money." What you're being told is that other people already booked the suite you wanted, or that the cheapest cabins have sold out.

DINING

How many people are reading these words in a bookstore after looking up "food" in the index? Food—quantity if not quality—is the common thread that, with water, symbolizes the cruise vacation. It's an odd reality—you can eat yourself into a stupor, feel 1,000 pounds heavier, yet still regret not making it to the pizza parlor at least once.

Mature travelers know that the food will be there. They also know that they do not have to eat it. Many of them eat it anyway, gain a little weight, and accept it. Only younger travelers act as if the cruise line forced them to gain five pounds.

A brief explanation on how cruise lines will cut food quality to save money can be found in Chapter 1: Inexpensive Cruises: Do You Get What You Pay For? Information here covers decisions that must be made at the time of booking.

Seating

Seating means a style of dining. Generally, the bigger the cruise ship, the more the dining is like a banquet. The smaller and more expensive the cruise line, the more a trip to the dining room resembles a meal at a good local restaurant.

OPEN SEATING: Show up when you're hungry; sit at any table with any dinner companions; leave after twenty minutes or four hours. Giving cruisers this kind of flexibility costs money, so it's found only on small and higher-priced lines. Beyond convenience, it also adds a considerable amount of freedom to a cruise.

SINGLE SEATING: The dining room has set hours, say 6:00 to 10:00, but you don't. While you'll have an assigned table and waiter used throughout the cruise, you show up when you want to eat as long as they're open. Single seating may also mean an established dining time similar to the description for two seatings.

TWO SEATINGS: The method used by the larger cruise lines, two seatings means that the dining room serves two meals each night. Passengers have set dinner times, tables, and waiters. Except for the fact that hundreds of people show up at the same time, it feels a bit like having a reservation. Most ships allow the rules to bend over breakfast and lunch, especially if they're also serving a buffet elsewhere and many people forgo the sit-down meal. At dinner, however, you show up on time or wait for the midnight buffet. Seatings cannot be adjusted. If assigned main seating and you wish to sleep in, for example, plan to visit the breakfast buffet rather than the dining room. Mealtimes, give or take a half hour, are:

Main or early seating
Breakfast: 6:30 A.M.
Lunch: 12:00 noon
Dinner: 6:30 P.M.

Late seating
Breakfast: 8:30 A.M.
Lunch: 1:30 P.M.
Dinner: 8:30 P.M.

Special Diets

Almost all special diets can be accommodated on a cruise. Most large lines offer, as part of every meal's menu, a "heart-smart," or "low-fat," or otherwise lean choice, and some kind of vegetarian — though not necessarily vegan — entrée. Kosher meals may even be offered on some lines without prior arrangement. With a limited amount of kosher food stocked, however, it's an all-or-nothing proposition should too many passengers request it.

All other special diets must be requested at the time of booking, though an amazing array of requests can be accommodated. Special diets that must be ordered ahead of time include dairy-free, gluten-free, low cholesterol, low salt, salt-free, vegan, or a specialized diet such as no MSG or sulfites or other ingredients used in preparation. Other special diets may also be available. Ask.

Since mainstream cruise lines offer perhaps seven entrées to all guests, it stands to reason that those twenty guests on special diets may receive food more akin to individually prepared restaurant fare, just as special airline meals seem less factory-produced than the generic food choices. Pragmatically, a cruise line cannot prepare hundreds of "special diets" ordered by people who simply want better food, and they deny that special diets are better than mass-prepared entrées. Still, they employ world-class chefs. It stands to reason that, at least on some lines, a special diet will compete evenly—or beat—food ordered off the regular menu.

Understanding the Fine Print

Tucked comfortably in the rear of every cruise brochure is a section called something like "The Fine Print," "General Information," or "What You Need to Know."

Read it.

The information covers some general topics, such as whether your electric razor will work in the bathrooms and how soon the ship sets sail after you arrive. But buried within the helpful information is negative news that, up to this point, went unsaid by the cruise line because it just didn't sound too nice. While the front of the brochure advertises a carefree vacation where "almost everything is included," the exceptions to that all-inclusive price are noted here. The scope and specifics of this section vary between cruise lines, but look for the following:

EMBARKATION: Explains times and procedures for getting on the ship. For most domestic cruises, passengers may start to board in the early afternoon and the ship will set sail in early evening. Guests must usually arrive at least a half hour before departure.

DEBARKATION: Cruise lines usually want guests out of their rooms early so they have time to clean and prepare for the next sailing. However, they (and you) are at the mercy of customs officials and the ship may not be cleared for debarkation for a few hours. With this in mind, they may advise you to book a return flight (if you book your own air) no earlier than noon or 1:00 P.M.

INSURANCE: Sometimes covered elsewhere in the brochure, this either explains the cruise line's personal insurance policy or highly recommends that you talk to your agent about coverage. See explanation at the beginning of the chapter.

DEPOSIT INFORMATION: At times, deposit information can be found beside the price list earlier in the brochure, especially if the line hosts many different types and lengths of sailings. This section also lists acceptable credit cards, generally American Express, Visa, MasterCard, and Discover.

CANCELLATION PENALTIES: Generally easy to read and understand, the cancellation penalties tell you how much you lose and when you lose it. For most lines, these are (almost) written in stone (see Insurance: A Necessary Evil, p. 85). Most lines require that your travel agent notify them in writing. If close to a penalty increase period, have your travel agent fax the request to the cruise line and then follow it up with a phone call, noting the full name of the person who received the fax.

AIRFARE RULES: This may be thrown in with the fine print or listed in a separate area that covers airfare costs. The cruise line makes it clear that they do not own the airlines and, therefore, are not responsible for their screw-ups. Because the airlines offer them sweet deals, the cruise lines cannot book any plane at any time, meaning this section leaves them an out should they not deliver the best times and most convenient flights.

AIR DEVIATIONS: Some cruise lines allow you to request a specific airline plus request seating assignments. For a fee of at least $35 plus any additional charges handed down by the airline, some lines will also allow you to change your flight dates and/or departure times.

POLICY STATEMENTS: Many times the ship has a policy against something, and the title of this section varies. Carnival, for example, had a problem with college students getting rowdy and drunk on spring break trips. Because March and April sailings tended to be wilder than others, word started to spread that older travelers should avoid Carnival in the spring. As a result, Carnival now requires guests under twenty-one to stay in a room with a guest who is over twenty-five. Other lines have instated similar policies. The cruise line may also have a policy against liquor on board, not because of any maritime law but because they want to maximize profits in their lounges and bars. (How well this is enforced inside a cabin varies, but some lines print their policy so there's no misunderstanding.) Policies may affect pregnant women (none over thirty weeks), visitors on board (most don't allow any), pets (only those who aid the handicapped), or children's ages (only four months or older).

TIPPING: Most brochures start off saying something like: "While tipping is at your discretion, we offer the following guidelines . . ." The numbers vary between luxury and budget cruise lines, but on an economy line or as a bare-bones recommendation, they break down to about $7.50 per person per day—$3.00 for the room steward, $3.00 for the waiter, and $1.50 for the busboy. Many cruise lines recommend more than the minimum. Others suggest a set amount for the week with the total divided among all crew. Windjammer, for example, recommends $50 per passenger.

CLOTHING: Explanations of formality go here along with weather forecasts (see Chapter 6).

SINGLE INFORMATION: Usually, information on traveling solo—such as the fact that it will cost 150 to 200 percent of the published fare—is found on the page that lists costs. Sometimes, however, it's found in the back of the brochure.

DISCLAIMERS: For valid legal reasons, the cruise lines include a list of things that say: "It's not our fault if . . ." These not-our-fault provisions include *problems created by noncruise line contractors*—the airlines that fly you to the port and the shore excursions at ports of call. Some onboard services also fall under this category, however, including medical services, spa services, and all noncruise line components that make up a post-cruise package. In truth, if you book a post-cruise hotel package through a cruise line, you're doing so because you trust their judgment. If that package falls short of expectations, you expect the cruise line to take some sort of responsibility. If that happens, they will probably go to bat for you as a goodwill gesture, but they'll also point to this clause and explain that it's not their responsibility.

Another not-our-fault clause will say that *the cruise line does not have to take you where it promised*. It essentially states that your itinerary could be thrown out the window if the captain wants to get creative. In practice, this rarely happens. Clients simply would not return to that cruise line. It does come into play, however, if the captain expects rough water. If a ship has a scheduled port of call in St. Thomas and Hurricane Zena is bearing down on the ill-fated island, the captain does not want to go there, and you do not want to go there. So you don't. If an island was hit by a hurricane only a few weeks before your scheduled visit, you'll usually be informed of itinerary changes before departure. Thanks to this clause, cancellation penalties still apply, however. After all, the cruise line cannot control the weather. Should you wish to switch cruises during the cancellation penalty period, most cruise lines don't view it as a change; they view it as a cancellation followed by a new booking — and charge penalties accordingly. This clause also covers changes in departure times should the ship choose to sail earlier or later than scheduled.

Another no-fault disclaimer will say *we're not responsible for theft*. Many newer ships provide a small safe inside cabins; all others offer a secure location at the purser's desk. On the one hand, theft is rare on a cruise ship because few passengers pay $1,000 to cruise and then rob the rich like a modern-day pirate. Also, there's nowhere to run. But if you do get robbed, they don't have to reimburse you for the loss thanks to this clause.

A final disclaimer may say *we can kick you off the ship at any time*, followed by a "and you don't get any money back." In practice, it's difficult to kick someone off a ship and it's reserved for only the worst problems. This disclaimer, however, makes it legally easier.

PASSPORT INFORMATION: For standard seven-day cruises, the brochure will cite all needed documentation for U.S. or Canadian citizens. It may be less clear for people boarding a ship in the U.S. who are citizens of a foreign country. Some information — visa requirements for selected round-the-world ports of call, for example — may change after the brochure has been printed. Updates concerning exotic destination requirements should come through your travel agent or the cruise line, but always double-check yourself.

BAGGAGE LIABILITY: Cruise lines have almost no liability for lost luggage — like $100 maximum per adult — though they may not mention this under the baggage liability section. Leave the diamonds, Rolexes, and Grandma's heirlooms at home for the kids to steal. If that doesn't seem wise, take out baggage insurance.

DISABLED ACCESS: In most brochures, this section usually says that the cruise line will try their best to accommodate those with disabilities or "special needs." They may explain a few specifics about guide dogs or wheelchair accessibility if the ship is distinctly unfriendly for those traveling on four wheels. Among other things, this clause may say something like "bring someone with you if you want to go" and "we're not responsible if you can't do everything that everyone else does." Specific concerns for wheelchair users include the size of cabin doors, size of bathroom doors, and accessibility of ports when the ship relies on tenders (water taxis) to transport passengers to dry land (see Chapter 3).

THE IF-YOU-WANT-TO-SUE-US-YOU-MUST-FOLLOW-OUR-RULES CLAUSE: Some cruise lines try to establish the ground rules should anything go wrong. It may, for example, say that all U.S. lawsuits must be filed in the state where the port of embarkation is located.

THE WE-CAN-CHARGE-YOU-MORE-MONEY CLAUSE: While part of every cruise line's fine print, cruise lines rarely charge passengers more money, though they reserve the right to do so if costs rise for port charges, fuel costs, airfare hikes, or other unexpected expenses. Unless a cost rise is truly dramatic, however, a cruise line usually accepts the loss, tells passengers what happened, and emphasizes how magnanimous they've been about the whole thing.

CRUISE RATES: Covers specifics on what is included in the cruise fare paid to the travel agent and what is not. This section also details port charges included in most cruise packages.

CRUISE LINE CREDIT: Almost all cruise lines now have cashless living, where you present a credit card upon embarkation, the cruise line creates its own credit card for use on board, and cash is not used for purchases, drinks, spa services, and anything else supplied by the ship. This section outlines the details and may explain how to apply for credit. If paying cash for everything, you should be able to give them your money and use the card, but ask before booking if explanations prove inadequate. Cruise lines don't like cash.

MAKING YOUR RESERVATION

Most cruise lines require just two cash outlays: a deposit and a final payment. For a complete description of standard deposits and the timing of final payment, see Chapter 4.

For most people, the deposit closes the decision-making process. Upon payment, the travel agent should either mail or hand you a breakdown of complete costs on an invoice created by the travel agency—the amount you've paid, the amount you still owe, and the day you owe it. Included on the invoice should be a final reminder of things you still need to do, such as obtaining a birth certificate or passport. If you've made special requests—a diet, type of airplane seating, nonsmoking preference, etc.—it should also be noted on the invoice.

Since the travel agency creates the invoice, it does not guarantee that special requests have made it to the cruise line. A travel agent sometimes makes mistakes or forgets to request something even though it's spelled out on the invoice she created. Should final documents arrive and your special requests are not noted somewhere in these cruise line-generated papers, ask the travel agent to reconfirm details while you sit at her desk. Many times, the details are confirmed but not mentioned in the documents, but it's better to find out now rather than later.

CONFUSING THINGS EXPLAINED

A lot of details just don't matter, but they're listed here anyway.

WHAT DOES "SHIP'S REGISTRY" MEAN? Sometimes called a ship's flag, this means almost nothing to passengers and everything to the cruise line's accountants. Ships must be registered to a single country even though they sail throughout the world. Registering brings certain financial obligations based on that country's rules. Therefore, most ships register with only a handful of countries—ones that offer liberal tax breaks and other considerations. Common ship's registries include the Bahamas, Panama, and Liberia.

WHAT LAWS APPLY? Because a ship can be docked in different countries as well as in international waters (meaning owned by no nation), the laws get tricky. Many times, U.S. laws apply if something occurs in a U.S. port or U.S. waters—twelve miles from the shoreline. Who has jurisdiction—and to what extent—has been a bone of contention in the cruise industry for years. Legal advice runs far, far beyond the scope of any travel guide, not to mention the fact that laws change all the time. If you have a specific legal question, contact a lawyer—preferably one who specializes in international law.

WHAT IF I GET ON THE SHIP AND DON'T LIKE IT? Generally, you're stuck. Carnival, however, has a cruise guarantee that allows you to get off at the first port of call. They'll fly you home and refund money for the part of the cruise you did not take, providing you inform them before arriving at that port. If considering this, make sure you understand Carnival's rules before you go.

CAN I FATHOM THE TENDER'S FUNNEL? No. A tender doesn't have a funnel and a fathom . . . well, it just doesn't apply. A fathom, tender, and funnel are, however, nautical expressions that you may run across while at sea. There are those—many, in fact—who believe that people who sail the high seas are obligated to know nautical lingo. Another camp, the one I'm in, believes that most cruise passengers want a unique vacation and, while willing to memorize the difference between port and starboard, feel no obligation to pretend their bed is a berth or the kitchen is a galley. Nevertheless, you may come across the following while on a cruise, and if your aft is on fire, you should know which way to run.

Aft: The back end of the ship.

Ahead: As in "full speed ahead," it means anything in front of the ship.

Alleyway: A hall or corridor.

Alongside: Something beside the ship, generally the pier on a cruise.

Amidships: The middle of the ship.

Astern: The area behind the ship (and the opposite of "ahead").

Bar: A place to buy piña coladas OR a pile of sand below the surface of the ocean.

Beam: The width of the ship at its widest point (the middle).

Bearing: A compass direction from the ship's current location to where it's headed.

Below: As in "below deck" or "down below," it refers to anything under the outside deck.

Bilge: Sounds like where they keep garbage, but refers to anything in the ship's lowest areas, generally below the waterline.

Boat stations: see muster station.

Bow: The forward part of the ship.

Bridge: Where they steer the boat.

Colors: The national flag flown by the ship.

Disembark: To leave the ship.

Dock: Pier or walkway; also the action of pulling up to a pier.

Draft: A measure of the amount of ship that's under water.

Embark: To board the ship.

Fathom: Nautical way to say six feet.

Funnel: The ship's chimney or smokestack.

Galley: Ship's kitchen.

Gangway: Any stairway or ramp that connects to land.

Gross Registered Tons: A measure of the amount of space within a ship. (It's a good way to compare the size of ships, but doesn't translate well into known quantities.)

Helm: The steering wheel but more complicated.

Hull: The main body of the ship that keeps water outside.

Knot: One nautical mile.

Leeward: The side of the ship protected from the wind.

Manifest: The list of passengers on board.

Muster station: The area on deck near a lifeboat. "Your" muster station means the area you go to with life preserver in hand in case of an emergency.

Nautical mile: 1/60 of a degree of the circumference of the world, equal to 1.15 land miles or 1853.25 meters.

Pilot: A professional steering person, notably in rough waters or into ports of call.

Pitch: The rise and fall of the ship's bow as it cuts through rough waters.

Port: When facing front, it's the left side of the ship. It's also a city's parking space for ships, as in the port of Miami. (It's also a rich wine.)

Rudder: Part of the underwater steering system.

Stabilizer: A finlike apparatus that extends from the ship into the water when at sea. Controlled by computers, the stabilizer counteracts waves to make the cruise smoother.

Starboard: If facing forward, the right side of the ship.

Stern: The far back of the ship.

Tender: A small boat that transports passengers from an anchored ship to nearby land.

Wake: The swell of water behind a moving ship.

Windward: The side of the ship currently hit with direct breezes.

Yaw: An erratic deviation from course in rough weather.

THE QUICK LIST

Like *Jeopardy!*, the Quick List is in the form of questions. It assumes you're sitting in a travel agency and reasonably close to confirming a reservation. There's nothing new here if you've read the rest of the chapter, but I've put it into a format that's easier to work with while seated in front of a travel agent. If answers cannot be found in the brochure, ask the travel agent to confirm it with a cruise representative and note his or her full name on your agency invoice.

1. Is that the total price I'll pay for the cruise? Does it include port charges? Airfare? Transfers?

2. Could I save any money by traveling at a different time? Could I save any money by traveling on another cruise line with equivalent service and amenities?

3. Should the cruise line drop the price of my cruise for any reason, does your office have a system to check existing reservations and automatically lower my rate?

4. What proof of citizenship do I need?

5. What is the last day I can cancel without penalty? At what point do I lose all my money if an emergency keeps me from traveling?

6. Does the cruise line offer insurance? Does your agency?

7. Will you get my airline seating assignments? My boarding passes? I don't want to fly on smaller airplanes (turboprops). May I request jet service only? Can it be guaranteed?

8. If I decide to change my itinerary and arrive earlier or stay later, may I do that? If so, what's the latest date that I can make changes?

9. How close is my cabin to the elevators? To the dining room? To other shipboard activities? To the disco? To the engine room?

10. How big is the ship's infirmary? How many doctors? How many nurses? Are they prepared to handle (fill in a medical condition)?

11. Does my cabin (if outside) have a lifeboat or public walkway between the window and the ocean?

12. Is my balcony (if you have one) separated from other cabins' balconies?

13. Do I have twin beds, a double bed, or what? If I want existing twin beds converted into a double, can I request it now?

14. Is my main (or early if applicable) dinner reservation confirmed?

15. May I be seated at a dining-room table for (two, four, six, or eight)?

The following may apply to you. If so, confirm details at the time of booking:

a. special diets

b. wheelchair accessible room, reasonably accessible ship, and help when flying

c. special restrictions, such as available tender service if confined to a wheelchair

d. special services such as oxygen or permission to board with a seeing-eye dog

e. dance hosts (if single, traveling alone, and with a yen to dance and talk)

f. onboard cash policies, especially if traveling without a credit card

g. money accepted in ports, especially if visiting exotic destinations

h. sports equipment availability or requirements if taking your own

i. parking costs if you're driving to the port of embarkation

j. religious services, especially on smaller ships

6

PREPARING TO SET SAIL

The final payment is in, documents have arrived, and final preparations begun. This is the easy part. Take along the required proof of citizenship, and you could board without further ado though you'd surely miss both toothbrush and clothes. While ship stores may not stock enough pants and dresses to assemble a complete wardrobe, you could buy what you need without going naked or missing out on basic hygiene, providing, of course, that you also took along at least one credit card with a reasonable balance left to tap.

Since most people prefer to pack a few favorite things to take along, however, this chapter covers the basics—info on how to make the home-to-sea transition smooth and painless.

TRAVEL DOCUMENTS

Complete information on needed documentation can be found at the end of Chapter 1. If down to the last few days before departure, it's probably too late to get a passport, though in selected cities you can get one in a single day—and it takes all day—if you can show that you're leaving soon. Proof of departure usually means an airline ticket dated sometime within the next week. (U.S. Passport Office at 202-955-0232 or *http://travel.state.gov/passportservices.html.*)

For most cruise destinations in the Caribbean or Alaska, a birth certificate is all that's required, though people who have a passport should take them simply because they're easy to carry and widely recognized. (If traveling in the U.S. only, such as with American

Hawaii or the Delta Queen Steamboat Co., no documentation is required.) One important note from Chapter 1 bears repeating: The birth certificate must be issued by the state—not the flowery one from the hospital. I know of only one person who couldn't find a birth certificate, and he went to the pier anyway, figuring it wasn't a big deal. And, against all rules, he got on the ship. (It *was* his honeymoon.) I've told that story to travel agents, and without exception, they sucked in their breaths and put a hand to their chests. Two told me similar stories, but their clients were not allowed to board.

MAKE COPIES. To cover all bases, make two copies of all travel documents—airline tickets, ship boarding passes, invoices, passports, etc. Give one copy to a relative or friend at home and take one copy with you, packing the copies in suitcases and keeping original documents in carry-on luggage. Should your original travel documents be lost or stolen, the copies can save a lot of guessing and explaining to cruise ship personnel, foreign governments, or U.S. embassies.

LETTERS OF PERMISSION. If traveling with grandchildren, bring along a letter signed by both parents giving you permission to take the kids out of the country. While most countries do not require this, some, such as Mexico, do. The law is meant to guard against kidnappings, especially those involving a noncustodial parent.

VACCINATION OR MEDICAL CERTIFICATES. Normally, only exotic cruises require some kind of medical vaccination or medical certificates. Also, bring along pertinent medical records that could be useful to the ship's doctors should something go wrong.

WHAT TO PACK, WHAT TO PACK . . .

Seasoned travelers pack very little. The women have a complete wardrobe of mix-and-match outfits that allow them to wear something different every day, created artistically with three skirts, three blouses, one dress, and a small bag of scarves, pins, and belts. The men pack two pairs of shorts, three pairs of pants, four shirts, one dark suit, and seven ties. They're efficient people. I admire them tremendously. Frequent travelers consider light packing a badge of honor, with the best of the best able to fit everything needed for a seven-day cruise into their carry-on luggage. Personally, I want to flip through eight shirts before deciding which one I want to wear; I don't like picking out a whole week's wardrobe before I go. How you pack depends on the type of person you are—and the amount of luggage you're willing to tote around.

With that said, less luggage is better. Cruise lines have few rules governing the amount of suitcases that may be brought on board, though the amount of drawer space inside a cabin varies tremendously. Still, most cabins have enough space for two people to unpack comfortably for a seven-day cruse. Suitcases usually slide neatly under beds with a bit of space left over for shoes and souvenirs.

The main constraint to an Imelda Marcos-sized collection of clothing comes from airlines that mandate limits such as "two suitcases and one carry-on bag per person." If the stack of suitcases by the front door keeps getting taller as you prepare to depart, check with the airline first. If taking a long cruise and you need everything, ask about the charges for extra bags.

These following guidelines apply to all mainstream cruise ships. High luxury ships may require more suits and a higher class of casual wear; economy lines require fewer suits and accept more T-shirts. A handful of cruise lines, usually touting themes such as "casual elegance" or "barefoot luxury," never require a jacket or tie. Still others, the soft adventure cruises, don't worry about a dress code at all, figuring people will dress for the weather and the activities rather than the social occasions. Still, 90 percent of the cruises out there adhere to the following guidelines:

FORMAL WEAR: Most seven-day cruises schedule at least two formal nights. For men, that means a tuxedo or dark suit—black or deep blue. Women will feel at home in either an evening gown or elegant dress. On a mainstream cruise, expect maybe 10 percent of the men to be in a tux, perhaps 80 percent to wear a dark suit, and 8 percent to wear a light suit. The remaining 2 percent of rugged individualists wear a suit without a tie, or a pair of khakis and the best shirt in their closet. On an economy cruise, the number of rugged individualists grows and the number of tuxes drops. The level of female elegance parallels that of the men.

For those who wish to rent a tux, check first with your travel agent to see if they offer that service onboard. Some companies rent tuxes specifically for the cruise line crowd. Floating Formals (*www.floatingformals.com* or toll-free 800-833-5621), for example, serves NCL and Costa Cruise Lines.

SEMI-FORMAL WEAR: Really, there is no such thing, but some cruise lines use this term for less-than-formal dinners. To dress informally, some men wear a suit and tie, while others wear a jacket sans tie. Women wear their nicest dresses, though you don't usually see evening gowns.

CASUAL WEAR: You wear one type of casual wear when you clean the garage; you wear another type for the neighbor's pool party. Simply put: You won't be cleaning any garages on a cruise ship. Really, though, almost anything goes during the day. If the cruise is tropical, people are heading to beaches, the swimming pool, or exercise room. Bathing suits with appropriate cover-ups fit right in. For nonbeach times, men tend to wear collared knit shirts, with a few people wearing decent T-shirts—but not ones with profane comments that relate to body functions. Women dress similarly and wear slacks or shorts and any kind of attractive top.

A subcategory of casual: For most dinners and other evening functions, "resort casual" is the buzzword. Simply put, resort casual means "don't wear those ugly garage-cleaning clothes." Men wear khakis or casual pants of any color—no shorts—along with a button-down shirt or a collared knit shirt. Some men wear the same thing they wear on a formal night minus the tie and jacket. Women wear fancy nonformal dresses as well as upscale slacks. Sandals are fine for women if dressy.

OTHER CLOTHING: Take at least a sweater, even if on a tropical cruise. Dining rooms and theaters get downright cold, especially if seated near an air vent. If traveling to a colder destination such as Alaska, consider taking a bathing suit "just in case." In all nontropical locales, peel-down clothing works well, meaning a decent T-shirt, button-down shirt or blouse, and coat. As the day warms up, layers come off.

SHOES: Everyone needs a good pair of walking shoes. During the day, sneakers offer support and good traction. On the larger ships, a trip from the dining room to the cabin could take ten minutes. Do that twice and you've had your exercise for the day—and that doesn't include the shore excursions or onboard activities. For occasions that call for something more high class than running shoes, women should consider only flat shoes or ones with medium-sized heels. Because walking tends to be done in short spurts on a cruise, it doesn't seem like real exercise. If you don't stay active at home, however, you'll feel it the next morning.

VALUABLES: Good jewelry and watches are more trouble than they're worth. Try to match an existing jewelry collection with similar fake pieces and call the cheap stuff your "travel collection."

SPORTS EQUIPMENT: Most cruise lines stock a limited amount of sports equipment (sometimes free, sometimes for rent), but take your own equipment if it can be transported easily and without the possibility of damage. Golf clubs can be a problem for airlines but do fit into cabin closets. If you want to take your own clubs, have your travel agent first check with the cruise line and, most importantly, the airline. When packing, assume someone working behind the scenes will throw them around.

ALL THAT OTHER STUFF: Hopefully, this list will complete the phrase "I should have brought my . . ."

• flashlight. Useful in a dark cabin when a mate is trying to sleep.

• hat. Straw hats work well in tropical climates.

• sunscreen. On most cruises, even in Alaska, you spend a lot of time outdoors.

• insect repellent. Alaska, surprisingly, has big bugs. Insect repellent is also useful on shore excursions and when in port.

• binoculars. The ocean is big and the horizon far away—especially valuable if whale watching.

• medicine. Take enough to last throughout the vacation.

• medical insurance information. Most insurance packages explain the procedure for reimbursement should something happen outside the country—assuming your insurance even covers it. Many do not.

• umbrella. The sun does not shine on all vacations.

• gum. Most ships don't stock it.

• sunglasses.

• backpack or fanny pack. Not only convenient for shore excursions or trips to the beach, backpacks or fanny packs are also harder to steal. Handbags become cumbersome.

- electricity converter. A few older ships do not have the same electrical system as the one used in the U.S. If so, the room steward probably has a converter you can use. But ask before arrival.
- living will. If you have a living will, consider taking it. Without a copy, a doctor will not know your wishes.

CARRY-ON LUGGAGE: This topic fits uneasily in the "what to pack" section since it deals with "where" more than "what"—but it has to go somewhere.

When packing, plan for the worst and pack your carry-on as if you may never see your luggage again. With many cruise vacations, you hand luggage to an airline reservationist at 6:30 A.M. and don't see it again until after the ship departs. If your luggage is lost, you should have all life's essentials in your carry-on luggage. The things you'll need during the day—handkerchiefs, a book, snacks, airline tickets, cruise documents, passport, all medicine (not just for the day), glasses, valuables, important toiletries, etc.—should be stored in carry-on luggage. Also consider a change of clothes. If you wish to clean up and change upon arrival, and the luggage has not yet arrived, it comes in handy. Some carry-on luggage sold in stores comes with a retractable handle and wheels, making it easier to cart around airports. Also, consider a backpack rather than traditional luggage if you think it will be easier to carry through airports.

MONEY—GREEN, FOREIGN, OR PLASTIC?

Virtually all ships are now cashless, meaning you give them your credit card number, and they give you a cruise charge card that may double as a room key and boarding pass. You buy anything you want—from casino chips to photos to toothpaste—by flashing that card. At the end of the cruise, you settle your account either by paying cash for the total bill or allowing the ship to charge the credit card. Few cruise lines now accept cash on board outside the casino or the purser's office. For travelers who don't want to use a credit card, the cruise line will also accept a cash deposit, allowing you to "charge" up to that amount. It's still possible to find a ship willing to accept a personal check with ID, but good luck. If you don't have a credit card, press your travel agent for specific info on what the cruise line will accept. Expect something like a mandatory

$250 deposit to get you started. While shore excursions operate under the auspices of a local company, they're bought on board and can be paid for through your shipboard account.

In most mainstream cruise ports of call, U.S. dollars work fine. Even Caribbean nations with a different currency usually accept greenbacks—in some countries, it's preferred, notably with near-the-port vendors that rely on cruise line business. In the U.S. Virgin Islands (St. Thomas etc.), the British Virgin Islands, and Puerto Rico, locals conduct all business with U.S. currency. Businesses everywhere accept traveler's checks, and most cruise ships cash them on board.

In cities that don't universally accept U.S. money, or if buying an expensive item, consider using a major credit card. While some small, independent vendors may not accept credit cards, most medium- to large-sized businesses do, and the exchange rate, if applicable, is usually better. It also offers a measure of protection since you can complain through the credit card company if problems arise later.

AIRPORT DEPARTURES AND ARRIVALS

By the time you booked a cruise, the travel agent should have explained airline policies, restrictions, and the penalties should you choose to change flights.

Arrive at least one hour before flights to domestic destinations such as Miami or Seattle. Arrive two hours before international flights. During a holiday season, especially Thanksgiving and Christmas, tack at least an extra half hour on to both those times.

If driving yourself to the airport, you might consider long-term parking at an off-site company. It will be located farther away than the airport long-term parking, but will perform the same function and charge less. They may even wash your car while you're gone or perform some maintenance work—all for a fee. Assuming the company actually keeps your car in a secure location, these guys can also be more convenient. Many allow you to park your car close to their registration desk and only a few feet from a shuttle bus; they'll valet park the car. In exchange for a tip of about a dollar per bag, they'll also help tote luggage. For a list of local companies that offer

this service, call the airport of departure and ask for recommendations.

When you reach the airport curb, skycaps will offer to take your
luggage. They'll check you and your bags in, meaning you can
avoid a long line inside the door (if there is one) and proceed
directly to the gate. The skycaps will cost you about another dollar
per bag. If you want to save on the tip or you have questions that
should be answered before you give up your luggage, proceed
inside dragging the suitcases as best you can, and get in line at your
airline's check-in desk.

If you must switch planes at an intermediary airport, the flight
crew may make an announcement before landing listing the gate
number where you'll find your connecting flight. Once you land,
follow those directions or check monitors in the terminal. They
should list a flight number, final destination city, and gate number.
There's no need to check in for your connecting flight. They
already know you're there.

AT AIRPORT NEAR PORT OF EMBARKATION: If arriving
in a foreign country, you'll have to pass through Immigration and
Customs, meaning you'll get your luggage back and someone will
ask you a few questions. As long as you're not smuggling, carrying
banned material such as fresh fruit or anything else declared inad-
missible, you should pass right through. If not flying into a foreign
country, follow the crowd to baggage claim. Get your luggage if
your cruise line does not provide plane-to-ship transfers for it,
though most do. In any case, look for a cruise line representative.
They're usually found somewhere en route to baggage claim in an
area that everyone must pass through. They'll be holding up a sign
with the ship's logo prominently displayed, and probably dressed
in some bright outfit that clearly says he or she is a cruise line
employee. Tell them who you are and let them take over. They'll
probably check your name off a list and direct you to a waiting bus
in which, with other passengers bound for the seas, you'll be transported to the ship. The cruise line may include a transportation
voucher with final documents if you're transferring from airport to
port by bus. If so, hand the voucher to the bus driver when you
board.

Airline Problems—and What to Do

The following problems are not unique to cruise vacations, nor do they happen often—but they do happen. Travel rarely goes smoothly, so take a sense of humor and anticipate that something, somewhere, will go a bit awry.

- **You're late for the plane.** If arriving within a half hour of departure, don't panic. Everything will probably be fine, and if not, airline staff will try to put you on another flight. If arriving after the plane has already left, personnel, theoretically, don't have to help you since you broke your contract with the airline. Throw yourself on the mercy of the local staff and ask to be included on the next flight out. Be polite. While courtesy and manners are ethically correct, in this case, they also do more good than demands and anger. If told that they "can't do anything," ask to see a manager. While they may be legally correct, they own the planes and can do whatever they want. If courtesy doesn't seem to be working, try complaining loudly—in front of other customers. Airlines hate to look less than friendly in front of paying customers.

- **The plane is canceled.** You may not know why they canceled the flight; it could be for safety reasons. They're certainly not going to announce that the wing fell off. If this happens, reservationists will try to get everyone on the next flight out. Make it clear that you have a ship to catch. If that doesn't pull enough weight to get you into town well before departure, ask the reservationist if you can call the cruise line. (A phone number should be in the documents you brought along; if not, make sure you write it down before leaving home.) If you booked your flight with the cruise line, it's now their problem. If you did not, and they can't help, it's your problem (see Chapter 3).

- **You're bumped.** "Bumping" means that the plane has more passengers than seats, no one volunteers to wait for a later flight in exchange for a free ticket or travel voucher, and the airline must force some people off the plane. This shouldn't happen to a cruise passenger, but if it does, insist upon a free ticket good for at least a year, and a seat on the first plane out. Then make sure you're booked on the next flight out.

- **You miss your connection.** If the first flight out is delayed, you may arrive at an intermediary airport too late to fly out on a connecting flight. This problem occurs more often than getting bumped or missing the plane, but is also easier to solve since it's (usually) a single connection to the port of embarkation. Reservationists will probably try to put you on that airline's next flight out, though it may be hours away. Politely demand the first flight out on any airline. (Note: if a plane leaves within the next fifteen or twenty minutes and you must run to catch it, especially on a competing carrier, there's a fair chance your luggage won't make it to the ship the same time that you do. You'll probably see it at the first port of call.)
- **A passenger is obnoxious.** Tell a flight attendant and ask to be moved. Airlines won't put up with this.
- **The airline lost your luggage.** You lose time with this one because you don't know your luggage is lost until everyone has left baggage claim. (If the luggage automatically transfers to the ship, you don't know it until that evening when you're at sea.) Immediately complain to the airline—an office should be located nearby in baggage claim—and give them your cruise information. While you could forgo the trip, it's not worth it. Go. You'll fill out a form; they'll give you a copy; and you'll probably see your luggage within a day or two.

CHECKING IN AT THE PIER

Checking in and boarding a cruise ship tends to be the second worst part of cruising. The worst part is getting off (disembarking) to be covered later. Assuming nothing goes wrong during the boarding process, embarkation is really not so bad. Expect, however, to waste time waiting in line and, at times, standing in thigh-to-thigh crowds.

If driving to the ship, watch for signs announcing locations as you get close. Most ports of embarkation have convenient parking, many times located directly across the street from the ship. They also have a luggage drop-off point close to check-in. The standard procedure is to pull in, drop off luggage and a spouse or friend, then pull across the street and park the car. Luggage should already be tagged (tags come with final documents) and ready for transport to your cabin. Most port parking lots have a chain-link fence and at least a roving security guard at night. Parking costs run about $7 to $8 per day in most U.S. ports. Ask your travel agent for specific information.

If you've arrived by cruise line transport from a hotel or airport, disembark and proceed through the main doors to check-in. Let the cruise line worry about your bags.

All ships require similar documentation from incoming passengers, but procedures vary slightly. To board, ship personnel need to see your proof of citizenship and any filled-out forms required by the countries. Figuring this is not the fun part anyway, many cruise lines also set up your shipboard credit account somewhere along the way. Generally, expect check-in to go something like this:

1. If embarkation begins at, say, 1:00 P.M., most passengers seem to arrive between 12:30 P.M. and 2:00 P.M. As a result, checking-in takes less time if you arrive a bit earlier or much later—but at least an hour before the scheduled departure. Arriving earlier has a few advantages: You get the paperwork out of the way, have time to get oriented on the ship, and enjoy the luncheon buffet somewhere around early afternoon when it was meant to be enjoyed. On the downside, you won't be the only passenger who chooses to arrive extra early and you'll still wait in line. Arriving late gives you relatively line-free boarding with minimum waits, but you'll miss out on onboard activities and lunch.

2. Multiple lines exist at check-in and are usually organized alphabetically. There may be separate lines for special groups, such as passengers who are not citizens of the port country or disabled guests. You may also enter a special, faster line if you booked a suite. To make check-in easier, fill out as much as you can before arrival—most forms will be included in the document packet given to you by your travel agent or handed out on the bus prior to arrival. If in doubt about any questions, leave them blank and ask the cruise line representative for instructions. When finished, you should have all the things you need to cruise. In some cases, the room key will be waiting in the cabin.

3. At some point, you pass through an X-ray machine similar to the ones used in airports. It's standard procedure to assure onboard security.

4. Either as part of the initial check-in process or somewhere nearby, the ship will offer to set up your onboard charge account. (A few do it on board.) You hand them a credit card (or cash if you must—see earlier section) and they deduct money from your credit card account. At this point, your credit card is not charged, but money is "blocked off." That means that if you have $1,000 worth of credit remaining on a card, and the cruise line blocks off $1,000 in credit, you cannot use that card for any other purchases. If you happen to be close to maxing out one card, you may want to bring a second card for charges made in ports of call.

5. Expect to have a picture taken somewhere along the way. Beyond smiling and posing, do nothing now. The picture will be posted on board and you'll have the option of purchasing it later (see Chapter 7).

6. You feel a bit of magic entering the ship, usually walking into an ornate entranceway surrounded by two lines of ship personnel in smartly pressed uniforms. Waiters pass out drinks, though you'll probably have to pay for it if you wish to indulge. Someone asks for your room number; you give it to him or her; a steward tells you to "follow me." You glance at a room or two as you pass, twist down a hallway, and finally come to an open door with your room number on it. The steward who brought you may give a quick overview of how things work. You may tip him or her if you wish, but it's not required. More information, including a roster of the day's scheduled activities, should be waiting for you.

7. Shortly after arriving in your cabin, your room steward should stop by and introduce himself. If you have special requests—an extra pillow, more towels—ask now. If something is wrong—an ocean-view room with an obstructed view, twin beds that don't convert as requested, etc.—complain now. As more passengers board, the cruise line's problem-solving options shrink. If the room steward cannot help, go directly to the hotel manager. Polite firmness works best. (If a room is noisy, you may not know it yet, however. Engine noises appear only when the engine is on, to state the obvious, and disco noises appear only when alcohol flows and people dance. Don't hesitate to complain later even if a problem does not show up right away.)

8. Take a tour of the ship. If hungry, start at the buffet usually served on a top deck. Carry a ship's diagram along or request one.

You might consider taking along the brochure used when you first made your booking since that many times has a better map than what they hand out on board.

9. As you tour, stop by the dining room, ask where you will be sitting, and confirm any special dietary requests. If you want to change locations, it's easiest now, accompanied by a $10 to $20 tip to the maître d'. On a few cruises, table assignments must be confirmed after your arrival. If so, make this the first stop.

10. Reserve what you can. Book desired shore excursions as soon as possible. The popular ones go fast. If you need any services while on board—hair salon, spa, massage, baby-sitting, etc.— make arrangements on the first day. Again, the best times disappear quickly. If an onboard ship credit account was not established before boarding, do so now.

11. Enjoy the cruise.

7

ONCE ON BOARD

If you want some idea of what life on an ocean cruise is like, read on. This is the nuts-and-bolts—the events and services planned for passenger enjoyment. If something must be considered prior to sailing or on the day of departure, look for information in earlier chapters. For all that last day information—disembarkation is the most un-fun part of a cruise—skip to the end of this chapter.

WHAT DO I HAVE TO PAY FOR?

Overall, upscale cruises include more items; economy cruises include fewer items. It's easy to find out if something is not included in your cruise fare while at sea—just ask. Before ordering a pizza at the small café by the pool, ask the attendant if pizza is free. That should not only net an answer of "yes" or "no," but also get you a price quote if the latter. If pizza costs nothing and dinner is one hour away, you may want a few bites to tide you over. If pizza costs $3 per slice and dinner is one hour away, you may prefer to wait, even if $3 is a negligible amount of spending money. There's no shame in that. And since the cruise lines decide what they include in your basic cruise fare, small fees for pizza are just a nickel-and-dime way to squeeze more money out of you. So ask, then say "no thanks," unless you want it. That'll show 'em.

A rule of thumb concerning shipboard costs: Most group services are included in the cruise fare, while most personal services are not. Evening entertainment, movies, and scheduled activities, for example, are free since they're open to all passengers. Massages, cocktails, and photos are not because they're personal—something of value only to one person or a family. A kids' program costs nothing during the day since it's open to all passengers. If a baby-sitter comes to the room or must be reserved in the evenings, however, it costs money. Shore excursions fall into the personal category.

For extensive information on costs, see Chapter 4. Generally, the following are not included in the prepaid price of a cruise: specialty food (honor bar or sometimes that pizza), liquor, beauty and spa services, phone calls, photos, special activities (painting class, book for a lecture series), casinos, in-room movies, golf, babysitting, and shore excursions.

YOUR CABIN

A small cabin may have bunk beds, drawers, and a bathroom. A suite may have room for dancing (not the waltz), a tub, a complete living room, a private balcony, and more. On almost all cruises, regardless of cabin booked, first-time cruisers, upon entering their cabin, usually say: "It's so small." Those in the Presidential Suite immediately compare it to a hotel suite and feel it doesn't quite measure up, even if they have four times the space of their bunk bed traveling companions. Space is at a premium on ships, and anyone who has used an airplane rest room understands the challenge.

On first arrival in your cabin, check layout, make sure everything works properly, and inform the room steward if things break along the way. Unlike a hotel maid, the room steward does more than simply clean the room. Their primary duty is fairly lofty—nothing less than making sure you're satisfied with the accommodations in every way. In that sense, their job has no boundaries. If you want a baby-sitter for the grandkids, the room steward may tell you whom to call. If you insist that he take care of it, he probably will. At the least, he'll do *something* because (a) no crew member wants to have a complaint registered against him, and (b) you will be tipping him at the end of the cruise and any extra service he performs may net him more money later.

For those who want someone to quietly take care of their needs while operating in the background, the room steward may be seen only in passing, with beds invisibly made or turned down only when you're at dinner or in a port of call. However, many travelers develop a personal relationship with their room steward, discussing his home country, children, and life at sea. If you want a friend, the room steward will be one. If you want to be left alone, he'll do that, too.

SAFETY DRILL

An eerie activity for first-time cruisers, the safety drill is a rehearsal so everyone knows what to do in case the ship must be evacuated. That evacuation could be a sinking, à la *Titanic*, a fire, or other disaster. A few first-timers, worried only about seasickness, suddenly have other concerns. It's ominous. However, it's also no big deal. Get over it.

The drill is mandatory under maritime law. Remember the fire drills in high school? Same thing here but wearing life jackets. In a quick-read version, you must (a) know where your life jacket is stored in your cabin, (b) grab it, (c) head for your muster station (or emergency boat station or separate meeting area), (d) put on your life jacket (sometimes the trickiest part of the whole exercise), and (e) wait for instructions from the crew.

The actual format for the emergency drill varies by cruise line. One line may require everyone to don life jackets and wait quietly while crew members call out names. Others may not require life jackets to be worn. Regardless, it's an important exercise, no different from knowing where the fire extinguisher is located in your kitchen or how to dial 911 in an emergency. It's also a good photo op if you've got grandkids strapped into bulky orange life preservers. Take the camera.

MEALS

On sailings with assigned mealtimes, the only meal without flexibility is dinner. In the evening, everyone wants a full-course meal, and without a buffet or snack bar offering food elsewhere on the ship, the dining room is the only game in your world. If you arrive late, you'll probably be seated, but because dinner service on a mega-ship runs like a finely tuned machine, you may find that you, the monkey wrench in the works, are served last, erratically, and rushed to completion.

At breakfast and lunch, however, an open buffet is usually served elsewhere on the ship, giving passengers a fast meal option if heading out to aerobics, a shore excursion, or other activity. Since many people opt for the buffet, it leaves plenty of empty seats in the dining room. Consequently, even with an assigned mealtime, you can usually show up early or late for breakfast and still be served, possibly at a different table. The same is true at lunch—even more so if in a port and most passengers choose to go ashore.

Should problems arise in the dining room, whether your fault for showing up late or someone else's fault, talk to the maître d' should the waiter be unable to help. If unlikable dining companions or inefficient service problems arise after the first meal or two, talk to the maître d'. If you wish to move to a different table or switch to an earlier or later dining schedule, slip him some money.

A SNAPSHOT OF DAILY CRUISE LIFE

Brochures all say something like "choose to do it all . . . or choose to do nothing at all." That's a bit of a lie. While "nothing at all" may work, you can't "do it all." Outside the fact that you'll kill yourself, there may be four or five activities scheduled at the same time.

A cruise has four main elements that sometimes flow together seamlessly and sometimes overlap. Food and meals create the first element followed by popular group activities such as the evening show or a port of call. The third element consists of specialty events—a lecture on Alaska, a how-to-play bridge class, or a slightly stale version of a game show—open to all but attended by only a small percentage of passengers. Personal services make up the fourth element. Those include the obvious spa and salon serv-ices, but also encompass personal entertainment such as the lounges, the playgrounds for kids, and the arcades for teenagers.

To overstereotype the typical first-time passenger's day: First-time cruisers tend to hit all meals, see all scheduled nighttime enter-tainment, and visit all ports of call—elements one and two. Their remaining free time generally breaks down in blocks of one- to three-hour increments—one hour on port days, three hours on at-sea days. During these breaks, they look at the daily schedule of events that the room steward slips under the door each night, find the activities scheduled during their free time, and go to whatever sounds appealing—element three. They may never get to element four, a personal service, because they never find the time. If they do, they have trouble scheduling a convenient time because they waited too long to do so and all the good times are gone. By the time the cruise ends, they're happy, exhausted, and slightly upset that they missed so much.

To overstereotype the seasoned passenger with two or more sailings under his or her belt: Seasoned cruisers eat dinner in the dining room, but may miss an evening program or two in lieu of an early night or cocktails and dancing. They plan to skip a port of call or two, either because they've already visited or because they enjoy the ship when 80 percent of the passengers have departed. Seasoned cruisers glance over the list of daily activities and note the ones that interest them before confirming anything in their mind. They may forgo a lunch in the dining room for a class, or they may opt for a lecture on St. Martin instead of an art auction. Many seasoned cruisers also build in time to read a book, watch the sun set across the ocean, or stare mindlessly at other passengers rushing to and from events. By the time the cruise ends, they feel they got their money's worth.

Mature travelers—even first-time cruisers—tend to be more like the seasoned passengers. They see the cruise as both adventure and stress-reducer.

Here's an eye-opener for some first-time cruisers: Many activities offered on megaships and economy lines seem more appropriate for college students on spring break. Expect men to participate in hairy chest or best-legs contests. Look for newlywed games for non-newlyweds as well as honeymooners. Partake if you must of sing-a-longs, cellulite lectures, talent shows, and even twist contests. Morbid curiosity draws many mature adults to the more outrageous activities.

GETTING AROUND

You walk far more on a cruise than you realize. An "I'm going to the gift shop" could include a fifteen-minute, round-trip hike. Add two miles for a shore excursion, three trips to the dining room, six other miscellaneous activities, and you've done yourself in. The best safeguard against burnout is a well-placed cabin, discussed earlier, and (hopefully) taken care of at the time of booking. While on the cruise, however, consider the following strategies:

PLAN AHEAD. It's easy to think of a cabin as home base and return to it often, but consider the entire ship your home. With a half hour to kill between the shore excursion lecture and your hair appointment, use the time to shop in a nearby gift shop, sit in the convenient deck chair, or look for last night's photos in the gallery right next door. Pack the things you use often — medicine, a camera, a novel, etc. — in your pocketbook or fanny pack.

TAKE A NAP. Heavy meals, extra walking, and a mild sunburn add up to complete exhaustion. A nap is one of life's greatest diversions and an afternoon journey to dream land makes the entire voyage more pleasant. It's good advice for all passengers, but only mature ones have the good sense to consider it.

SWIM DOWNSTREAM. Expect heavy crowds and elbow-to-elbow elevators for shows, meals, and port excursions — anytime most passengers go the same direction at the same time. Elevators can become extremely crowded and slow, stopping at every floor to pick up passengers who find no room to enter. While tough to avoid completely, consider going early or late to dinner. Early works well if you can find something close to the dining room to while away the time, or if you don't mind waiting twenty minutes or more for the show to start; at least you'll get good seats.

When visiting a port of call, disembark later. If you do decide to get off early, wait at least a few minutes after the announcement that you're cleared to disembark. Paperwork must be filed and it takes a while for a ship to be cleared for entry; during this time, a throng of waiting people may clog nearby hallways and doors. If it's first-come/first-served for a tender (boat) assignment when the ship cannot dock in port, waiting may create a delay, however, as the first seats go early.

STUDY THE DECK PLAN. Getting lost wastes time and energy, but on the megaships, it's not unusual to use one route to get to the dining room, only to find out on the last day that you could have saved steps by going a different direction. It also helps if you can combine trips to the store, gym, and dining room into one easy round-trip plan that minimizes backtracking.

TAKE A DAY OFF. Pick one day in the middle of the cruise and call it your "day off." Plan only relaxing activities, such as a massage or show, and spend most of the day reading or playing games. You may miss one major activity or two, but you'll enjoy the pace better when you go back to "work." It can also be a psychological pickup since the daily itineraries tend to ebb and flow in the same way each day.

SHORE EXCURSIONS

The easiest, safest, and recommended way to see most islands and world destinations is by booking a shore excursion through the cruise line either before sailing or, if not possible, once on board. In some ports, however, you can explore most of the nonbeach areas simply by getting off the ship and walking, especially if shopping is your primary goal. If disabled, the ship's crew can also advise you on options—and problems—with different itineraries, including which shore excursions can accommodate you and what problems can be expected. They can also make special arrangements.

Take only what you need, including your boarding pass, and leave extra credit cards and valuables in the room safe. If arriving at a beach destination, crew members usually hand out towels as you exit. As you shop, keep a receipt for all purchases—it may be important when you return home and pass through customs (see Disembarking in this chapter).

CRUISE LINE SHORE EXCURSIONS: One advantage: You book these ahead of time and don't waste time in port. Second advantage: If it's worth seeing, there's probably a shore excursion that takes you there. Third advantage: A bus probably picks you up near the ship. Fourth advantage: You may get to disembark earlier than other passengers. Fifth advantage: Cruise lines do not simply hire the land tour company that offers them the most money;

tours are part of the entire cruise experience and they weed out the losers. Sixth advantage: The cruise line's insurance carrier probably covers you while on shore excursions, but if that's a concern, confirm it with the cruise line.

First disadvantage: It's usually more expensive to take a cruise line sponsored excursion since both cruise line and tour operator take their cut. Second disadvantage: You see what everyone else sees and hear what everyone else hears. Third disadvantage: Since many people travel on a cruise ship–sponsored shore excursion, each tourist attraction will be most crowded during your visit. Fourth disadvantage: A rigid tour schedule may force you to spend more time in one area than you wish—and less time in another. Fifth disadvantage: Someone is always late for the bus and you end up waiting.

Most get-to-know-the-area shore excursions provide general knowledge about the port and country with a few recycled insider facts—perfect for a first visit but old by the second. If interested, book these early in the cruise, preferably soon after you board the ship.

PRIVATE SHORE EXCURSIONS: Anyplace where 5,000 tourists disembark every Tuesday (your ship and others), someone will have a boat, bus, or taxi, and they will be standing in front of it offering tours. Safety and security are always a concern, and the best advice is to ask a crew member for advice before disembarking. That's not meant to raise any unnecessary red flags, but common sense— common among mature travelers—should not be left on board. The number one rule for any private shore excursion: Get back to the ship on time. If you break rule number one and literally miss the boat, immediately contact the cruise line's local representative.

SHOPPING: Megaships tend to visit ports also frequented by other megaships, and a touristy downtown district filled with T-shirt shops usually thrives nearby. Onboard lectures about a port many times concentrate on shopping, and everywhere you look, someone is handing you a discount coupon for merchandise. Like anything else, the best advice comes from those who have visited before, especially if looking for something specific such as china or linens or electronics.

In many Caribbean countries, you haggle to get a good price on merchandise from local vendors, such as those in Jamaica, though stores along a main street may post prices and stick to them.

If haggling, consider it a game and enjoy it. The rules: If you stare at something longer than a half second, a vendor will say, "I can give you a good price on that." You say, "I'm just looking," and if actually interested, go back to the item before you're ready to leave. Let the vendor make an offer. Look thoughtful, as if slightly interested but disappointed with the price quote. Then, if the vendor's "discount" was 20 percent less than the posted price, offer perhaps another 20 percent off that price. Based on the vendor's response, work toward something acceptable. If close to agreement but negotiations seem frozen, thank them and start to walk away. If you're just bluffing, stop back in a minute and buy it at the final price they offered. Many times, they'll cave in on the price since people who leave tend not to come back, finding something very similar at another vendor's booth. If you and the vendor are far apart on the cost, you'll know it early in the negotiations.

Note on name brand items: In almost all countries, a copyrighted name cannot be duplicated. With that said, it's done all the time. Before buying an "incredible deal," make sure that that Rolex is a Rolex, that Sony is a Sony, and that diamond in your new ring doesn't melt in the noonday sun. Many times, prices for items in ship stores come close to those on land, and should something go wrong, you can complain.

Note on "recommended" stores: Many tour leaders receive a kickback from a store owner if they schedule a "break" for fifteen minutes or so directly in front of their souvenir stand. If the guide says it has the "cheapest prices in all of St. Thomas," it might be true—or not. The same may be true of recommendations from the cruise line, so comparison shop.

RENTING A CAR: In many countries, cars and roads differ from those in the U.S., and the stress of memorizing new rules may take the pleasure out of renting a car. Requirements vary, too. On the other hand, a self-driven tour is the best way to stop at a secluded restaurant or take pictures of everyday residents. If interested in a car, ask your travel agent about the details when you book your cruise. Alternately, check at the shore excursion desk to see what the ship can offer.

TAKING A TAXI: A taxi makes sense if you plan to visit a specific beach, casino, or restaurant. You can also turn it into an inexpensive, personalized tour of the island or town. Before getting off the ship, ask ship personnel which cab companies are reliable, then look for one near the ship, taking care to avoid unmarked taxis. Expect competition from different drivers offering rides and, without appearing too interested, casually walk over to one that seems friendly, can communicate in a language you know, and drives for one of the recommended companies. Then negotiate a price. The key in most ports is to tell the driver where you wish to go and ask how much it will cost. If you simply wait for a fee to be quoted at the end of the tour, as you do in U.S. cities, it could be far more expensive. If going to a specific destination such as an out-of-the-way beach, ask if they will return to pick you up—and make their tip worthwhile. If a taxi breaks down and you return to the ship late, however, wave good-bye. The cruise won't wait.

EXPLORING ON FOOT: Many ports can be explored on foot, though that obviously limits you to stores and attractions nearby. On megaships, this also tends to keep you in elbow-to-elbow crowds, but in smaller ports generally frequented by smaller ships, you may only have a few blocks to explore. Wear good walking shoes, sunscreen in the tropics, and spend a few minutes inside a local restaurant or bar to get a feel for the local life.

STAYING HEALTHY: If there is any danger in drinking the local water or eating local food, ship personnel post ample warnings. In most ports, spots frequented by tourists are fine. Most times—Mexico, for example—roadside vendors should be avoided. Generally, if the water should not be consumed, don't eat anything that has water on it, such as salads and, to state the obvious, ice. (Creatures of habit, we order a Coke to be safe and forget that ice is, in reality, frozen water.) Also spend more time washing hands in foreign ports. Even if generally clean, changes in diet and activity levels may leave the body more open to sickness.

PRIVATE ISLANDS

Many Caribbean brochures say something about a "day at our own private island, (Something) Cay." For these, cruise lines either rent or buy an island, strip out most native buildings, if any, and re-create a paradise reminiscent of *Gilligan's Island*. They serve beach barbecues, sell frozen drinks with little umbrellas, and string hammocks between palm trees. NCL has Great Stirrup Cay, Royal Caribbean has CocoCay, Princess has (obviously) Princess Cay, Holland America has Half Moon Cay, Premier has Salt Cay, and Disney has Castaway Cay. Disney also owns one of the few islands with deep-water access, meaning the ship docks at a pier. Guests may come and go as they please, returning to the ship as needed. On most other islands, a tender (smaller boat) transports guests between ship and shore.

Generally, a private island day provides cooped-up Northerners with a great way to tan, relax, swim, and explore the tropics. For those who prefer to stick a toe in the clear water, shop for ten minutes, and then say, "Thank you very much, I'm done now," it's also a great time to do things on the ship.

Private islands can present two challenges: getting there and, once ashore, walking. The tender transfer can present a problem for wheelchairs (see Chapter 3), and it also makes scheduling difficult. Twenty minutes to the island, twenty minutes back, and twenty minutes for loading/unloading passengers makes each transfer of guests take about one hour. Even with two tenders, it takes a while to transfer an entire shipload of passengers. Later, of course, they all must return. Early in the day, crowds can get thick in hallways and nearby public rooms as people wait to go ashore. When ready to return from the island, crowds begin to line up at the dock.

Most islands have at least minimal access for wheelchairs, though once main walkways end, sand paths or covered trails prove the norm—and are impassable. Even main walkways can be tricky once 5,000 toes start tracking grains of sand across the concrete. Even for the ambulatory, however, some islands demand a lot of walking. Most islands usually have some kind of beach close to the point of arrival, but these tend to get crowded and have the most kids. They also run out of beach chairs or hammocks minutes after the first tender arrives. Most islands have other beaches too, but all require walking—sometimes a lot of it. The island, for example, may have an active ocean on one side and a passive ocean on the other. A passive side faces other islands or seas and is usually where the ship drops anchor; an active side faces the open ocean and has bigger waves. To reach the good waves, you have to walk across the island. An adults-only beach may be in one area and the ruins of an old rum distillery in another. More walking. Some islands even have hiking trails for an excursion into a natural tropical setting. More walking. Add to this the fact that you must cross sand — always more strenuous — and you can quickly reach your exercise quota for the day. Many people sightsee first and save swimming for last, giving them a workout, a rest, and a chance to cool off before returning to the ship to prepare for the evening's activities.

ENTERTAINMENT

Onboard entertainment comes in second only to food in attracting guests to cruising. The big guys show pictures of Las Vegas-style dancers with bathing suit outfits and sprays of feathers cascading from their heads. Rather than plays or concerts, most big-time entertainment events use a vaudeville style, and it's common to have a bevy of musical numbers interspersed with magicians, comedians, or puppet shows.

Do not expect Broadway-quality entertainment on a cruise ship. Expect decent lighting and sound with jokes, songs, and dancing that appeals to all age groups. There may be a strong Caribbean influence if traveling in the Caribbean, a strong European influence in Europe, or a specific thematic style on cruise lines such as Disney, American Hawaii, or the Delta Queen Steamboat Co. Songs may be lip-synced rather than live; orchestras could be taped rather than backstage. Costumes may be bigger than life, and a single performer may make ten costume changes each night. Expect to see the same entertainers a night or two later in a different show singing different songs and clad in different costumes.

Ships with two dinner seatings often have two shows scheduled — both identical — timed roughly a half hour after each group finishes eating. Those dining at first seating then watch the show as the main seating diners eat.

Many lounges are smaller entertainment venues. A single comedian may perform late at night, for example, if his material is a bit off-color and inappropriate for children. But he may be very good, an up-and-coming star honing his craft as he prepares for the big time. A jazz trio in a small lounge may also be excellent, having accepted a three-month booking to prepare for a gig in New York. While the smaller performances may not offer the "wow" factor of the main production, the individual performers may be more talented.

SERVICES

Casinos, coiffures, and crunches—onboard options offer an array of activities.

CASINO: Casinos remain highly profitable for cruise lines and only Disney chose not to include one—a major decision for the seafaring mouse. Most major cruise lines do not operate their own casinos; rather, they subcontract the service in exchange for a cut of the profit. Once on board, casinos are usually easy to find; indeed, you almost can't help finding them. Many times, you must walk through the casino to get from one frequently visited room to another. And, in passing, even non gamblers tend to check their pocket for change and drop a quarter into the nearest slot machine.

Games such as blackjack offer the same odds on a ship as they do anywhere else. Discussion arises on how "loose" the slots are on a cruise ship, however, meaning how often they let you win. While slots and video games seem to offer rather random payouts, the amount of money returned to players is predetermined and doled out through a computer software program. Overall, passengers lose. On a case-by-case basis, though, someone wins. At the same time, three other "someones" lose.

Companies that run cruise casinos claim that the odds of winning money on board are at least equal to the odds of winning in Las Vegas or other gambling meccas where one casino competes with another down the street. They claim that consumers are now savvy and would not gamble on a cruise if they did not have a fair chance of winning. But the cruise lines don't have to compete, of course: You either play in their playground or you don't play at all. Also, many cruise gamblers do not frequent Las Vegas or gamble much, meaning the operators don't have as much incentive to pay back a lot of money.

Advice: assume the odds of winning do not compare well to other gambling venues in the U.S., at least for slots and other programmable games. That's advice—not a provable fact. The actual percentage returned to guests is a secret. For most passengers, gambling is a diversion—fun and exciting—but few expect to become King Midas.

One more item: most ports with legalized gambling pay out no more—and usually less—than the cruise ship slots and games. If you want to gamble, go to Vegas; if you want to have fun gambling, take a cruise.

You must be at least eighteen to gamble on a cruise ship, but no one seems to check once at sea. Also, casinos close when in port thanks to the rules of the host countries that, mainly, want you to gamble in their own casinos—or not at all.

BEAUTY SALONS: Make reservations early, doubly so if planning to have work done prior to a formal dinner. Services are similar to beauty salon offerings within the U.S. While prices vary, expect to pay (before tip) about $20 for a simple cut and style. Prices escalate from there. Tips run about 15 percent, at your discretion, and may be charged to your room.

SPAS: Again, make reservations early. Spa novices may be downright scared of some offerings that sound like a torture by Captain Nemo. Even confirmed spa-goers are usually unaware of some treatments. (Confusion usually sets in when, for example, the staff says that they'll tone your skin with seaweed. Obvious questions include: "Why seaweed?" and "Does it really do anything?" Answers: "I don't know" and "Yes.") Ignorance is the norm, however, and the staff answers the most basic questions without laughing in your face. The best time to get answers is the day of arrival when they host an open house.

People with a health condition that might be aggravated by a treatment or exercise should notify cruise staff; in most cases, they'll ask you first. The 15 percent rule of thumb applies to tips—higher or lower depending on your satisfaction.

All services tend to fall into one of three categories—massage, skin improvement, or exercise.

Massage everyone understands; Swedish, aromatherapy, reflexology, and other types of massage tend to confuse, however, with the differences between them somewhat unclear to the layman or laywoman. While therapists may take me to task, in general, any massage is good. Unless you need a massage to combat a specific physical problem, pick the one that appeals to you. A massage also does something to the mind, taking tension not only from muscles but also brain cells. If you've never had a professional massage, consider this one of the mandatory extras worth paying for on a cruise. Different massage styles last different lengths of time, but they average about $40 to $50 per half hour.

Skin improvement includes all those lotions, masks, and baths that do something to the skin. Some offerings use chemicals developed in laboratories; others use the seaweed mentioned earlier along with ivy, clay, and other natural ingredients. These may attack specific problems you have, such as cellulite or water retention, or simply improve the appearance of your skin.

Exercise services range from personal training to body-fat analysis. Personal training includes a study of your current body followed by recommendations of exercises that will improve it. If you already exercise daily, the trainer will suggest ways to tone as-yet-unworked muscles. If you don't exercise, the personal trainer will get you headed in the right direction. The body-fat analysis and other tests may be used by the trainer or taken independently. On some ships, professional sports trainers also offer advice or lessons in their area of expertise such as tennis or golf.

While personal trainers can cost about $50 per hour, exercise rooms cost nothing to use and generally remain open throughout the day. Cruise ships now compete on how much they offer to fitness buffs, and on the megaships, expect to find a range of cutting-edge equipment with expansive views of the ocean. Many ships also have tennis, basketball, and/or volleyball courts, Ping-Pong tables, dartboards, and shuffleboard.

SHOPPING

The megaships sell almost everything in a series of shops that are eerily mall-like. The basics of life—toothbrushes, sunscreen, etc.— can be found somewhere, as well as the usual range of tourist merchandise sporting the ship's logo—the T-shirts, refrigerator magnets, and other paraphernalia. Shops also stock a range of clothing, more for women than men, and more for resort casual occasions than formal attire. They also sell liquor, jewelry, collectibles, shoes, makeup, and perfume. Liquor tends to be extremely affordable, mainly because it's duty-free (tax-free). Don't expect to consume it right away, however. Most ships deliver liquor purchases to your room at the end of the cruise and force you to drink in their bars and lounges while at sea. (Unless you buy a bottle in port and sneak it into your cabin. It's not illegal—just against policy.)

Also expect to find shops stocking a nutshell version of island products waiting to be discovered when you visit a port of call. For example, one of the shopping draws in Nassau, Bahamas, is the straw market, a tightly packed area where vendors sell handmade crafts. Many are indeed made of straw, but you'll also find wood carvings, clothing, and other things. On board, one small section of a store will probably stock similar items. In most (but not all) cases, the products offered on board will be slightly more expensive than a similar land product, assuming you negotiated the land price down to its lowest level. The quality of the onboard offerings may be a bit higher, however. Most people shop on board after they return from a port excursion, perhaps because they forgot a gift for the grandchildren or weren't comfortable haggling in the market. A better idea, however, is to shop for items before visiting a port—but don't buy anything. It not only provides an overview of the type of goods you can expect to see, but with an approximate cost in your mind, it makes haggling easier. Also, it's sometimes difficult to make purchase decisions at your first port of call when you still have three islands to visit—who knows what better deals you'll find there? Compare products on board first, see where they were made, and then make preliminary decisions about port shopping.

The same rule applies to major purchases—electronics, jewelry, etc. you plan to buy. Rather than comparison shop on board before arrival in a port, however, price shop before departure at hometown stores. If planning to buy a camcorder in Barbados, for example, check the local camcorder prices by brand, taking note of special features. You may find that the Sony camcorders sold in Barbados differ from the ones you checked out, but both have similar features, and you'll know whether it's a bargain.

Another shopping draw on board many ships is the *art auction*. To state the obvious: They auction off art. Expect to see some better-than-usual pieces on display and, to catch your eye, a famous name or two, though many times only print number 300 out of a complete run of 500. Expect also to see supremely mediocre stuff. Understand the rules before you bid—it probably comes unframed—and purchase anything you find pleasing. Whether or not it's a bargain depends on the number of people who attend and the competition for a specific piece. It only takes two interested parties to make the price go through the roof.

If there's a downside to port shopping, it's the possibility of *scams*—something you won't have to worry about on board. If an item costs slightly more on board than its counterpart in a port, it may be worth the extra money. When holding a diamond ring in a port city store and considering paying $1,200 for it, the slight chance of a scam may kill the deal in your mind. If that sounds like you, either become an expert on the product you wish to buy, purchase it from the cruise line, or shop in a cruise line-guaranteed shop that, working through the cruise line, has agreed to refund dissatisfied customers within thirty days of purchase (see Shore Excursions in this chapter).

For those who love *sales*, ships do discount merchandise, especially toward the end of a cruise. Keep one eye on the shop's schedule, though. They usually close when docked.

Whether buying things on the ship or on shore, keep receipts. They may come in handy when passing through Customs upon your return to U.S. shores (see section on Disembarking at the end of the chapter).

RELIGION

Megaships tend to offer more religious diversity than smaller ships, mainly because they have more people. Almost all ships offer some type of Christian nondenominational service on Sundays; many also offer a Jewish Sabbath service on Fridays, though they may not have an onboard rabbi to take charge. Larger ships also conduct Catholic services on a regular basis throughout the cruise. If you want guarantees, ask your travel agent to confirm that your preferred religious service will be offered before putting down a deposit.

KEEPING IN TOUCH

Pick your favorite form of communication and you'll find it on the ship—telephone, e-mail, fax, or letter. Letters remain cost effective. Telephones, e-mails, and faxes will set you back more—substantially more. On most ships, you can call home from your cabin after dialing a few extra numbers to get through.

Ships have two systems for telephones. The original system, still used on cruises, involves the ship's radio. You place a call, it's waylaid to a nearby body of land, then transferred to U.S. shores. The new system used on most ships, however, now shoots your voice through space where it bounces off a satellite before connecting—with crystal-clear clarity—to loved ones. The traditional method is the cheapest but not quite as clear, nor can the ship's radio be accessed from your cabin. The satellite method is more convenient and more expensive. Expect to pay at least $7 per minute (quick addition: over $100 for a fifteen-minute call). Calls are charged to your onboard account. A fax service, using the same system, costs roughly the same.

Newer ships also offer e-mail service, a great way to stay in touch since it's cheaper than a phone call. Since notes can be written on a computer without being on-line, and sent simultaneously to more than one person, the amount of satellite time actually used to send the e-mail is minuscule. Pricing varies by ship—it may standardize after e-mail has been around for a while—but could be an hourly charge or a simple fee per e-mail system, perhaps $3 or $4 per electronic letter.

To receive e-mail on board, you may have to set up a new, temporary e-mail account, meaning you can't use your existing e-mail address. One exception: Many Internet host companies allow users to check their e-mail through their main Web site. AOL, the nation's largest Internet connection company, does this, for example. The shipboard cost may be higher, however, since you must be actively on-line at all times on the Web site. If you must pay for Internet time by the minute, download all messages, write responses off-line, and then reconnect. Since hundreds of e-mails can be sent or received in seconds, it may soon become the preferred form of communication, and some ships are already experimenting with offering it as a free service.

If you want to call loved ones on the cheap, wait until arrival in a port of call and use a nearby pay phone. To shave more money off the deal, check out prepaid calling cards before leaving home—many work in foreign countries. Beyond price savings, a calling card is also more convenient.

Friends and family may call you on the ship by dialing 800-SEA-CALL. They'll be asked which ocean you're in (if they don't know that, they shouldn't be allowed to call) and the name of your ship. Look for details in the packet of information that comes with your cruise documents—many times the cruise line gives you a calling instruction card to leave with family or friends. Calls from the U.S. come in by satellite, and prices are comparable to similar calls sent from the ship. If they really are loved ones, warn them.

A cheaper alternative is a similar program that delivers a telex (note) directly to your room, again sent by satellite. Family and friends may call 800-MARISAT for more information or to send the telex.

For cell phone users: There are no towers at sea, so don't expect a cell phone to work in the middle of the Atlantic. You must be less than thirty to forty miles from shore or in port for a cell phone to work. And while technology changes faster than it takes to type this sentence, current U.S. cell phones do not work in most other nations. If traveling the Caribbean, for example, you'll need a new temporary phone number to hand out to relatives and friends if you plan to rely on your cell phone. Before departure, call your local cell phone service provider to see if they can help. Also, Cable and Wireless Caribbean Cellular, a company that serves the Caribbean, offers info on their Web site, and they'll arrange for service while you're away. Go to *http://www.caribcell.com/cruising.htm*. The site also has links to other countries that have their own cell phone systems. Generally, cellular service costs less than ship-to-shore calls but more than using a pay phone while in port, though the system does not work unless relatively close to land.

Letters and postcards, the traveler's tried-and-true method of contact, can be "mailed" from the guest services (purser's) desk. U.S. stamps do not work, but local stamps can be purchased in the correct amount and through the appropriate nation. The crew will then officially mail the letter in the next port of call.

PHOTOS

A professional photographer seems to be everywhere while at sea. As pictures develop, they're displayed in a room built for just that purpose. You stop by, look for your group, and buy ones that appeal to you. Ships charge nothing to take your picture and develop the prints; if you want to take them home, however, they charge at least $6 per four-by-six print. Most people pose at every opportunity, figuring that if they get a good shot with everyone smiling, it's worth the money. The photographer and cruise line figure that too.

When looking for your photo, events are usually grouped together. The captain's party, for example, may be in one section. If you participated and had your picture taken, you scan all the photos looking for a familiar face. It's tedious, but you scan anyway. If something seems ideal—meaning the person paying has never looked better—you may be able to get them enlarged. Their cost, of course, will also be enlarged.

TIPPING

Tipping throughout the cruise is covered in Chapter 4 with a breakdown of all expected amounts, though day-to-day requirements reflect systems on land. The tipping process unique to the cruise industry, however, takes place on the final evening of the voyage when waiters, room stewards, and busboys receive their gratuity. The maître d' may also be tipped but at your discretion. The suggested minimum amount to tip on an inexpensive cruise, again, is:

Room steward: $3 per day, or $21 per week, per person.

Waiter: $3 per day, or $21 per week, per person.

Busboy: $1.50 per day, or about $11.00 per week, per person.

For some odd reason, it's okay to tip half the adult amount for a grandchild, though having raised three kids, I can't imagine why—they're twice the work.

On a handful of ships, such as Holland America and the luxury cruise lines, tipping is not required—just highly encouraged. Many people leave something more. There may be not so subtle hints such as more than one reminder on the last day that tipping is not required "unless you want to do so to reward exceptional service." If you do wish to leave a tip on these lines, refer to the above guidelines and round down.

On lines where you should leave a tip, don't fret about doing it right. The people you tip will help. The daily bulletin will probably explain the process, as will the cruise director at the disembarkation briefing. They'll even provide envelopes to use, generally passed out on the last day with the words "Busboy," "Waiter," and "Room Steward" clearly printed on the sides. You simply take the tip money, put it into the appropriate envelope, and hand it over at dinnertime.

To make the whole process easier, set aside tip money before leaving home. Use the above guidelines, round up a bit, put the money in a separate envelope, and don't leave it on the kitchen table. For the waiter, for example, the baseline amount is $21 per week. Round up to $25 per person ($50 per couple) and pack it. When the last day of the cruise rolls around, add a few dollars for truly outstanding service or subtract a bit if necessary. Most times, the $50 you prepacked will seem fair. Pack more if sailing on a luxury line.

In addition to a tip, many cruise lines ask departing passengers to fill out a comment card with specific questions on food, service, and other amenities. The cards are very important to the cruise lines since departing passengers will go out and recommend (or trash) the cruise line to their friends. If a significant amount of people complain about the same thing, cruise lines listen. As a result, some crew members may ask you to give them a good review—or worse, tell a sob story about how they must get top marks just to keep their job. If that happens, pay no attention. Cruise lines don't want this type of behavior, though it occurs sometimes. In the end, rate the service honestly.

WHO'S WHO

The cruise line pays a lot for advertising to convince you to travel on their ship. You, in turn, pay good money for the vacation. Given that, it's my opinion that you're under no obligation to memorize anything, either ship terms or the rankings of staff. Nevertheless, many people want at least rudimentary information on who's who, and who does what at sea since every common object and person seems to have a completely different, somehow nautical name.

The big guys: The captain runs the ship. While he's (most are men) a figurehead at times, hosting his own table in the dining room and throwing parties, he's not on board just for show—all important decisions rest in his hands. Below the captain fall three subcategories—four if you count the medical staff usually employed by an outside firm. The hotel manager (or chief purser) runs all resort-related activities including the rooms, the restaurants, and the onboard entertainment. A chief engineer oversees all mechanical functions of the ship; and a staff captain oversees the maritime concerns, such as getting the ship from here to there without incident. On a typical cruise, 95 percent of the people you meet work under the hotel manager.

Captain: Sea CEO.

Chief engineer: Person who makes sure the ship actually cruises somewhere.

Chief steward: Oversees the stewards who keep rooms cleaned and passengers happy.

Cruise director: In charge of onboard entertainment. At times, he or she works unseen; many times, he or she introduces shows and conducts lectures.

Executive chef: In charge of all onboard food service.

Head chef: In charge of all food service in a single restaurant.

Hotel manager: Oversees all passenger services—the ultimate person to complain to if things go seriously wrong with a cabin or meals.

Maître d': In charge of a single dining room's operation.

Purser: The purser is in charge of something (there's more than one); many times it's a financial position and he or she works under the hotel manager.

Staff captain: Second-in-command under the captain and generally in charge of navigation.

Steward or cabin steward: Maintains a block of cabins.

As in any business, titles vary. On one ship, someone may have three assistants; on another, the same position may operate independently. Most crew members are happy to tell you what they do.

PROBLEMS

When at sea, you're (almost) on your own. Problems caused by human error should all be solved the same way they are on land — complain. If food is bad or something leaks in your cabin, first talk to your personal attendant, either the waiter or the steward. If that does not work, go one step higher, to either the dining-room maître d' or the chief steward. If still unsatisfied, go to the hotel manager.

Given the number of passengers, the crew expects to hear a few complaints from those people who grumble and moan for a living. If you keep your complaints politely forceful and explain things in a nice way that illustrates your inconvenience, you stand a better chance of seeing corrective action. This isn't meant to be a lesson in manners; rather, the crew tends to help more if you're viewed as an inconvenienced passenger rather than someone else they "have to deal with."

Other problems experienced on board, and suggested solutions (if any), include:

Jet lag: If flying through several time zones to reach a point of departure, the change can disorient hardy individuals and even weaken immune systems. If possible, arrive a day or two before departure to get used to the change. It also helps to adapt your body to the departure city's zone before leaving home by either going to bed later or earlier. (Eastbound flight time changes tend to cause more jet lag problems than westbound flight time changes.)

Air conditioning: Expect the too-hot/too-cold experience. You may want a heating pad in the theater and wish to go naked in the dining room. Pack a sweater with the tank tops.

Casino losses: Don't gamble.

Disembarkation: See the next section.

Departure without you: If you miss the boat — literally — look for a local representative of the cruise line. You'll have to pay for your own overnight room, if applicable, and airfare to the next port of call, but the cruise rep will help make the arrangements. The same rule applies if you miss the ship in a port of call during the cruise.

Lost and found: Contact the purser's desk for any lost and found items. If the loss is not discovered until after your return home, have your travel agent contact the cruise line directly. (Don't get your hopes up.) If you left something on a tour bus, also go to the purser's desk, but really don't get your hopes up. If the item was expensive, you can call the local tour company directly, either from the ship, the next port, or home. The longer you delay, however, the greater the chance you'll never see the item again.

Seasickness: See Chapter 1.

Security: See Chapter 1.

Injury: The ship's infirmary can handle most minor medical procedures. For more information, see Chapter 1.

Shore excursion troubles: If booked through the cruise line, upon return to the ship, immediately complain to the shore excursion desk. If booked on your own, also complain to the shore excursion desk, but don't expect them to be able to offer much help. They can, however, warn future passengers of problems should they hear a series of complaints.

Luggage does not arrive: Tell the room steward and the purser's desk. While your bags may not arrive before the next port of call, they should be able to get you information on its whereabouts and supply you with enough supplies to keep you clean and dressed.

Noisy neighbors: Feel free to ask them to keep it down, but the easiest solution is to tell the room steward. For a major problem, complain to a higher authority.

Not-as-promised: If you arrive on the ship and find something missing—something stated in the brochure or implied by your travel agent—find the source of the problem and complain appropriately. If the fault lies with the travel agent, there's not much to do about it on the ship since, to them, the travel agent is an independent contractor. Raise the roof when you arrive home. If it's a he-said/she-said situation and your travel agent swore she booked you something important—a special diet or accessible room, for example—it's worth a call to your travel agent while still on board. If the travel agency has any pull at all with the cruise line, things should get corrected.

Dining-room troubles: See the maître d'.

Inferior food: If brochure pictures do not equal served food, complain to the maître d'. Go higher up the chain of command if nothing changes. Realistically, you should expect anything promised in the brochure—a lobster dinner, for example—but not every night.

Large groups on board: If a large group, such as a ten-cabin family reunion with many small children, takes up your entire hall, complain to the steward. If a cabin change will solve the problem, talk to the hotel manager. If a group of hundreds has, unknown to you, booked most of the ship, complain to the proper authorities while on board, to your travel agent upon your return home, and after that, write a letter to the cruise line. At the least, you may receive an offer for a discounted future sailing.

Changed itinerary: A cruise ship can, by contract, go anywhere it wants. However, they rarely delete a port without a good reason. Those "good reasons" can include recent hurricane damage, political trouble, or incoming bad weather. For good mental health, it's best to go with the flow on this one.

Bad airline schedule: If booking space through the cruise line, you generally must take what they give you. If motivated, however, you can try a few things. First, beg your travel agent to call the airline. If that doesn't work, call the airline yourself. If that doesn't work and you're reasonably close to the airport, go to the airline's reservations desk before the day of departure and ask nicely for a change. If that doesn't work, complain loudly. If that doesn't work, insist on talking to "your manager." This might work—but no promises. Remember that it's their plane, however, and they established "the rules" and signed the contract with the cruise line.

Overcharged on your bill: Complain to the purser but expect to wait in line (see next section).

You hated the cruise: First, if you truly hated cruising, let me apologize. If it's my fault, write to me. More likely, however, you hated your specific cruise, perhaps because of unexpected and unusual inconveniences. If the company failed to provide the cruise they promised, write them a letter through your travel agent. Be as specific as you can about the problems, including names of people you spoke with while at sea. If justified, the line may offer you a credit toward a future cruise. They rarely refund money. Each line has different procedures—check the cruise contract first.

DISEMBARKING

While I understand why the final day of a cruise is fraught with problems, I also find it sad that many cruisers' last impression is one of waiting for hours in public rooms with an array of carry-on luggage spread about their feet while nearby children—*other* people's children—whine and cry. From a marketing angle, satisfied cruisers should not confront so much stress, at least not on the ship (save it for the airport), especially at a time when they're mentally planning their next cruise vacation.

But that's the way it is on most lines, and certainly the way it is on the mainstream lines. (And why must you "disembark" a ship? You "get off" a train and an airplane. Maybe because "getting off" a train or plane is a lot easier than "disembarking"?)

BRIEFING: The first phase of disembarking takes place the day before arrival when the cruise director hosts a briefing. He'll cover tipping, your final bill, packing procedures, Customs and Immigration requirements, and the internal system for getting passengers off the ship. It's boring compared to the past week's lectures, but also important since information varies from ship to ship and even sailing to sailing. In addition, disembarking a foreign port creates a whole new set of regulations to be followed. U.S. Customs will then be cleared after the plane flight home.

PACKING: All suitcases must be tagged (the cruise line will supply luggage tags) and placed in the hallway the evening before arrival back home. Sometime during the night, they disappear, but they must be claimed the next morning before passing through Customs either locally or at the airport upon your return home. This can prove awkward if you tend to have full carry-on luggage. If traveling to a cold weather destination from a Caribbean cruise, for example, you must carry the last night's clothes, all the medicine and toiletries you need that evening and the next day, plus a winter coat and other heavy things. When reunited with your luggage after the cruise, transfer any unneeded gear.

BILL PAYING: If paying by credit card, do nothing but check the bill left in your cabin the last night of the cruise. It's probably correct—you hope. If mistakes are found or you choose to pay in cash, take the bill to the purser's (guest relation's) desk and wait in line.

And wait. You won't be the only passenger with a billing question. If complaining about an overcharge, ask to see a copy of all receipts and compare them to your own. Once the bill has been adjusted, ask for a final—and correct—copy for your records.

OTHER LAST DAY ACTIVITIES: The gift shop probably closes the last evening and does not reopen. Buy any last-minute souvenirs before arrival in port and pick up photos—it's your last chance. If you plan to cruise again, check any discounts being offered for guests who rebook on board.

CUSTOMS DECLARATION FORM: To reenter the U.S. either through a home port or international airport, you will fill out a Customs Declaration Form—one per family—on which you list all out-of-country purchases. (You "declare" everything you bought.) As the law now reads, you may bring $400 worth of duty-free goods into the country, including as part of that allowance one liter of alcohol and/or one carton of cigarettes. There are exceptions to the rule. The duty-free exemption is $600 if from a Caribbean Basin Economic Recovery Act country, and $1,200 if returning from American Samoa, Guam, or the U.S. Virgin Islands. Other exceptions apply to what you purchased (like some art) rather than where it was purchased. (Like any good government-controlled oversight department, Customs rules can be difficult to comprehend.)

It's important to keep those shopping receipts mentioned earlier. A Customs agent could value a watch at $550, even though you paid only $395. Without receipts, it's his word against yours—and he wins. With the receipt, the watch will be valued at the price paid.

A note about lying to Customs agents: Lying is a sin. Beyond that, it's illegal. Beyond even that, it's done all the time. How, people rationalize, will that Customs agent know that I bought this diamond ring in the Cayman Islands? After all, I could have brought it with me. While true, Customs agents, should they choose to check you closely, have made a career out of spotting people doing just that. For most passengers, it's not worth the gamble. With that said, most cruise passengers tend to glide off the ship, barely touched by Customs agents. How you handle lying is up to you and your conscience.

If Customs officials overvalue your purchases at the port, or if anything else goes wrong, such as claiming you bought something in St. Thomas that you actually brought from home, you can contest their decision later—in writing—through the U.S. Customs Service.

For more Customs information, write to:

The Department of the Treasury
U.S. Customs Service
Washington, D.C. 20229

Or visit their Web site at *http://www.treas.gov* and look under "Treasury Bureaus."

MORNING OF DISEMBARKATION: The fact that you must get off the ship leaves a cloud hanging over your head. Getting off, after all, means returning to a normal life where chocolates don't appear on the pillow and polite requests go unfulfilled. Add to that the changed schedule on board—you get up and eat earlier—and the day starts badly. Then it gets worse.

BREAKFAST: Served in the main dining room, ships usually move the serving hours earlier to give the crew time to prepare for the next onslaught of passengers. If you want to eat, you must be there at the crack of dawn. Since they simultaneously ask you to be out of your cabin as early as 8:00 A.M., that also means you must shower and pack before eating. The day may feel like it's half over by 9:30.

CUSTOMS PAPERWORK: The Customs Declaration Forms already mentioned must be turned in at an announced spot where they will be studied (or ignored) by Customs agents if returning to a U.S. home port. A note about the process: Customs agents are all-powerful and may do whatever they wish. As a pragmatic matter, of course, they cannot closely inspect every returning passenger. If your perfume somehow smells like cocaine and a dog sniffs it out, however, they can and will expect you to answer questions and wait around while they paw through every personal item you have. Again, a thorough inspection is very rare—but that's their right. (And you have none.) Nonresidents of the U.S., including those with a green card, must meet with Immigration officials and bring their entire family to the interview.

WAITING TO DISEMBARK: Once out of their room and finished with breakfast, most folks just want to get off the ship and go home. Passengers and families tend to line nearby hallways, lounges, and rooms, their carry-on luggage spread out around them, their children whining, their morning shower wearing off, even though most ships divide passengers into groups—generally by color-coding luggage—to avoid a massive exodus at one time. As a color is called, those in the group disembark. (Generally, those with early plane flights get to leave first.) Take a book. It's not fun, but it's the norm, and correct mental preparation can make it less taxing. Much of this heartache can be avoided if you opt for smaller and/or upscale cruise ships.

RETURNING HOME: If you drove to the pier, have one person get the car, drive to the doors where luggage is stacked, and pick up your traveling partner and the baggage. If flying home on cruise line booked air, you'll receive instructions on boarding a waiting bus. If you booked your own air, but with transfers to the airport, you'll ride the same buses. If taking a post-cruise tour or package, you'll receive special instructions—if not, ask before getting off the ship. If suddenly on your own, taxis will be waiting nearby.

8

CRUISE LINE AND SHIP PROFILES

Assume that a truly average ship exists somewhere. The S.S. *Average* serves good food most of the time with great food occasionally and bad food sporadically. Cabins on the S.S. *Average* have twin beds that convert to a queen-sized bed plus a small desk and chair; they may or may not have a balcony. Service is polite and adequate, neither five-star nor rude. Ports of call are interesting. People dress for dinner two nights per week, with 90 percent of the men wearing a dark suit for the occasion.

That ship, the S.S. *Average*, is the baseline for all the following descriptions. Differences between the S.S. *Average* and the noted cruise line are the major deviations that come into play in any book-or-reject decision. If food is not mentioned at all, for example, consider it average and fitting the above description.

WHAT THE PROFILES TELL YOU . . .

Profiles are organized by cruise line, such as Royal Caribbean or NCL, with the individual ships listed later. Descriptions draw a distinction between "luxury," "mass market," and "budget." Luxury, as used here, means more pampering and more services at a higher cost. (Slightly different, "upscale" is used to reflect more formal service.) Mass market means a middle-of-the-road price, generally large ships, and universal appeal. Budget may mean the same thing, but at a lower cost and, usually, older ships.

To simplify the size rankings, the following descriptions are based on the ship's GRT (Gross Registered Tons–a measurement of interior space):

Yacht-plus: Less than 5,000 GRT—from 50 passengers or less to a maximum of 250.

Small: 5,000–30,000 GRT—from about 250 passengers to a maximum of 800.

Medium: 30,000–50,000 GRT—from about 750 passengers to a maximum of 1,500.

Large: 50,000–70,000 GRT—from about 1,300 passengers to a maximum of 2,200.

Mega: 70,000–100,000 GRT—from about 1,800 passengers to a maximum of 2,500.

Mega-plus: 100,000-plus GRT—from about 2,300 passengers to 3,100—and more as new ships enter service.

The per diem rate in the ship profiles is based on the choice made by most people—an outside cabin:

Cheap: Less than $100 per day

Inexpensive: $100–$150 per day

Moderate: $150–$200 per day

Expensive: $200–$250 per day

Top dollar: Over $250 per day

Knowing the year a ship was built can be a good guideline to style and possible problems, but may also be deceptive since some older ships have had multimillion-dollar upgrades.

LARGE MAINSTREAM CRUISE LINES

In reality, no clear dividing line exists between the large cruise lines and the small cruise lines, a judgment made even less clear when one jumbo line owns another company. Carnival, Royal Caribbean, Princess, and others are, undeniably, kings of the cruise market. Companies such as Windjammer and Crown Cruise Line obviously exist on the small end. Others, however, fit uneasily in a middle ground. It becomes a judgment call.

Carnival Cruise Lines

UNIQUE TRAIT: Fun and glitzy—a resort that just happens to float.

MATURE AUDIENCE APPEAL: Either high or low, you love it or hate it. Those who enjoy a Las Vegas vacation should consider Carnival first, and the line says that 30 percent of all passengers are over fifty-five. It's also an excellent choice for an inexpensive cruise with younger family members. Carnival offers an AARP discount on some sailings—up to $200 per cabin for selected voyages of ten days or longer; $100 per cabin for most seven-day cruises; and $50 on three-, four-, or five-day sailings. Some restrictions apply.

CRUISE STYLE: As "The Fun Ships," Carnival advertises—and delivers—a break from everyday life. Expect every nuance associated with a cruise, but with a few more individual items priced as extras rather than included in the basic cruise price. Under the category of "you get what you pay for," buffets lean toward fast-food fare. Shows are glitzy, casinos bright, and (most) staff in-your-face friendly. Lounges have off-the-wall themes, such as a ten-foot-high can of baked beans in the *Fantasy's* "Cats Lounge." People party and more than a few drink. With hundreds of entertainment options, most folks find plenty of activities to fill their days.

PASSENGER/CREW RATIO: An average of 2.3 passengers per crew member.

MARKETS: Primarily the Caribbean, Mexico, and Alaska.

MEDICAL STAFF: Carnival's mega-plus ships travel with two doctors and four nurses; all others have one doctor and two to three nurses.

DISABLED ACCESS: The newest ships have good wheelchair access to most areas with the exception of selected outside decks. All ships also have accessible rooms that generally include lower peepholes in the door, lower telephones, grab bars in the shower, wider doorways, and a television remote control. Check when booking since accommodations vary from ship to ship. For the deaf, most rooms may be converted to include a portable TTY and visual notifications for door knockings, smoke alarms, phones, and television closed captioning. On the newer ships, elevators are even voice-controlled. The reservations department has a "Special Needs Desk" that should be consulted when calling about a disability.

TRAVELING SOLO: In their lowest category cabin with bunk beds, Carnival charges single passengers 150 percent of the listed brochure rate; in all other categories, singles pay a hefty 200 percent. The company does have a guaranteed share program, though they match people based only on gender. Your roommate could be a born-to-party twenty-something. No ship has dance hosts.

NOTE: For an inexpensive party atmosphere, Carnival is the mature traveler's best choice. If seeking the sublime or a seagoing experience, look elsewhere. Expect a few off-color entertainers and contests, notably late at night, and a passenger list heavy with younger adults and, in certain seasons, children. One strong advantage to Carnival: a vacation guarantee. If dissatisfied with the cruise, they'll fly you home at the first non-U.S. port of call and refund money for the unused portion of your cruise. If this appeals to you, read the rules carefully before departing—they contain a few caveats.

While Carnival suggests that passengers book through a travel agent, they will accept direct bookings either through their Web site or by phone. The company also has a master Web site posting information on all their cruise lines—Carnival, Holland America, Windstar, Cunard, Seabourn, and Costa—in one location, *www.leadership.com*.

Contact:

3655 NW 87th Ave.
Miami, FL 33178-2428
800-CARNIVAL
www.carnival.com

Carnival's fleet	Size	Cost/outside cabin	Year built
Celebration	Medium	Inexpensive	1987
Conquest	Mega-plus	N/A	Oct. 2002
Destiny	Mega-plus	Moderate	1996
Ecstasy	Mega	Inexpensive	1991
Elation	Mega	Moderate	1998
Fantasy	Mega	Inexpensive	1990
Fascination	Mega	Inexpensive	1994

Carnival's fleet	Size	Cost/outside cabin	Year built
Glory	Mega-plus	N/A	July 2003
Holiday	Medium	Inexpensive	1985
Imagination	Mega	Inexpensive	1995
Inspiration	Mega	Inexpensive	1996
Jubilee	Medium	Inexpensive	1986
Legend	Mega	N/A	July 2002
Paradise	Mega	Inexpensive	1998
Pride	Mega	N/A	Nov. 2001
Sensation	Mega	Inexpensive	1993
Spirit	Mega	N/A	Feb. 2001
Triumph	Mega-plus	Moderate	1999
Tropicale	Medium	Inexpensive	1981
Victory	Mega-plus	Moderate	2000

Celebrity Cruises

UNIQUE TRAIT: The upscale side of mass-market cruising, Celebrity has high-end artwork, above average accommodations, and formal-yet-friendly service.

MATURE AUDIENCE APPEAL: High. Celebrity ships fall into the "mass-market cruise line" category, but are a notch higher than competitors. Since parents and twenty-somethings tend to be drawn to other lines, it also favors older adults, notably on sailings longer than seven days. The line also draws a number of business-age adults.

CRUISE STYLE: Celebrity's sense of style is refined yet friendly, big in size yet intimate. The food served is distinctly above average, and all-in-all, the cruise line offers a lot of bang for the vacation buck. Celebrity falls comfortably in the (usually mature) market niche that wants a superior standard cruise yet is not interested in the crème de la crème luxury leaders' smaller ships.

PASSENGER/CREW RATIO: 2.1 passengers per crew member.

MARKETS: Primarily sails in ports relatively close to the U.S., including the Caribbean, Atlantic, and Alaska.

MEDICAL STAFF: At least one doctor and one nurse per cruise.

DISABLED ACCESS: All ships have cabins adapted for wheelchair use, and the line accommodates a wide range of disabilities. Bus tours also adapt to wheelchair guests at no extra charge. For specific information, the line's Special Needs Desk has its own toll-free number: 800-242-6374.

TRAVELING SOLO: No guaranteed share program. Single supplements 200 percent of the posted fare. Celebrity also offers dance hosts (gentleman hosts) fleet-wide and on all sailings.

NOTE: Celebrity Cruises is owned by Royal Caribbean, allowing the larger line to offer this upscale product alongside its standard mass-market cruises. Suites come with butler service. The food does not disappoint.

Contact:

5201 Blue Lagoon Dr.
Miami, FL 33125
800-437-3111
www.celebrity-cruises.com

Celebrity's fleet	Size	Cost/outside cabin	Year built
Century	Mega	Moderate	1995
Galaxy	Mega	Moderate	1996
Horizon	Medium	Moderate	1990
Infinity	Mega	Moderate	2001
Mercury	Mega	Moderate	1997
Millennium	Mega	Moderate	2000
Zenith	Medium	Moderate	1992

Disney Cruise Line

UNIQUE TRAIT: It's Disney—quality, imagination, and special effects.

MATURE AUDIENCE APPEAL: If traveling with grandkids begging to go to Walt Disney World, the line's cruise/tour package is your best bet for giving them what they want with a minimum amount of stress. Pick the four-day cruise and take the three-day theme park vacation first. For mature adults traveling alone, however, Disney appeals only to those who love Disney. The line, however, does have an adults-only beach on its private island, a no-children restaurant on each ship, and a multi-lounge entertainment area.

CRUISE STYLE: It's Disney. The ships, however, have a surprisingly traditional feel, welcome in today's world of resort-style lines. (Albeit with hidden images of Mickey Mouse in the moldings.) Disney defines family cruising, and while it tries to appeal to all adults, it does so with mixed results. Kids: best in the business. Adults: adequate to good.

PASSENGER/CREW RATIO: 2.5 passengers per crew member.

MARKETS: Both three- and four-day Caribbean cruises offer a one-week vacation by rounding out the days with a theme park add-on. In 2000, the line initiated seven-day cruises to the eastern Caribbean.

MEDICAL STAFF: One doctor and one nurse travel on all cruises.

DISABLED ACCESS: Fourteen cabins per ship have wheelchair access, and all public rooms are fully accessible. The line also accommodates most other medical problems. Check with your travel agent at the time of booking.

TRAVELING SOLO: Disney has no deals for single travelers and, depending on category, charges a single supplement of 175 to 200 percent above the brochure rate.

NOTE: If choosing the one-week vacation that includes Disney World and a cruise, guests conveniently check-in only once. A single key works both hotel room and ship's cabin, and both you and your luggage transfer easily via bus between airports, ships, and resorts. In layout, both the *Disney Magic* and *Disney Wonder* are identical; in style, the *Magic* has classic decor (think *Titanic*), while the *Wonder* favors art nouveau (think Captain Nemo's *Nautilus*). For the best rates, book in low season (early fall, early January) and as far in advance as possible. Programs for younger age groups — three of them based on the child's age — cannot be beat. Uniquely, passengers eat in different restaurants each night. Disney has no casinos in its fleet . . . at least not yet.

Contact:

210 Celebration Place, Suite 400
Celebration, FL 34747-1000

800-WDW-CRUISE
www.disneycruise.com

Disney's fleet	Size	Cost/outside cabin	Year built
Disney Magic	Mega	Expensive	1998
Disney Wonder	Mega	Expensive	1999

Holland America Line-Westours

UNIQUE TRAIT: Classic cruising for older adults. A big player in Alaska with complimentary land packages.

MATURE AUDIENCE APPEAL: High. Known for years as the cruise line for older adults, Holland America has fought that image by boosting its children's programs and adding other kid-friendly perks—but with limited success. As a result, it's a good choice for adults traveling alone or with the grandkids. In Alaska, packages also include extensive land excursions. The line estimates that at least half its passengers are over fifty-five, but that number goes higher on cruises longer than seven days.

CRUISE STYLE: As one of the two cruise lines with a strong Alaska presence, the company owns and operates its own land tours (Westours) to seamlessly integrate a vacation from ship to shore to train. Overall, Holland America shies away from the silly games played on Carnival (owner of Holland America) and others. The result: a traditional cruise line (almost 130 years old) with smiling and efficient staff. The ambience is distinctly historical and calmer than that on many cruise ships, perhaps the big reason older adults seek out Holland America's less glitzy, yet more enriching, cruise experience. The ships also have a distinctly Dutch influence, explaining how the "Holland" got into "Holland America."

PASSENGER/CREW RATIO: About 2.5 passengers per crew member, varying by ship.

MARKETS: The line has a strong presence in Alaska and the Caribbean, but they make forays elsewhere on earth including an occasional round-the-world cruise.

MEDICAL STAFF: One doctor and three nurses per ship. All are emergency medicine board certified.

DISABLED ACCESS: Public areas and elevators on all ships are, according to the company, accessible to wheelchairs. The *Statendam,* *Maasdam, Ryndam,* and *Veendam* each have six wheelchair-accessible staterooms, while the *Rotterdam*—the line's most accessible ship overall—has twenty-three. Ships also have TDD equipment for hearing-impaired guests. *Rotterdam* has Braille elevator directories and a closed loop listening system in its main show lounge.

TRAVELING SOLO: Guaranteed share offered. Single supplements vary by ship and itinerary. They start at 135 percent of the double rate, but most run 150 percent. Dance hosts travel on cruises of fourteen days or longer.

NOTE: "Tipping not required" means just that—but most people leave something anyway. Assume a basic level of service is included in the cruise price, and if staff deserves something over and above that amount (they will), leave more. Consider cruising on one of Holland America's theme cruises that feature country music, 1950s rock 'n' roll, big band sounds, or Dixieland sounds. Last-minute deals can be found through a travel agent, on the company Web site listed below (click on "Best Values"), or mailed to your home if you've cruised with them before. The company will accept direct bookings by phone or through its Web site.

Contact:

300 Elliot Ave. W.
Seattle, WA 98119
800-426-0327
www.hollandamerica.com

Holland America's fleet	Size	Cost/outside cabin	Year built
Amsterdam	Large	Moderate	2000
Maasdam	Large	Moderate	1993
Nieuw Amsterdam	Medium	Moderate	1983
Noordam	Medium	Moderate	1984
Rotterdam	Large	Moderate	1997
Ryndam	Large	Moderate*	1994
Statendam	Large	Moderate*	1993

*Listed "Moderate" rates are close to the "Inexpensive" category.

Holland America's fleet	Size	Cost/outside cabin	Year built
Veendam	Large	Moderate*	1996
Volendam	Large	Moderate	1999
Westerdam	Large	Moderate*	1988
Zaandam	Large	Moderate*	2000
Not-yet-named "dam" 1	Mega	N/A	2003
Not-yet-named "dam" 2	Mega	N/A	2004

*Listed "Moderate" rates are close to the "Inexpensive" category.

Norwegian Cruise Line

UNIQUE TRAIT: Lots of theme cruises—lots of activities. Mass-market appeal.

MATURE AUDIENCE APPEAL: Strong if longer than seven days or on theme cruises highlighting your favorite dance era, sport, or other pastime. NCL appeals to a cross section of people, however, including younger adults and families.

CRUISE STYLE: A mixed bag. From ship to ship, NCL has less consistency than other cruise lines. That's not a criticism, but a favorable experience on one NCL ship—based on your personal taste—may not translate to a favorable experience on a different ship simply because they both sail under the NCL name. In general, though, NCL offers good service that only on rare occasions falls short.

PASSENGER/CREW RATIO: 2.5 passengers per crew member, though their newest ship—as yet unnamed—is supposed to have only two passengers per crew member.

MARKETS: Primarily the Caribbean, but with a presence in Alaska and Europe, Australia, Bermuda, Europe, Hawaii, and South America.

MEDICAL STAFF: The *Norway* has three doctors and three nurses; the *Norwegian Sky* has two doctors and three nurses; all other ships have one doctor and two to three nurses.

DISABLED ACCESS: All ships offer wheelchair accessibility in cabins and throughout the ship, and they can generally accommodate other disabilities. They emphasize the need to plan for accessible facilities at the time of booking, but if needed, even provide refrigerators in rooms.

TRAVELING SOLO: Going it alone can be expensive — the line generally charges a 200 percent single supplement. They occasionally offer single specials, however. (They offer a lot of specials.) Call the line directly for more info. They do offer "gentleman hosts" on selected sailings — generally on cruises longer than seven days, notably ones to South America, Europe, Bermuda, and Hawaii, as well as transatlantic crossings, repositioning cruises, and sailings with a big band dance theme.

NOTE: NCL books over the Internet from "in-house cruise professionals," and if reservations seem to be slowing, the line quickly discounts fares. The company itself has gone through some major transitions that included low profits and ownership changes. It's now owned by Star Cruises and things seem to have settled down. In the past, service ranged from "wonderful" to "okay," and appears to be regaining consistency. With that said, their newest ship, scheduled to debut in October of 2002, may redefine the cruise industry — yet another confusing addition (but a good one) to a dissimilar fleet. The new mega-liner will, in NCL's words, "challenge land-based vacations for market share." Restaurants will have open seating in two main dining rooms offering different menus. If neither one appeals to you, visit the not-yet-built ship's round-the-clock buffet or eat in one of the five small gourmet restaurants. In other words, NCL plans to take the regimented clock-checking out of a cruise, making it more like a traditional vacation where you eat what you want when you want. If successful, the company will convert selected existing ships to the new system.

Contact:

7665 Corporate Center Dr.
Miami, FL 33126
800-327-7030
www.ncl.com

NCL's fleet	Size	Cost/outside cabin	Year built
Norway	Mega	Moderate*	1962
Norwegian Dream	Medium	Moderate	1992

*Prices can come close to "Inexpensive."

NCL's fleet	Size	Cost/outside cabin	Year built
Norwegian Majesty	Medium	Moderate*	1992
Norwegian Sea	Medium	Moderate*	1988
Norwegian Sky	Mega	Moderate	1999
Norwegian Sun	Mega	N/A	Sept. 2001
Norwegian Wind	Medium	Moderate	1993
Norwegian not-yet-named	Medium	N/A	Oct. 2002

*Prices can come close to "Inexpensive."

Princess Cruises

UNIQUE TRAIT: As their brochures will tell you, this was the cruise line that inspired *The Love Boat*. Big and well run, Princess offers something for everyone and, for the most part, delivers on that promise.

MATURE AUDIENCE APPEAL: Princess draws thousands of older adults looking for a well-rounded sea cruise—but it appeals to all generations. Other lines—Holland America or Delta Queen, for example—host more older adults, per capita, but Princess's style appeals to a wider audience. Princess also has a strong Alaska program.

CRUISE STYLE: When Princess's newer ships enter a harbor, people notice, thanks to sleek lines and an overall feel that looks like the next generation of sailing vessels. The line has good kids' programs, but without most cruises (avoid summer and holidays) being overrun by teens and their younger siblings. "Balance" may be the best way to describe Princess. It has glitz, but not too much; it has traditional oceangoing ambience, but only a little; it has good food, but not true gourmet; it has large open spaces, but also small intimate nooks. Quality control remains consistently high from ship to ship. Because Princess does not go after a single market niche, it's hard to point to a single facet and say, "It's the best cruise line for . . ." However, there's a supreme compliment in that statement that seems to masquerade as a lukewarm review. Passengers rarely depart a Princess cruise ship complaining that something went wrong, and it's a strong contender for best mass-market cruise line. While the company continues to press its *Love Boat* connection, however, it does not actually offer a more romantic experience than the competition. (They all have their romantic moments—the moon, the stars, the ocean . . . nature sets the mood once accompanied by the distant strains of an orchestra.) It's also ideal for family reunions.

PASSENGER/CREW RATIO: 2.2 passengers per crew member.

MARKETS: While strong in Alaska and the Caribbean, Princess's fleet sails throughout the world. Many repeat passengers simply opt for different destinations on each sailing.

MEDICAL STAFF: All ships have at least two doctors and three nurses, with up to five on the *Grand Princess*—less on the *Pacific Princess*. A list of services can be found on their Web site.

DISABLED ACCESS: Princess claims to have the highest number of wheelchair-accessible staterooms in the industry, with doorways wide enough for most chairs and bathrooms featuring roll-in showers and handheld detachable shower heads. Ships also have wheelchair transportation gangway mechanisms, ramps, elevators with Braille call buttons, and, on many ships, audible arrival sounds. Kits make every cabin adaptable for most special needs and can include telephone amplifiers, visual smoke detectors, door knocker sensors, text telephones, and other aids.

TRAVELING SOLO: No dance hosts, but they do offer a guaranteed share program. Single fares range from 160 percent to 200 percent for a suite or top-end cabin.

NOTE: Princess has very aggressive plans for expansion over the next four years. With fully six ships not yet completed, the cruise line will actually add more passenger space than it currently has in the water. The strength of a cruise depends mainly on the staff, and Princess management has mastered the art of hiring and, presumably, firing. The line also hosts an extensive Web site with detailed information on every facet of Princess cruising.

Contact:

10100 Santa Monica Blvd., Suite 1800
Los Angeles, CA 90067
800-PRINCESS
www.princesscruises.com

Princess's fleet	Size	Cost/outside cabin	Year built
Crown Princess	Large/Mega	Moderate	1990
Dawn Princess	Mega	Moderate	1997
Grand Princess	Mega-plus	Moderate	1998
Ocean Princess	Mega	Moderate	1999
Pacific Princess	Small	Moderate	1971
Regal Princess	Mega	Moderate	1991
Royal Princess	Medium	Moderate	1984
Sea Princess	Mega	Moderate	1998
Sky Princess	Medium	Moderate	1984
Sun Princess	Mega	Moderate	1995
Golden Princess	Mega-plus	N/A	Apr. 2001
Not-yet-named Princess 1	Mega-plus	N/A	Jan. 2002
Not-yet-named Princess 2	Mega	N/A	Oct. 2002
Not-yet-named Princess 3	Mega	N/A	June 2003
Not-yet-named Princess 4	Mega-plus	N/A	July 2003
Not-yet-named Princess 5	Mega-plus	N/A	May 2004

Royal Caribbean International

UNIQUE TRAIT: Huge ships, astounding construction, and unique things to do—skating rinks and miniature golf courses, for example.

MATURE AUDIENCE APPEAL: Royal Caribbean (RCCL) seems like the ideal cruise for adults age thirty to fifty-five plus their children, but it's also good for any older adult who wants a complete cruise vacation and doesn't mind a few kids nearby. The line has made an aggressive effort to make its ships bigger and bigger, so by benefit of size alone, RCCL has mass appeal.

CRUISE STYLE: If seeking a resort vacation with knock-your-socks-off activities, Royal Caribbean delivers. The fact that it also floats is, many times, secondary to what happens between bow and stern. RCCL actively competes in the "our ships are bigger than

your ships" contest, and is the current winner. The fact is, most
ports of call are interesting, but you don't "wow" friends once you
return home with historical facts and descriptions of vistas and volcanoes. But tell them that you went on *Voyager of the Seas*—which
has a nine-hole miniature golf course, full-size basketball court,
rock climbing, in-line skating, Olympic size pool, and ice skating
rink—and they'll suck in their breath. Then tell them about the
ship's "boulevard" that's four decks tall and longer than a football
field. It looks like a city street. Really. It has cafés, shops, and
strolling musicians—and RCCL has two more similar-sized sister
ships hitting the waters soon. The cruise line may not be the best
choice for those who want to be one with the sea, but it's a top choice
for the resort cruise of the twenty-first century. For food aficiona-
dos, expect good but not gourmet items at most meals.

PASSENGER/CREW RATIO: Average of 2.7 passengers per
crew member.

MARKETS: Mainly the Caribbean with ventures into Europe and
other areas. In 2000, RCCL announced a land-based Alaska tour
program that will compete head-to-head with established players
Princess and Holland America. The company also announced a
Universal Studios-cruise partnership to combine an Orlando vacation with a cruise.

MEDICAL STAFF: Numbers vary, but at least one doctor and
two or more nurses per ship.

DISABLED ACCESS: Almost all RCCL ships accommodate
almost all disabilities. Some cabins accommodate wheelchairs and
most can be adapted for the hearing impaired, blind, and other
physical challenges.

TRAVELING SOLO: No guaranteed share program. Single
occupancy rates are 200 percent of the brochure rate.

NOTE: Royal Caribbean has the smallest cabins in the industry,
though newer ships come with more cabin space. If you plan to
spend time in the cabin, think twice. Most people, however, actually don't—there are just too many pleasurable things found elsewhere. All the newer ships have private balconies on many outside
cabins, an extra that can make even the smallest cabins feel much
bigger. Crew members encourage passengers to get involved, and
the line schedules some silly activities that can (and should?) be
avoided, along with adult-friendly offerings.

Contact:

1050 Caribbean Way
Miami, FL 33132
800-ALL-HERE
www.Royalcaribbean.com

Royal Caribbean's fleet	Size	Cost/outside cabin	Year built
Adventure of the Seas	Mega-plus	Moderate	Apr. 2001
Enchantment of the Seas	Mega	Moderate	1997
Explorer of the Seas	Mega-plus	Moderate	2000
Grandeur of the Seas	Mega	Moderate	1996
Legend of the Seas	Mega	Moderate	1995
Majesty of the Seas	Mega	Moderate	1992
Monarch of the Seas	Mega	Moderate	1991
Nordic Empress	Medium	Moderate	1990
Rhapsody of the Seas	Mega	Moderate	1997
Sovereign of the Seas	Mega	Moderate	1988
Splendour of the Seas	Large/Mega	Moderate	1996
Viking Serenade	Medium	Moderate	1982
Vision of the Seas	Mega	Moderate	1998
Voyager of the Seas	Mega-plus	Moderate	1999
Not-yet-named of the Seas #1	Mega-plus	N/A	2 0 0 2
Not-yet-named of the Seas #2	Mega-plus	N/A	2 0 0 3

SMALL MAINSTREAM CRUISE LINES

To restate: The dividing line between "large mainstream" and "small mainstream" is arbitrary. In general, however, the following cruise lines offer the full-blown cruise experience—casinos, shows, abundant food, and ocean breezes—but they have only a limited number of ships. Many times, they satisfy two ends of the spectrum—the budget crowd or the luxury cruiser. As such, they tend to serve certain needs (saving money or a desire for stunning service and food, for example) better than the already listed mainstream lines.

If seeking a traditional style of cruise but on the most luxurious, top-dollar lines in the market today, you have four choices: Crystal Cruises, Cunard, Radisson Seven Seas, or Seabourn. (For a sailing ship, Windstar also fits into the luxury category.) If seeking a traditional style cruise—but cheap—you have five options: Cape Canaveral Cruise Line, Commodore, Mediterranean Shipping Cruises, or Regal.

American Hawaii Cruises

UNIQUE TRAIT: Hawaiian themed food and entertainment— and the only line based in the fiftieth state.

MATURE AUDIENCE APPEAL: High. Most passengers, in fact, are older adults. To see the Hawaiian islands with a minimum of packing/unpacking/walking, this is the way to go.

CRUISE STYLE: Hawaiian . . . but I said that already. It's similar to other mainstream lines, but the South Pacific theme works its way into everything—meals, entertainment, designs, etc. Their one ship is not new or lavish, and has a traditional ocean liner layout—a bit confusing with many-sized cabins—but elegant at the same time.

PASSENGER/CREW RATIO: 2.5 passengers per crew member.

MARKETS: Hawaii.

MEDICAL STAFF: One doctor and one nurse. This ship has a medium-sized medical facility, but quick access to top-notch U.S. hospitals since it's never far from land.

DISABLED ACCESS: Limited in many areas due to lips and thin hallways common in older ships. Wheelchairs can be a maximum of twenty-seven inches wide, and the port in Kona uses a tender (small ship) to ferry guests to shore and may be inaccessible for wheelchairs.

TRAVELING SOLO: The *Independence* has a few single cabins for those unwilling to pay a single supplement. For most cabins, the single supplement is 160 percent of the double rate, going up to 200 percent for suites. Dance hosts accompany most sailings.

NOTE: If planning a first trip to Hawaii, there's no better way to get a feel for the life on many islands. People who love to cruise, however, generally go somewhere else on their next trip. People who love Hawaii generally pick one or two islands on their second trip and stay on land.

Contact:

1380 Port of New Orleans Place
Robin Street Wharf
New Orleans, LA 70130-1890
800-513-5022
www.cruisehawaii.com

American Hawaii's fleet	Size	Cost/outside cabin	Year built
Independence	Medium	Expensive	1951

Cape Canaveral Cruise Line

UNIQUE TRAIT: A cheap three-day cruise for Floridians or people vacationing in Orlando.
MATURE AUDIENCE APPEAL: Choose the line for budget reasons only, and expect a heavy dose of younger adults, people on tight budgets, and families with children.
CRUISE STYLE: Cape Canaveral is somewhat like the bigger lines, but everything is watered down. (Pun intended.) Since many passengers thought they could never afford a cruise, however, the atmosphere can be boisterous and positively exhilarating. The fun centers around free things like the sun, the water, and the party ambience.
PASSENGER/CREW RATIO: 2.3 passengers per crew member.
MARKETS: The Bahamas and, sometimes, Key West.
MEDICAL STAFF: Varies, but limited.
DISABLED ACCESS: Almost none.
TRAVELING SOLO: While not made for the solo traveler, some people do travel alone. If looking for a rich widow or widower, however, look elsewhere. Single supplement: 150 percent of regular fare for cruise only, 200 percent for cruise and land.
NOTE: The *Dolphin IV*, their only ship, is one of the oldest still sailing the seas. The disco is small, the casino crowded, the swimming pool overworked. But don't reject if offhand. Think of it like Burger

King—good for what it is, providing your expectations are realistic. (It's also reasonable advice concerning the food—fine but not gourmet.) Think of it as the best cruise on the market if it's the only one you can afford.

Contact:

7099 N. Atlantic Avenue
Cape Canaveral, FL 32920
800-910-SHIP
www.capecanaveralcruise.com

Cape Canaveral's fleet	Size	Cost/outside cabin	Year built
Dolphin IV	Small	Cheap	1956

Commodore Cruise Line

UNIQUE TRAIT: An inexpensive cruise from New Orleans that offers a slapstick good time. Also known for its theme sailings.

MATURE AUDIENCE APPEAL: If you live in the lower Midwest, Commodore is your hometown line and you'll sail with her because she's there. While it attracts many older travelers and repeat guests, also expect a full slate of families and younger adults. They generally have more older travelers in the fall and winter with families preferring the summer months.

CRUISE STYLE: Fun, fun, gambling, dancing, and fun. As with many older ships, a single decorative theme doesn't run through everything, but the ships' ages create some huge rooms, some tiny rooms, and the feel of historic cruising. Commodore also invented, and mastered, the theme cruise concept. In addition to the usual fare, cruises offered in 2000 included Trucker's Cruise, Irish Cruise, Cajun Fiddler Bank, Women in Jazz, and Magical Halloween.

PASSENGER/CREW RATIO: 2.2 passengers per crew member.

MARKETS: Eastern Caribbean including Mexico and Key West.

MEDICAL STAFF: One doctor and one nurse.

DISABLED ACCESS: *Enchanted Isle* has two accessible rooms, elevators, and accommodates passengers in most public areas. *Enchanted Capri*, however, is not recommended.

TRAVELING SOLO: Single supplements range from nothing (you pay the regular double rate) to 200 percent of the brochure rate. The *Enchanted Isle* and *Enchanted Capri* also have single cabins. Dance hosts travel on the *Enchanted Isle* in nonsummer months.

NOTE: A cruise is a balancing act. Commodore cuts corners—it has to at these prices—but still takes customer service seriously. Ships may be older, lobster less noticeable, and entertainment less grandiose; but for a fair price, Commodore delivers a hefty amount of cruise vacation for your travel dollar. Don't look for the upscale style of Seabourn or the newness of Royal Caribbean, but expect a cruise product that delivers more than you expect. The line offers varying deals, such as "second passenger cruises free for all early bookings." Book as cheaply as possible (off-season, early, four people per inside cabin, etc.) and it can cost as little as $357 per person for a full seven-day cruise—a little over $50 per day. Sometimes, third and fourth passengers sail free.

Commodore is one of the few cruise lines that allows passengers to cruise stand-by, just showing up at the New Orleans pier and taking a chance. They also discount last-minute cruises on-line at *www.bid4vacations.com*.

Contact:

4000 Hollywood Blvd.
South Tower, Suite 385
Hollywood, FL 33021
800-237-5361
www.commodorecruise.com

Commodore's fleet	Size	Cost/outside cabin	Year built
Enchanted Isle	Small	Cheap/Inexpensive	1958
Enchanted Capri	Small	Inexpensive	1975

Costa Cruise Lines

UNIQUE TRAIT: All Italian all the time.

MATURE AUDIENCE APPEAL: High if you're Italian, medium if not. Caribbean sailings come with a $100 savings, per cabin, if one passenger is sixty or older.

CRUISE STYLE: Italian says it all. It's not just the food or decor; it's the whole atmosphere. Costa celebrates Italy's art, cuisine, and style in a robust way. Under the Italian surface, the cruise line has many of the same amenities as its competitors, but the international flavor sets it apart. On St. Patrick's Day, everyone's Irish; on a Costa cruise, everyone's Italian. Even the Irish.

PASSENGER/CREW RATIO: 2.2 passengers (varies per ship) per crew member.

MARKETS: *CostaRomantica* and *Costa Victoria* mainly sail the Caribbean; other ships serve the European market.

MEDICAL STAFF: At least one doctor and one nurse on every cruise.

DISABLED ACCESS: Two ships in the line, the *CostaRiviera* and *CostaMarina*, have no accessible cabins.

TRAVELING SOLO: Single supplements range from 150 percent for a stateroom to 200 percent for a suite. Some ships also have single cabins.

NOTE: Costa's Italian theme actually breaks from the usual mold. Food is Italian, but they offer heart-healthy entrées in addition to the usual artery-clogging favorites. *CostaRomantica* has big cabins by cruise line standards. Costa kids' programs appeal to adults traveling with grandchildren. For a set fee of $199, children seventeen or younger can cruise. Through a "Friends and Family" fare, cabins (a minimum of two) save $100 off the cruise fare.

Contact:

World Trade Center
80 SW Eighth St.
Miami, FL 33130-3097
800-462-6782
www.costacruises.com

Costa's fleet	Size	Cost/outside cabin	Year built
CostaRomantica	Mega	Inexpensive	1975
CostaVictoria	Large	Inexpensive	1996
CostaAllegra(Europe)	Small	Moderate	1992
CostaAtlantica (Europe)	Large	Moderate	2000

Costa's fleet	Size	Cost/outside cabin	Year built
CostaClassica (Europe)	Medium	Moderate	1992
CostaMarina (Europe)	Small	Moderate	1990
CostaRiviera (Europe)	Small/Medium	Moderate	1963

Crown Cruise Line

UNIQUE TRAIT: Moderately upscale cruising to Bermuda from Philadelphia or Baltimore.

MATURE AUDIENCE APPEAL: Expect varied ages of passengers with a slight lean toward older adults.

CRUISE STYLE: Crown is a Commodore cruise (owned by the same company) with a slightly higher cost, slightly upscale style, and much newer ship. Crown works hard to please passengers, and decent food and service make it a good value for the vacation dollar.

PASSENGER/CREW RATIO: 2.5 passengers per crew member.

MARKETS: In the winter, the southern Caribbean (sailing out of Aruba). In the summer, Bermuda but with trips into Canada.

MEDICAL STAFF: One doctor and one nurse.

DISABLED ACCESS: The *Crown Dynasty* has four accessible rooms, elevators, and accommodates wheelchair guests in virtually all passenger areas.

TRAVELING SOLO: Single rates can go from the standard double rate to 150 percent—higher for suites. Dance hosts travel on some sailings. Ask when booking.

NOTE: The North Atlantic can be rough, and a small ship may rock more than a larger ship or one sailing the Caribbean. If you have a strong fear of seasickness, you may want to consider a different itinerary your first time out. Crown Cruise Line works with Apple Vacations, a Northeast tour company, unlike most cruise lines that handle all their bookings in-house.

Contact:

4000 Hollywood Blvd.
South Tower, Suite 385
Hollywood, FL 33021

800-237-5361
www.crowncruiseline.com

Crown's fleet	Size	Cost/outside cabin	Year built
Crown Dynasty	Small	Moderate	1993

Crystal Cruises

UNIQUE TRAIT: One of five truly upscale, luxury cruise lines serving the North American market.

MATURE AUDIENCE APPEAL: High. Younger adults, generally, opt for a less costly cruise, though most sailings do have a few families with children. The line says that at least 70 percent of passengers have passed that magical fifty-five-year milestone. Recognizing the mature traveler, they schedule activities deemed older-adult-friendly, such as "unintimidating computer classes," bridge, golf clinics, etc. They use larger type on menus and can accommodate most special diets—but confirm unique needs at the time of booking. When describing optional shore excursions, they also list activity levels required.

CRUISE STYLE: Pay more but get your money's worth. Crystal is the upscale cruiser's first choice if also seeking the largest ships in the luxury niche, as well as a range of scheduled activities. Crystal, more than other lines, takes the best vacation elements found on megaships and enhances them with the luxury service expected by high-income passengers. Attention is paid to details. Many passengers who end up booking Crystal first insist upon a luxury cruise, then choose the line because it has larger ships and more things to do.

PASSENGER/CREW RATIO: 1.7 passengers per crew member.

MARKETS: Worldwide including Alaska and the Caribbean.

MEDICAL STAFF: One doctor and two nurses.

DISABLED ACCESS: The line highly recommends that wheelchair passengers travel with someone who can help, but both ships offer virtually full accessibility. Amplifying headsets for cabin phones are offered upon request.

TRAVELING SOLO: Crystal has a sliding payment scale based on cabin category. Least expensive cabin categories cost 125 percent of the full cruise fare, then rise to 135 percent, 150 percent, and, finally, 200 percent for the largest penthouse. On occasion, they also offer a single deal that's only 10 percent higher than the standard double rate. For information, check their Web site or talk to your travel agent. Four dance hosts travel on each ship, with more scheduled for special events, such as a big band cruise.

NOTE: Rule of thumb: First-time cruisers with money in the bank—and not sure if they'll like cruising—should consider Crystal. If all goes well, consider the other luxury lines for future cruises if seeking less people or smaller ports of call. Even on a second, third, fourth, etc. sailing, however, you can't go wrong with Crystal. Like their big cruise line brothers, Crystal also offers occasional theme cruises—Arts & Culture, Big Band & Jazz, Health & Fitness, Golf, and Wine & Food—as well as a round-the-world itinerary.

Contact:

2121 Avenue of the Stars, Suite 200
Los Angeles, CA
800-820-6663
www.crystalcruises.com

Crystal's fleet	Size	Cost/outside cabin	Year built
Crystal Harmony	Small/Medium	Top dollar	1990
Crystal Symphony	Small/Medium	Top dollar	1995

Cunard

UNIQUE TRAIT: The very definition of classic luxury cruising and invisible British service. Think *Titanic* without the iceberg.

MATURE AUDIENCE APPEAL: Most passengers are fifty-five to seventy-five with an income of $100,000 plus (according to Cunard). Since the line emphasizes the gentility of cruising rather than drinking contests, its style also fits more mature tastes.

CRUISE STYLE: Quiet, reserved, and still reminiscent of the caste system in British culture. *Queen Elizabeth 2* (*QE 2*) is the best ship, hands down, for those who consistently dress for dinner and appreciate the fine art of good manners and proper breeding. The line correctly states that people "are buying into an anticipated experience" that includes the line's 170-year history. Expect high tea rather than a wet T-shirt contest, formal dinners rather than tank tops and jeans, and service so reserved that you won't know anyone is there until one minute before you decide to ask for something. Unique in the industry, the *QE 2* also has separate dining rooms, with the best ones used only by those who paid top dollar for their cabin or suite, a remnant of an era where the bluebloods did not mix with the lower class.

PASSENGER/CREW RATIO: 1.7 passengers per crew member.

MARKETS: Worldwide and round-the-world, though the *QE 2* is known for her transatlantic crossings.

MEDICAL STAFF: *Caronia* has one doctor and two nurses. *QE 2*, medically, is one of the best ships at sea with two doctors and three nurses.

DISABLED ACCESS: *QE 2* has four cabins built for disabled passengers. Both *Caronia* and *QE 2* have additional cabins accessible by those partially disabled. The *Queen Mary 2* will offer greater access but does not hit the water until 2003.

TRAVELING SOLO: The *QE 2* has over seventy single rooms for those traveling alone plus dance hosts on all cruises. They enlist additional dance hosts for a round-the-world cruise.

NOTE: In the near past, Cunard had a number of ships that didn't compare easily. Under Carnival (the line's new corporate owner), however, the line added the *Caronia* and seems to be creating a clear marketing niche, so that anyone who traveled the *QE 2* can reasonably expect a second cruise on the *Caronia* to compare favorably. In 2003, Carnival will launch the *Queen Mary 2*, slated to be the world's largest passenger ship and the first true ocean liner (meaning built for speed and distance) built in the past thirty years. Expect more ships to enter the Cunard fleet. The *QE 2* also schedules theme cruises that, while seemingly un-British, include very British themes, such as Gardens of Great Britain, Food & Wine of Old and New Worlds, British Theatre, British Comedy, Great Authors of the Century, and *QE 2* Goes to the Movies. (Okay, the last deviates a bit from the U.K. theme, as does an occasional jazz cruise.) Passengers may book a cruise directly through Cunard.

Contact:

6100 Blue Lagoon Dr., Suite 400
Miami, FL 33126
800-7CUNARD
www.cunardline.com

Cunard's fleet	Size	Cost/outside cabin	Year built
Caronia	Small	Expensive	1973
Queen Elizabeth 2	Mega	Expensive	1969
Queen Mary 2	Mega-plus	N/A	2003

Delta Queen Steamboat Company

UNIQUE TRAIT: Pure Americana, they're laden with history and tradition—steamboats, paddlewheels, and a taste of Mark Twain's Midwestern life.

MATURE AUDIENCE APPEAL: Extremely high; as a matter of fact, a huge percentage of Delta Queen passengers have white hair, no hair, or frequent dates with Lady Clairol. It's also an ideal choice for those wary of seasickness since there's no sea.

CRUISE STYLE: For youngsters, Delta Queen cruises are a history lesson; for mature travelers, it's the real thing—a confirmation of the American dream, undistilled by lying politicians, corporate pollution, and other modern maladies. Food follows the theme with Cajun and Southern delicacies part of the mix.

PASSENGER/CREW RATIO: 2.5 passengers per crew member.

MARKETS: Historically home on the Mississippi and its tributaries, the *Columbia Queen* recently debuted in the Pacific Northwest.

MEDICAL STAFF: Advanced medical care and even a helicopter airlift are easily arranged since Delta Queen steamboats never stray far from major U.S. cities that border the river. No doctor or nurse accompanies a cruise, but the crew knows CPR and other first aid procedures.

DISABLED ACCESS: The *Delta Queen*, an older ship, cannot be accessed. Elevators and wide hallways can be found on the *Mississippi Queen* and *American Queen*, however, with the latter offering the best ship-wide accessibility. A limited number of accessible state-rooms are also available.

TRAVELING SOLO: The *American Queen* has a few single rooms, and all steamboats have a guaranteed share program. Single supplements generally run 175 percent of the double rate, but go to 200 percent for suites. The line also has dance hosts (gentleman hosts), though the men work as part of the crew and are not single men who dance in exchange for a reduced or free cruise.

NOTE: In truth, Delta Queen is not a cruise ship company, and more than one seafarer probably considers its inclusion here an offense. It's also too small to list first, but mature traveler appeal is very high, and steamboats are a floating vacation option worth considering. The line also schedules theme cruises such as Dixie Fest, Kentucky Derby, Cajun Culture, Civil War, and special holiday sailings.

Contact:

Robin Street Wharf
1380 Port of New Orleans Place
New Orleans, LA 70130-1890
800-215-0805
www.deltaqueen.com

Delta Queen Steamboat's fleet	Size	Cost/outside cabin	Year built
American Queen	Small*	Top dollar	1995
Columbia Queen	Small*	Top dollar	2000
Delta Queen	Small*	Top dollar	1927
Mississippi Queen	Small*	Top dollar	1976

*All are smaller than traditional ocean liners but larger than yachts. Along a riverbank, however, they seem bigger.

Mediterranean Shipping Cruises

UNIQUE TRAIT: Italian-style cruising at a bargain price.
MATURE AUDIENCE APPEAL: The line does not encourage children with programs and other parent-friendly offerings, so it tends to have more adults. Still, it's not exclusively a draw for post-fifty travelers who can usually afford something a bit better.

CRUISE STYLE: The line's single Caribbean ship—it has three more in Europe—is, in many ways, a scaled-down Costa cruise (see earlier description). It's a bit less Italian, a bit less formal, a bit less upscale, and—the main selling point—cheaper in price.
PASSENGER/CREW RATIO: 2.1 passengers per crew member.
MARKETS: One ship in the Caribbean and three in Europe.
MEDICAL STAFF: One doctor and at least one nurse.
DISABLED ACCESS: Poor in the Caribbean. The ship has the traditional older-ship pitfalls for wheelchairs—small doors and lips in doorways.
TRAVELING SOLO: 150 percent of stated fare in all but the highest cabin categories.
NOTE: The line's single Caribbean ship was once the *StarShip Atlantic* owned by Premier Cruise Lines (*The Big Red Boat*), and is unchanged since its Premier days—minus the red paint. Mediterranean Shipping Cruises is not a bad deal per vacation dollar spent—and you spend relatively few of those vacation dollars. Just don't expect five-star luxury. Or four-star luxury.
Contact:

420 Fifth Ave.
New York, NY 10018
800-666-9333
http://www.msccruisesusa.com

Mediterranean Shipping's fleet	Size	Cost/outside cabin	Year built
Melody	Medium	Cheap	1982
Monterey (Europe)	Small	Inexpensive	1952
Rhapsody (Europe)	Small	Inexpensive	1977
Symphony (Europe)	Small	Inexpensive	1951

Radisson Seven Seas Cruises

UNIQUE TRAIT: The best cruise line for harried executives that want "the best" without the strict formality.
MATURE AUDIENCE APPEAL: Most passengers won't see their fortieth birthday again. Radisson is also ideal for adults who,

the day they retired, hung a tie and jacket in the closet—forever. Children are accepted, but parents are politely encouraged not to bring them.

CRUISE STYLE: On a formal cruise such as the *QE 2*, the cruise line has an obligation to provide top service and entertainment, but passengers also have a responsibility to bring refined manners to the table both literally and figuratively. The difference on Radisson is more psychological than physical. The cruise still does its part, but as in their hotel chain, they use the tried-and-true maxim "the customer is always right." Cuisine, service, and onboard amenities are at the top of the pack, but passengers feel a bit more freedom to be themselves—or, at least, their "vacation selves."

PASSENGER/CREW RATIO: Average of 1.4 passengers per crew member.

MARKETS: Only two ships serve the North American market, the *Radisson Diamond* and the *Seven Seas Navigator*. The others sail in Europe and the Pacific, and the line sometimes charters an expedition ship to explore Antarctica. The line receives a lot of return passengers, notably those who enjoyed the Caribbean last year, for example, and now trust Radisson to keep them just as happy as they explore Tahiti, or Alaska, or Europe.

MEDICAL STAFF: At least one doctor and one nurse.

DISABLED ACCESS: All ships offer wheelchair access in most passenger areas. TDD guests may also use a dedicated phone line for reservations: 800-906-2200. They also offer "Room Accessibility Kits" that adapt any room or suite, on request, with tools for the deaf such as flashing lights on room door or telephone, amplified phone volume, and closed caption television programming.

TRAVELING SOLO: Single travelers pay a supplement but the percentage varies based on itinerary and ship. Dance hosts (and bridge instructors) travel on some trips; specifically, the *Seven Seas Navigator* cruises in Asia, Australia, and the South Pacific. The *Navigator* and *Radisson Diamond* also have dance hosts on their Panama Canal and Costa Rica voyages.

NOTE: Radisson takes its hotel style and market niche to sea with its cruise line. Most guests are adults, but compared to other highscale lines, they attract younger adults and business meetings. They accept direct bookings.

Contact:

600 Corporate Dr., Suite 410
Fort Lauderdale, FL 33334
800-477-7500
www.rssc.com

Radisson's fleet	Size	Cost/outside cabin	Year built
Hanseatic (cold climates)	Small	Top dollar	1993
Paul Gauguin (Pacific)	Small	Top dollar	1998
Radisson Diamond	Small	Top dollar	1992
Seven Seas Mariner	Medium	Top dollar	Mar. 2001
Seven Seas Navigator	Small/Medium	Top dollar	1999
Song of Flower (Europe/Asia)	Small	Top dollar	1984

Regal Cruises

UNIQUE TRAIT: Cheap—and sailing out of Tampa in the winter and New York in the summer.

MATURE AUDIENCE APPEAL: Heavy demand comes from all ages within driving distance of the ship, though most people along Florida's Gulf Coast *are* older adults. For less kids, choose a cruise over seven days long.

CRUISE STYLE: There are fifty-two weeks in the year, and if you could spend one of those weeks cruising—at a price roughly equal to what it would cost to stay home—would you go? Maybe, maybe not. But a lot of people find the trade-off worth it. And, given that reality, you pay McDonald's prices but get a product that, most times, surpasses expectations. But don't expect everything to.

PASSENGER/CREW RATIO: 2.8 passengers per crew member.

MARKETS: Cruise lengths vary but include the Caribbean and the East Coast of the U.S.

MEDICAL STAFF: At least one doctor and one nurse.

DISABLED ACCESS: Poor. The age of this ship creates many obstacles.

TRAVELING SOLO: Single rates offered but they vary.
NOTE: Regal is like a regular cruise only smaller and less intense. Food costs them less to buy, mainly because it's hamburger rather than filet, but you can eat gobs of it. Showgirls may not kick as high, but they kick. The ocean is just as blue-green as on any other cruise line.

Contact:

4199 34th St. S.
St. Petersburg, FL 33711
800-270-SAIL
www.regalcruises.com

Regal's fleet	Size	Cost/outside cabin	Year built
Regal Empress	Small	Cheap	1953

Royal Olympic Cruises

UNIQUE TRAIT: Greek cruising.
MATURE AUDIENCE APPEAL: Most passengers are older than fifty, with many retired. Mature travelers fill almost the entire passenger list on cruises longer than seven days.
CRUISE STYLE: In the Caribbean, Royal Olympic offers many of the same amenities as its larger kin. While the smaller ship means less shows and less activities, it's well run and comfortable. The Greek crew operates in the background, and it's not as Greek as, say, Costa is Italian. Still, Greek food (love the pastries), dancing, and culture are an intimate part of the vacation. The line also has a measure of stability. Many crew members sign on for life, greeting returning passengers by name. Service is top-notch. Royal Olympic also schedules a number of scientific or educational theme cruises that offer a lot more for the mind than the fare dished up by some competitors.
PASSENGER/CREW RATIO: 2.2 passengers per crew member.
MARKETS: Caribbean and eastern Mediterranean with longer cruises to South America and other world ports.
MEDICAL STAFF: One doctor and at least one nurse on board.

DISABLED ACCESS: Difficult on the older ships, but the *Olympic Voyager* is more accessible.

TRAVELING SOLO: Each cruise includes at least two dance hosts. Travelers in suites pay double the regular cruise rate, but all other cabins charge 150 percent. The line also has a guaranteed share program.

NOTE: Royal Olympic sails the Caribbean only in the winter and, while it may change ships from year to year, currently uses its new ship, *Olympic Voyager*, in American waters. In the eastern Mediterranean, it's the area's largest cruise operator.

Contact:

805 Third Ave.
New York, NY 10022
800-872-6400
www.royalolympiccruises.com

Royal Olympic's fleet	Size	Cost/outside cabin	Year built
Odysseus (Europe)	Small	Expensive	1962
Olympic Countess (Europe)	Small	Expensive	1976
Olympic Explorer (Europe)	Small	Expensive	Mar. 2001
Olympic Voyager	Small	Expensive	2000
Stella Solaris	Small	Expensive	1953
Triton (Europe)	Small	Expensive	1971
World Renaissance (Europe)	Small	Expensive	1966

Seabourn Cruise Line

UNIQUE TRAIT: The upscale and luxurious bed and breakfast of the high seas. It competes head-to-head with Silversea.

MATURE AUDIENCE APPEAL: High. Few younger adults can afford it, appreciate it, or take the necessary time off work. The cruise pampers you to the max and quietly transports you from port to port—and that's why most guests choose Seabourn. Seabourn says its typical passenger is thirty-five to sixty-five with an average age around fifty and an income of $200,000 plus.

CRUISE STYLE: This is the type of place that famous faces may go to be politely ignored by everyone. Group activities take a backseat to individual needs, and the line caters to people who "are used to being in control of any situation." Simply put, it's one of the most luxurious cruise lines on the market today, with the highest cuisine, finest wines, and servers who mysteriously know what you need before you've figured it out. That very niche, however, means fewer people can pay for or appreciate Seabourn. Consequently, the line uses only smaller ships that, while giving each guest ample personal space, have less public space and activities. While luxurious, Cunard can arguably be called more upscale if you consider the British standard of formality the litmus test of high society. Food on Seabourn compares easily to the world's finest restaurants, and dining-room seating is open, meaning guests eat when they want and with whomever they please.

PASSENGER/CREW RATIO: 1.3 passengers per crew member.

MARKETS: Worldwide.

MEDICAL STAFF: *Goddesses I* and *II* have one doctor each. *Legend*, *Spirit*, and *Pride* have one doctor and one nurse. *Seabourn Sun* has one doctor and two nurses.

DISABLED ACCESS: Seabourn has "limited access for guests with disabilities." *Seabourn Sun* has four accessible cabins; and *Legend*, *Spirit*, and *Pride* have four suites each that accommodate wheelchairs. Both *Goddesses* are inaccessible. (Isn't that always the way?)

TRAVELING SOLO: Dance hosts travel on each cruise with more scheduled on round-the-world itineraries. Single rates vary by cruise and itinerary but in the off-season run only slightly higher (10 percent to 25 percent) than double rates.

NOTE: Most rooms are outside suites, so forget saving money by booking that cheaper inside cabin. Seabourn also recently came under the Carnival marketing umbrella and now works side by side with Cunard, with each line shooting for a slightly different type of luxury passenger. Cunard is more of a mainstream cruise line based on its ship's sizes and itineraries. Seabourn, on the other hand, visits out-of-the-way ports of call and, with smaller and more expensive ships, has more of a vacation atmosphere and exclusivity. The line's smaller ships may also rock more in turgid seas, meaning a greater possibility of seasickness. If concerned, consider their largest ship the first time out, the *Seabourn Sun*. The line has a no-tipping policy and accepts direct bookings.

Contact:

6100 Blue Lagoon Dr., Suite 400
Miami, FL 33126
800-929-9391
www.seabourn.com

Seabourn's fleet	Size	Cost/outside cabin	Year built
Seabourn Goddess I	Yacht-plus	Top dollar	1984
Seabourn Goddess II	Yacht-plus	Top dollar	1985
Seabourn Legend	Small	Top dollar	1992
Seabourn Pride	Small	Top dollar	1988
Seabourn Spirit	Small	Top dollar	1989
Seabourn Sun	Medium	Top dollar	1988

Silversea

UNIQUE TRAIT: Luxurious and upscale, but not with a British formality. Silversea competes directly with Seabourn.

MATURE AUDIENCE APPEAL: Almost all passengers remember when rock 'n' roll started and know the difference between Kmart sheets and Frette bed linens. Silversea estimates that 75 percent of its passengers are fifty-five or older.

CRUISE STYLE: Relaxed formality (the line recently revised its dress code and now allows men to forgo the tie but not the jacket for nonformal meals), worldwide itineraries, top service and cuisine, and exotic ports of call. It's made for top executives and retirees who want on-the-spot service served with a smile. The ship itself is stylish but modern. Cabins are spacious by sea standards.

PASSENGER/CREW RATIO: 1.3 passengers per crew member.

MARKETS: Caribbean, U.S., worldwide, and round-the-world.

MEDICAL STAFF: One doctor and one nurse on each cruise.

DISABLED ACCESS: *Silver Wind, Silver Cloud,* and *Silver Shadow* accommodate wheelchairs almost everywhere, though there is no elevator access to *Silver Shadow's* observation deck.

TRAVELING SOLO: Single supplements start as low as 110 percent but can go to 200 percent of published fares depending on cabin category selected. Silversea schedules dance hosts "more than twenty sailing a year." If single and interested in dancing, confirm that dance hosts will be on board before making a deposit.

NOTE: A relative newcomer to the cruise business, Silversea has a clear vision and has taken concrete steps to achieve its goals. The entire fleet is new and, while small, not all *that* small. Gratuities, liquor, and airfare are included in the price, giving passengers a comprehensive package without the nickel-and-dime expenditures found on mainstream lines.

Interesting note: A new type of ship, *ResidenSea*, hits the water at the end of 2001 and will be managed by Silversea. Rather than a cruise ship, however, it operates much like a condominium. Owners buy units and pay a monthly maintenance/activity fee. As with condominiums, some people will rent out their unit when traveling elsewhere while others will live at sea full-time. *ResidenSea* will continually circle the globe with extended stays in world ports.

Contact:

110 E. Broward Blvd.
Fort Lauderdale, FL 33301
800-722-9955
www.silversea.com

Sliversea's fleet	Size	Cost/outside cabin	Year built
Silver Cloud	Small	Top dollar	1994
Silver Shadow	Small	Top dollar	2000
Silver Wind	Small	Top dollar	1994
Silver Mirage	Small	Top dollar	June 2001

SMALL SPECIALTY CRUISE LINES

The small cruise lines roughly compare to a bed and breakfast — fewer guests and an experience that is an apples-and-oranges comparison to the big lines. Of course, some are top-shelf B&Bs, and others a room you rent by the day. Generally, these smaller lines offer a sea trip rather than a resort experience. Ships may not be new and, if sailing in the open sea, trips rougher. Expect to enjoy lectures by local experts, ports of call unseen by big ships, and less formality. The bread and butter of these lines is the older traveler, but almost without exception, a certain *type* of older traveler. You love it or hate it. Those who love it go again and again. Those who hate it don't even read this section.

Alaska's Glacier Bay Tours and Cruises/Voyager Cruise Line

UNIQUE TRAIT: Alaska up close and personal in small ships, one of three such lines in Alaska.

MATURE AUDIENCE APPEAL: High, as it is with most Alaskan itineraries. Many passengers are over fifty-five, though ones who exercise a bit and remain more active than their peers. Selected sailings, however, require less physical exertion. Elderhostel usually offers a few programs through Alaska's Glacier Bay Tours each year.

CRUISE STYLE: An Alaskan adventure. The line specializes in avoiding the tourist areas frequented by cruise ships and delving into the heart of nature. Activities may include kayaking and hiking. The small size of the ships means few onboard activities beyond the occasional local act—but that makes a see-Alaska itinerary the focus. Food is hearty, plentiful, and best described as "real food for real people."

PASSENGER/CREW RATIO: 3.2 passengers per crew member.

MARKETS: Alaska.

MEDICAL STAFF: None.

DISABLED ACCESS: Poor. Ships have no elevators and many doors have lips.

TRAVELING SOLO: The single supplement is 175 percent of the double rate.

NOTE: Alaska's Glacier Bay Tours and Cruises requires different amounts of physical exertion per ship. *Executive Explorer* and *Wilderness Discoverer* offer itineraries reminiscent of their larger cruise line brethren and demand less physical activity. On these two ships, up to 80 percent of the passengers are older than fifty. On *Wilderness Adventurer* (soft adventure cruises), 56 percent of travelers are older than fifty; on *Wilderness Explorer* (active adventure), 31 percent are older than fifty.

Alaska's Glacier Bay is also the only line owned by a cooperative of Alaska Native shareholders. The ships are extremely small by cruise standards and hold only fifty to eighty-four passengers each. As a result, however, passengers and crew many times form more intimate friendships than on some other lines. The company usually works through travel agents but will accept direct bookings, and free videos may be ordered through their Web site.

Contact:

226 Second Avenue W.
Seattle, WA 98119
800-451-5952
www.glacierbaytours.com

Alaska's Glacier Bay fleet	Size	Cost/ outside cabin	Year built
Executive Explorer	Yacht-plus	Expensive	1986
Wilderness Adventurer	Yacht-plus	Expensive	1983
Wilderness Discoverer	Yacht-plus	Expensive	1993
Wilderness Explorer	Yacht-plus	Expensive	1969

American Canadian Caribbean Line

UNIQUE TRAIT: Unique ship construction takes passengers to areas not visited by any other line.

MATURE AUDIENCE APPEAL: Most passengers are older adults with a sense of adventure in their bones. The line appeals to adults looking for camaraderie (i.e., not much personal space on board) and unique itineraries that don't go to ports where the megaliners go. Kids under fourteen cannot cruise. ACCL claims that up to 75 percent of its passengers are older than fifty-five.

CRUISE STYLE: ACCL compares to a hike or canoe trip without the usual backpack and self-cooked meals. People eat together, family style, and entertain themselves by playing cards or talking. There's no bar—you can bring your own liquor—and personal happiness is your responsibility. Unless planning to dine out while in a port, leave the suit and tie at home. The ships have a unique docking system. They pull the bow (front of the ship) up to the shoreline and passengers disembark directly, no dock necessary.

PASSENGER/CREW RATIO: 4 passengers per crew member.

MARKETS: The Caribbean, Central America, and, in summer, the upper U.S. and Canada.

MEDICAL STAFF: None, though crew is CPR certified.

DISABLED ACCESS: Wheelchairs do not fit on ships but they do have stair-lifts.

TRAVELING SOLO: If looking for a mate, hunt elsewhere. If looking for a good time, the at-one-with-the-earth atmosphere encourages conversation. Some single cabins offered at 175 percent of the full rate.

NOTE: ACCL is "family owned and operated." A cruise may be booked through a travel agent or directly with the line.

Contact:

461 Water St.
Warren, RI 02885
800-556-7450
www.accl-smallships.com

ACCL's fleet	Size	Cost/outside cabin	Year built
Grande Caribe	Yacht-plus	Moderate	1997
Grande Mariner	Yacht-plus	Moderate	1998
Niagara Prince	Yacht-plus	Moderate	1994

American Safari Cruises (Alaska Yacht Safaris)

UNIQUE TRAIT: Alaska up close and personal in small ships, one of three such lines in Alaska, but the smallest and most luxurious.

MATURE AUDIENCE APPEAL: High. Steep prices, an intimate atmosphere, and an all-inclusive style attracts only the affluent—mainly the post-fifty cruiser.

CRUISE STYLE: The traveler who wants to see the "real" Alaska from the comfort of a hot tub with a dry martini in one hand has no choice but to sail with Alaska Yacht Safaris. The word "yacht" is the key. Passengers—no more than twenty-two at any one time—receive, essentially, a private cruise. It's more of a personal tour than a group experience, though you do get to know those few other passengers well.

PASSENGER/CREW RATIO: 2 passengers per crew member.

MARKETS: Alaska in summer, rivers and western U.S. year round.

MEDICAL STAFF: None.

DISABLE ACCESS: Difficult without elevators to offer transport between floors.

TRAVELING SOLO: No special deals offered.

NOTE: They also call themselves American Safaris.

Contact:

19101 36th Avenue W., Suite 201
Lynnwood, WA 98036
888-862-8881
www.americansafaricruises.com

American Safari's fleet	Size	Cost/outside cabin	Year built
Safari Quest	Yacht-plus	Top dollar	1992
Safari Spirit	Yacht-plus	Top dollar	1981

Clipper Cruise Line

UNIQUE TRAIT: With a U.S. staff, these small ships offer a casual cruise that's a cut above some other small ship lines.

MATURE AUDIENCE APPEAL: Once again, the vast majority of passengers have celebrated their fiftieth birthday in the near, or not so near, past. Clipper estimates that only 5 percent of passengers are younger than forty-nine.

CRUISE STYLE: Clipper appeals to older adults with above average incomes who don't equate quality with lifting a pinkie while drinking tea or wearing a tux to make a meal somehow better. People who want the small ship adventure—out-of-the-way ports of call, unusual itineraries, and small crowd ambience—love the line if, simultaneously, they don't want to "rough it." As with other small cruise lines, the itinerary entertains; the ship's crew does not. Food can be described as great nongourmet cuisine. Clipper says that, despite its name, it's "philosophically much closer to a tour operator than a cruise line. It just happens to use ships as a means to an end— to explore and discover secluded areas best reached from the water."

PASSENGER/CREW RATIO: 3.4 passengers per crew member.

MARKETS: *Nantucket Clipper* and *Yorktown Clipper* serve Alaska, the Caribbean, and major U.S. rivers. Other ships pretty much skirt the world—including Antarctica.

MEDICAL STAFF: One doctor per ship on any sailing outside U.S., Canadian, or British waters.

DISABLED ACCESS: Only the *Clipper Odyssey* can reasonably accommodate wheelchairs (it has an elevator), and even that ship has only one truly accessible cabin.

TRAVELING SOLO: Most departures offer a set single rate of 150 percent based on a category two cabin. At times, they also offer a guaranteed share program. You may call for more information, but all bookings must go through a travel agent.

NOTE: The higher cost for a Clipper cruise reflects, in part, a higher pay structure for the line's American staff. For most passengers, money is no object anyway. They want the small ship experience and simply pay a bit more to lessen potential hassles and make sure food rises above the "tasty meat loaf like Mom used to make" level of dining. They look first at all the small ship lines and then choose Clipper because, while it costs more, it offers personal service.

Contact:

7711 Bonhomme Ave.
St. Louis, MO 63105
800-325-0010
www.clippercruise.com

Clipper's fleet	Size	Cost/outside cabin	Year built
Clipper Adventure (World)	Small	Top dollar	1976
Clipper Odyssey (Pacific)	Small	Top dollar	1989
Nantucket Clipper	Yacht-plus	Expensive	1984
Yorktown Clipper	Yacht-plus	Expensive	1988

Club Med

UNIQUE TRAIT: A resort and/or camp that floats under sails.

MATURE AUDIENCE APPEAL: A few older adults love Club Med, but its push to get people to participate in activities send more than a few people into the arms (cabins) of the competition.

CRUISE STYLE: The sea part of the adventure compares uneasily to Windstar, though the latter has a different, more upscale, attitude. Club Med's single ship is less a cruise than an extension of the popular Club Med vacation concept found throughout the world. Megaliners may be resorts without saying so, but Club Med says so. French-based, the ship has a strong international influence — a plus to some travelers — and U.S. money must be converted to French francs. Entertainment, per the camp atmosphere, is more amateur fun than professional performance.

PASSENGER/CREW RATIO: 2 passengers per crew member.

MARKETS: Caribbean in the winter, Mediterranean in the summer.

MEDICAL STAFF: At least one doctor and one nurse.

DISABLED ACCESS: Limited.

TRAVELING SOLO: The single supplement varies by sailing, though Club Med also offers a share rate if you're willing to bunk with a same sex roommate.

NOTE: Club Med owns some family resorts, but their ship is not one of them. If traveling with grandkids, they must be at least ten years old. The ship has camp counselors (only they're called G.O.s) who tend to push people toward activities suitable for twentysomethings, though participation is still voluntary. Club Med also charges a one time membership fee of $30 per family and an additional fee of $50 per adult, per year ($20 for children 12 and under) simply to join the "club" — money paid above and beyond the cruise fare. (Strange, huh?)

Contact:

40 W. 57th St.
New York, NY 10019
800-4-LESHIP
www.clubmed.com

Club Med's fleet	Size	Cost/outside cabin	Year built
Club Med II	Small	Moderate	1999

Cruise West/Alaska Sightseeing

UNIQUE TRAIT: Alaska up close and personal in small ships, one of three such lines in Alaska.

MATURE AUDIENCE APPEAL: As with all small Alaskan cruise lines, almost everyone is over fifty. They offer up to a $400 per couple discount for AARP membership, $100 discount for making final payment early, and varying discounts for AAA members.

CRUISE STYLE: Ships are good-looking and clean, but the grandeur of Alaska is still 95 percent of the entertainment. Passengers get extremely close to the glaciers and wildlife.

PASSENGER/CREW RATIO: 3.8 passengers per crew member.

MARKETS: Alaska and, in the winter, California and Mexico.

MEDICAL STAFF: Generally none, but one doctor cruises on Mexican itineraries.

DISABLED ACCESS: The *Spirit of '98* has one wheelchair accessible cabin and elevators. Otherwise, access is poor.

TRAVELING SOLO: Some ships have rooms with only one bed, though the total cost still equates roughly to the double rate for one of their largest cabins. Special single rates may be offered at times.

NOTE: The *Spirit of '98* has a turn-of-the-century decor that plays well against the ruggedness of the Alaskan wilderness. The *Spirit of Endeavor* feels more upscale than the other ships. Cruise West also operates a land tour program under the Alaska Sightseeing name, and coordinating a cruise and tour is easy to do. Cruise West, while seeming to imply the western U.S., is a family-owned business. The owner? A man actually named Charles B. West. A coincidence? The line accepts direct bookings.

Contact:

Fourth and Battery Building, Suite 700
Seattle, WA 98121
800-426-7702
www.cruisewest.com

Cruise West's fleet	Size	Cost/outside cabin	Year built
Spirit of '98	Yacht-plus	Top dollar	1984
Spirit of Alaska	Yacht-plus	Top dollar	1980
Spirit of Columbia	Yacht-plus	Top dollar	1979
Spirit of Discovery	Yacht-plus	Top dollar	1971
Spirit of Endeavor	Yacht-plus	Top dollar	1983
Spirit of Glacier Bay	Yacht-plus	Top dollar	1976

First European Cruises

UNIQUE TRAIT: Comparable to mainstream cruise lines, but featuring a French influence and international crew.

MATURE AUDIENCE APPEAL: New to the Caribbean in 1999, the line attracts more than a few older adults but appeals to all age groups.

CRUISE STYLE: First European offers all the basics: casino, good food, Las Vegas-style shows, plenty of ports to visit, and good service.

PASSENGER/CREW RATIO: 2.3 passengers per crew member.

MARKETS: Caribbean and Europe.

MEDICAL STAFF: At least one doctor and one nurse.

DISABLED ACCESS: All three ships can accommodate a "limited number of disabled passengers," though the *Mistral*, being newer, has better accessibility. Collapsible wheelchairs required.

TRAVELING SOLO: Single supplement of 150 percent to 180 percent depending on date and itinerary.

NOTE: Most Americans choose something a bit more U.S.-sounding—and "First European" is a misnomer given the lines Caribbean presence. Therefore, it appeals to Europeans who want to experience the Caribbean, but U.S. citizens seeking a heavy international flavor will also enjoy the trip.

Contact:

95 Madison Ave., Suite 1203
New York, NY 10016
888-983-8767
www.first-european.com

First European's fleet	Size	Cost/outside cabin	Year built
Azur	Small	Expensive	1971
Flamenco	Small	Expensive	1972
Mistral	Medium	Expensive	1999

Lindblad Expeditions

UNIQUE TRAIT: Small ship educational ventures with light physical activity.

MATURE AUDIENCE APPEAL: Over 75 percent of all passengers are fifty-five plus.

CRUISE STYLE: Most small ship cruises include destination-specific learning in their programs, but Lindblad truly brings learning to the forefront. The family atmosphere comes, in part, from the small number of people and casual dining, but passengers also share a passion for the world. Only two ships — *Sea Bird* and *Sea Lion* — serve North America. The others can be found anywhere from Saudi Arabia to the South Pacific.

PASSENGER/CREW RATIO: 3 passengers per crew member (1.7 passengers per crew member on *Caledonia Star*).

MARKETS: Two ships serve North America, but Lindblad cruises and tours worldwide.

MEDICAL STAFF: One doctor per ship. Unique in the cruise industry, medical services are free.

DISABLED ACCESS: Ships and shore excursions are not wheelchair accessible.

TRAVELING SOLO: Lindblad has a decent singles program, charging 150 percent of the double rate for a single cabin. The line also has a guaranteed share program. If you cannot be matched with a same-sex roommate, you get a room to yourself at the normal double rate.

NOTE: Ships all have Zodiacs, a kind of inflatable boat, that can transport passengers to almost any shore too shallow for a boat to access. The cruises, however, make up only a part of Lindblad's offerings, and the company also schedules tours with a similar educational theme. While the style appeals to a limited percentage of older adults, those who fit their niche return again and again. In

addition to company-owned ships, Lindblad extensively subcon-
tracts ships for selected cruises including the *Hapi, Amadeus II,
Temptress Explorer, Coral Princess I* and *II*, and *Cezanne*.
Contact:

720 Fifth Ave.
New York, NY 10019
800-397-3348
www.lindblad.com

Lindblad's fleet	Size	Cost/outside cabin	Year built
Caledonian Star (worldwide)	Yacht-plus	Top dollar	1966
Polaris (Galapagos)	Yacht-plus	Top dollar	1960
Sea Bird	Yacht-plus	Top dollar	1982
Sea Lion	Yacht-plus	Top dollar	1981
Swedish Islander (Scandinavia)	Yacht-plus	Top dollar	1995

Sea Cloud Cruises

UNIQUE TRAIT: A true luxury yacht.
MATURE AUDIENCE APPEAL: High. It rocks, literally, but
passengers enjoy fine service while still at one with the sea. Families with small children avoid it.
CRUISE STYLE: Elegant, upscale, and luxurious on the *Sea
Cloud*. Topped with massive sails, this oversized yacht features
ornate wood paneling, gold faucets, and the classic styling of a traditional ship made and used exclusively by the well-heeled aristo-
crats of the early twentieth century. Guests dress for dinner and
enjoy it.
PASSENGER/CREW RATIO: 1 passenger per crew member.
MARKETS: Caribbean and Europe.
MEDICAL STAFF: One doctor and, on some sailings, one nurse.
DISABLED ACCESS: Poor. Ships have steep steps and no elevators.

TRAVELING SOLO: Single supplements vary depending on the ship and itinerary, but, according to the line, "are rarely 200 percent of the double rate."

NOTE: One ship, the *River Cloud*, sails only on the rivers of Europe. The *Sea Cloud*, however, plies Caribbean waters and, built in 1931, is the largest private sailing ship ever built. It has hosted dignitaries such as the Duke and Duchess of Windsor and Franklin D. Roosevelt. The result: small ship luxury that is not just re-created; it's original. A new ship, *Sea Cloud II*, will attempt to duplicate the feel of its older sister ship.

Contact:

32-40 North Dean Street
Englewood, NJ 07631
888-732-2568
www.seacloud.com

Sea Cloud's fleet	Size	Cost/outside cabin	Year built
River Cloud	Small	Top dollar	1996
Sea Cloud	Small	Top dollar	1931
Sea Cloud II	Small	Top dollar	2000

Star Clippers

UNIQUE TRAIT: True clipper ships that re-create history.

MATURE AUDIENCE APPEAL: The line has no kid-friendly amenities to give Mom and Dad a rest, so fewer families travel with Star Clippers—but it's not exclusively enjoyed by older adults.

CRUISE STYLE: Outside: historically accurate sailing ship that re-creates the travels of our ancestors. Inside: modern cabins with all conveniences. Cabins have VCRs, among other things, and penthouse suites come with a butler. During construction, original drawings of nineteenth-century clipper ships were used to guarantee accuracy of the ships' size and style. It's perfect for people who want to step back into the past, though the ships' massive sails towering over the ocean impress even those who know nothing about nautical history.

PASSENGER/CREW RATIO: 2.3 passengers per crew member.

MARKETS: The *Star Clipper* and *Royal Clipper* sail the Caribbean in the winter, while their sister ship, *Star Flyer*, tours the Mediterranean. The line also visits other world ports.

MEDICAL STAFF: The line has an LPN (licensed practical nurse) on board for all cruises and a doctor on transatlantic crossings.

DISABLED ACCESS: No ship has an elevator, and given the back-to-the-sea style of cruising, those in wheelchairs may prefer a different line.

TRAVELING SOLO: Single supplement of 150 percent, though the line also has a guaranteed share program

NOTE: Ships have stabilizers to negate the rolling of the seas, but due to their size are not the best choice for those prone to seasickness. The crew adds the special touch to the line—they're proud to sail a true historic re-creation and excited about the sea and its history. That excitement comes across in lectures and hands-on experiences that can include raising the sails. The line also has an open bridge policy, meaning guests feel as if they're part of the adventure.

Contact:

4101 Salzedo St.
Coral Gables, FL 33146
800-442-0553
www.star-clippers.com

Star Clipper's fleet	Size	Cost/outside cabin	Year built
Star Clipper	Yacht-plus	Expensive	1992
Star Flyer (Europe)	Yacht-plus	Expensive	1991
Royal Clipper	Yacht-plus/Small	Expensive	2000

Windjammer Barefoot Cruises

UNIQUE TRAIT: Nonformality under tall sails for little money.

MATURE AUDIENCE APPEAL: Children under six are not allowed on board, and whether older adults enjoy the cruise depends more on Windjammer's style and dress code than it does on your age. Most passengers are only semimature travelers.

CRUISE STYLE: The line's tall sailing ships (exception: *Amazing Grace*) create that one-with-the-sea feeling and passengers, if they wish, may act almost as a crew member. Ships are steeped in history and past owners, depending on exact ship, include notables such as the French government, Gloria Vanderbilt, and E. F. Hutton. The difference between Windjammer and other sailing cruise lines, however, rests more with its attitude and resulting dress code. Anything classier than a T-shirt is optional. Windjammer is the only small sailing ship line that simultaneously offers a high-party atmosphere.

PASSENGER/CREW RATIO: 2.5 passengers per crew member.

MARKETS: Caribbean.

MEDICAL STAFF: None.

DISABLED ACCESS: The line makes no accommodations for travelers with disabilities.

TRAVELING SOLO: A guaranteed single room costs 175 percent of the double rate, but Windjammer promotes its guaranteed share program and many people take advantage of it.

NOTE: While *Amazing Grace* is recommended for the slightly more sedate crowd, the line is known as a good place to have a party. People seeking a short-term romantic encounter tend to book passage because of the line's relaxed atmosphere. There are few planned activities—people tend to make their own fun. People who like this style of cruising usually *love* this style of cruising, and the line has a high return rate of passengers. For last-minute deals, check out their Web site.

Contact:

1759 Bay Rd.
Miami, FL 33139
800-327-2601
www.windjammer.com

Windjammer's fleet	Size	Cost/outside cabin	Year built
Amazing Grace	Yacht-plus	Inexpensive	1955
Flying Cloud	Yacht	Inexpensive	1935
Legacy	Yacht-plus	Inexpensive	1959

Windjammer's fleet	Size	Cost/outside cabin	Year built
Mandalay	Yacht	Inexpensive	1923
Polynesia	Yacht	Inexpensive	1938
Yankee Clipper	Yacht	Inexpensive	1927

Windstar Cruises

UNIQUE TRAIT: A small ship with towering sails—the most luxurious of the lot for people who can afford the best but reject the luxury cruises' pomp and circumstance.

MATURE AUDIENCE APPEAL: Windstar doesn't appeal to older adults alone, but does appeal to adults only. Average cruisers tend to be well off, down to-earth, and age thirty to sixty-five.

CRUISE STYLE: Luxurious without being upscale, Windstar appeals to those who want to be one with the sea, hate crowds, yet can still afford the best in the small sailing ship bunch. The staff, service, and food tend to be upscale while, simultaneously, not putting the same demands on passengers. (Jackets not required for dinner.) Gourmets may argue the fine points between Windstar food and that served on other luxury lines, but Windstar is on a par with the best of them. Even deckside barbecues have a certain feeling of luxury not found elsewhere.

PASSENGER/CREW RATIO: 1.7 passengers per crew member.

MARKETS: The Caribbean and Mediterranean Seas.

MEDICAL STAFF: At least one doctor on each ship.

DISABLED ACCESS: The *Wind Surf* has elevators, but otherwise offers limited access.

TRAVELING SOLO: Single travelers pay a 175 percent single supplement.

NOTE: Ships visit a lot of ports and, as a result, have few shipboard activities. All but the *Wind Surf* (over twice as big as the others) are virtually identical in design, even though all still fit into the "small" size category.

Contact:

300 Elliot Ave. W.
Seattle, WA 98119
800-258-7245
www.windstarcruises.com

Windstar's fleet	Size	Cost/outside cabin	Year built
Wind Song	Small	Top dollar	1987
Wind Spirit	Small	Top dollar	1988
Wind Star	Small	Top dollar	1986
Wind Surf	Small	Top dollar	1990

World Explorer Cruises

UNIQUE TRAIT Another small ship adventure into Alaska, but one of only two that is relatively inexpensive. Also one of the best in educational facilities.

MATURE AUDIENCE APPEAL: The line encourages kids to come along. It's a good choice if taking the grandchildren, and World Explorer reports that only 8 percent of guests are over fifty. AARP members can enjoy discounts of up to 20 percent below the published rates.

CRUISE STYLE: Educational—it actually offers a college credit study program. Low-key attentive service doesn't disappoint, and food is plentiful and good though not gourmet. The emphasis is on the ports and scenery, complemented by an extensive library heavy with Alaska-related titles.

PASSENGER/CREW RATIO: 2.3 passengers per crew member.

MARKETS: Alaska.

MEDICAL STAFF: One doctor and one nurse on all cruises.

DISABLED ACCESS: The ship was not built for disabled passengers, but it has an elevator and reasonable access (lips on many doors, however) for those in wheelchairs. If disabled, the line requires that you travel with a nondisabled companion.

TRAVELING SOLO: 150 percent of basic fare in most cabin categories with dance hosts (surprisingly) on selected Alaska sailings.

NOTE: Soft adventure shore excursions (meaning not too physically challenging) allow passengers to experience Alaska up close. The ship also offers fourteen-day Alaska excursions.

Contact:

555 Montgomery St.
San Francisco, CA 94111-2544

800-854-3835
www.wecruise.com

World Explorer's fleet	Size	Cost/outside cabin	Year built
Universe Explorer	Small	Moderate	1957

CRUISE LINES NOT SERVING THE NORTH AMERICAN MARKET

Abercrombie & Kent

Abercrombie & Kent cannot be pigeonholed into a single description—they literally cover the globe visiting all seven continents and more than 100 countries. They are also not a cruise company, though they offer a number of sailings both as part of a longer tour and by themselves. Prices tend to be upscale, but those who can afford exotic itineraries find value for their vacation dollar. Their ocean-going vessels are owned by other lines—*Sea Cloud* is one—and leased by Abercrombie and Kent.

Contact:

1520 Kensington Road
Oak Brook, IL 60523-2141
800-323-7308
www.aandktours.com

Bergen Line

Bergen says it offers the world's most dramatic scenery, and since it travels the fjords and seas of Norway, it may not be exaggerating. It also says that it's the ideal "alternative to the traditional cruise for the independent, seasoned traveler." That's also true. With eleven ships that stop in remote towns, the ships double as supply lines to civilization for Norwegians in distant ports while comfortable passenger areas allow them to do double duty as cruise ships. Older ships are yacht-plus in size but newer ones are small and carry almost five hundred passengers. Prices can be inexpensive depending on season of the year, and the line offers a discount to passengers sixty-seven and older.

Contact:

405 Park Avenue
New York, NY 10022
Brochures: 800-666-2374
800-323-7436
www.bergenline.com

Classical Cruises/Travel Dynamics

Classical Cruises sails three yacht-plus-sized ships in the Mediterranean with longer trips to European and African ports. It has, perhaps, the most diversified fleet in the industry, even if it is small—one sailing ship, one twinned hull ship, and one traditional ship. The emphasis is on education and deluxe accommodations; due to the size of the smallest ships, every cabin is a small suite. Prices are top dollar.

Contact:

132 East 70 Street
New York, NY 10021
Brochures: 800-252-7745
www.classicalcruises.com

Eurocruises (Delphin Seereisen GmbH. Fred Olsen Cruise Lines, Kristina Cruises)

Eurocruises defies definition, mainly because it represents a cross section of cruise companies in Europe. In one sense, it's a marketing company—a front to bring European lines to an American audience. Other companies that sail only in and around Europe own the ships; Eurocruises then markets the ships and sailings that appeal to a U.S. traveler. If included in the Eurocruise roster, the ship staff either speaks English or lists it as one of their official languages. Eurocruise's offerings range from river vessels to ocean liners to old world cruising ships. Many are small. Prices range from inexpensive to moderate with a few choices approaching the top dollar range.

Contact:

303 West 13th Street
New York, NY 10014
Brochures: 800-661-1119
www.eurocruises.com

Marine Expeditions

Marine Expeditions emphasizes the "expedition" part of its name and, for those who want to visit the colder areas of the northern hemisphere, they deliver the (frozen) goods. From Greenland, the company's three ships visit areas including the Arctic and northeastern Canada. One ship hauls a maximum of 100 passengers and fits into the yacht-plus category. The company's two other ships also fit into the yacht-plus categories but border on small and carry a maximum of 128 passengers each. Marine Expeditions passengers want to see wildlife and, using Zodiacs (inflatable boats), the crew makes it happen. All sailings can vary somewhat depending on whale and other wildlife sightings. Atmosphere is relaxed, educational, and passengers tend to have adventurous attitudes. Marine Expeditions.

Contact:

890 Yonge Street 3rd floor
Toronto, Ontario, Canada M4W 3P4
800-263-9147
http://www.marineex.com

Orient Lines

Orient Lines cruises almost everywhere but North America and the Arctic—though it does visit Antarctica. The company has two ships; one fits the small category and carries about 800 passengers; the second fits the moderate category and carries around a thousand. Prices—notably with airfare from the U.S. thrown in—run from expensive to top-dollar. Not all trips remain on the water, and the company offers a number of cruise tours that include land stays, tours, and other inclusive options. Their ships are similar to smaller mass market U.S. cruises. Their newest acquisition, in fact, was part of the NCL fleet until summer 2000.

Contact:

1510 SE 17th Street
Fort Lauderdale, FL 33316
800-333-7300
www.orientlines.com

P&O Holidays
P&O has been around for 160 years and, today, has an interest
in almost every kind of sea transportation—including passenger
cruises. Owner of Princess Cruise Lines, P&O's absence from the
American market may be a desire not to compete with its successful U.S. cruise product. The line has a distinctly British flavor, but
it emphasizes the traditional lack of British formality, perhaps to
differentiate itself from the more formal service of the *QE2*. The line
owns and operates four ships and flies the British flag. While one
ship in the fleet fits easily into the small size category, the remaining three all come in at the high end of large or the low end of mega.
Costs run from moderate to expensive depending on ship, cruise,
and exchange rate.

Contact:

Princess Tours
2815 Second Avenue, Suite 400
Seattle, Washington 98121
206-336-6000 (in U.S.)
www.pocruises.com

Quark Expeditions
Quark Expeditions *is* Antarctica. The company's two ships fit
into the yacht-plus and small categories, and carry a maximum of
50 and 100 passengers respectively. Unlike general cruise lines,
however, ships can handle the cold climate of an Antarctic summer
(North American winter). For top-dollar prices, passengers learn
the continent's history, visit historical sites, and see a range of
wildlife unseen outside a zoo. The touring itinerary, by definition,
requires some physical exertion but can be enjoyed by most mature
travelers. Some cabins come without baths.

Contact:

980 Post Road
Darien, CT 06820
800-356-5699
www.quark-expeditions.com

Renaissance Cruises
Renaissance Cruises almost disappeared from North American radar screen when the company decided to remove travel agents from the booking process by taking away their commission. With a major expansion underway, however, that tactic did not work and the rules changed. A few agents, however, have no plans to start booking Renaissance again. The line began as an upscale, small-ship fleet (and still has a few of those yacht-plus, all-suite vessels) but now operates as a mainstream line. They have eight medium-sized ships in the water that explore most world ports outside the North American continent—with an emphasis on the Mediterranean. The company claims it will have 5,742 berths (beds) soon, making it the fifth largest cruise line in the world. It's a good choice for mature travelers who wish to explore the far reaches of the world on a traditionally styled cruise ship. The company offers moderately priced cruises, but that may change as they swallow the cost of agent commissions.

Contact:

1800 Eller Drive, Suite 300
Ft. Lauderdale, FL 33335-0307
800-590-8863
www.renaissancecruises.com

Society Expeditions, Inc.
This cruise line's single yacht-plus ship can cut through ice and glide over coral reefs. Depending on season, they can be found in the Arctic, Antarctica, or South Pacific. The line also visits Alaska but, unlike the mainstream lines, departs from Anchorage and many times explores the fiftieth state's northern regions rather than the more familiar Inside Passage. Prices run into the top-dollar range.

Contact:

2001 Western Ave., Suite 300
Seattle, WA 98121
800-548-8669
www.societyexpeditions.com

Star Cruises
Star Cruises is a big player in the Asia-Pacific market offering ships that look and feel like the companies that serve North American markets. Their twelve ships do not easily fall into size categories, however, and range from yacht-plus to mega-ships. Likewise, prices cannot be easily summarized and exact costs depend on ship and itinerary—with the more expensive options offering more amenities than those that save a few dollars. With that said, if you wish to visit the Pacific and countries to the east, Star has the most options. Star Cruises is now one of the three largest cruise lines in the world and the company claims that it now controls 70 percent of the market in the Asia-Pacific area.

Contact:

1 Centerpointe Drive, Suite 380
La Palma, CA 90623
714-994-1616
www.starcruises.com

Temptress Adventure Cruises
With rates from the moderate to expensive range, Temptress Adventure Cruises offers in-depth tours to Central America, the Caribbean, and the Pacific Ocean from a home base in Costa Rica. The line's two ships, both yacht-plus in size, have only outside cabins. Trips concentrate on ports and culture thanks, in part, to the fact that there's just not much room onboard for shows.

Contact:

6100 Hollywood Blvd., Suite 202
Hollywood, FL 33024
800-336-8423
www.temptresscruises.com

Voyager Cruise Line

Voyager Cruise Line is, in another life, Glacier Bay Tours outlined earlier. In the winter months when it's too cold to tour Alaska, the company—a Juneau-based Alaska Native corporation—relocates its ship to the Sea of Cortez and Mexico's Pacific coast. Details on ships can be found under Glacier Bay Tours.

Contact:

520 Pike Street, Suite 1400
Seattle, WA 98101
800-451-5952
www.voyagercruiseline.com

9

PORTS OF CALL

A port's im-*port*-ance (get it?) usually varies by geography. On an Alaskan cruise, ports usually take second stage to nature. Passengers want to see whales, glaciers, mountains, and, oh, some towns along the way. On a Caribbean cruise, people may want to see a specific island but willingly forgo it in favor of a different itinerary, simply because the cruise is better or cheaper or longer. Ports count, but they're not all that important. (Ports, however, may be extremely important in other world destinations, especially to U.S. travelers.)

Most Caribbean cruises sail from Miami, Fort Lauderdale, Port Canaveral, or Tampa. A few, notably those covering the southern Caribbean, sail from San Juan, Puerto Rico. (Some cruise lines dock in smaller Caribbean islands, such as Star Clippers, Seabourn, and others.) Selected sailings on the mainstream lines may also cruise from smaller U.S. ports. Carnival, for example, sometimes sails from Charleston, SC, and Newport News, VA. NCL sails from Houston; Regal from Port Manatee, FL; and Commodore from New Orleans. In the summertime, most of the major cruise lines dock a ship in New York City, Boston, or Philadelphia. If you live within driving distance of these cities, the money saved on air transportation could more than compensate for a high season rate.

This chapter does not cover all world ports. This chapter doesn't even cover all Caribbean ports. It does, however, cover all major Caribbean ports frequented by 90 percent of the cruise lines as well as the major North American ports of departure. Note that the interesting ports frequented by smaller ships are virtually ignored. In the Bahamas, for example, major cruise ships stop in Nassau or Freeport. A small cruise ship may, however, visit the Abacos Islands, a different experience altogether. Indeed, even side-by-side islands in the Abacos have distinctly different styles.

HOME PORTS TO THE CARIBBEAN

Miami

Cruise departure central, Miami hosts more ships than any other U.S. port, and funnels as many as 4 million passengers per year from shore to ship and back again. Carnival Cruise Lines, Cunard, Norwegian Cruise Line, and Royal Caribbean International all operate cruise vessels from the port of Miami. As a city, Miami has an electric tourist base found nowhere else as well as pockets of abject poverty.

GETTING THERE: Because Miami handles so many passengers, it's good at moving people around. For those driving to the ship, the port has plenty of parking located near all the major terminals at a cost of $8 per day. For those flying, the cruise lines themselves offer free transfers if arranged ahead of time. If transfers have not been arranged, lines of taxis await those who want personalized service for a cost of less than $20.

LOCAL SITES: If you have a few hours to kill on the morning of departure, South Beach or Bayside Marketplace offer diversions close to the terminal (though too far to walk). Bayside Marketplace has restaurants and shopping, much of it unique and offered by smaller vendors. South Beach, on the other hand, houses the art deco district, and has many sidewalk restaurants. The place to "see and be seen," it's less electric and more relaxed during daylight hours. Have a drink and watch young buff guys skate past. Other tourist sites include Miami Beach itself, the Bass Museum of Art (305-673-7533), Vizcaya, a palatial Italian villa (305-250-9133); and the Miami Seaquarium (305-361-5705).

PORT INFORMATION:

Port of Miami
1015 N. America Way
2nd Floor
Miami, Florida 33132
305-371-7678
http://www.metro-dade.com/portofmiami
portofmiami@co.miami.dade.fl.us

CITY INFORMATION:

Greater Miami Convention and Visitors Bureau
701 Brickell Avenue, Suite 2700
Miami, Florida 33131
305-539-3000
http://www.miamiandbeaches.com

Fort Lauderdale

Located only forty-five minutes north of Miami, Port Everglades—
the official name of Fort Lauderdale's port—actually covers three
cities and some countryside. Only 13 percent of it lies within Fort
Lauderdale itself; 75 percent sits within Hollywood, Florida. Still,
from a visitor's point of view, it's a Fort Lauderdale port.
GETTING THERE: Located at the end of State Road 84 (only it
becomes Spangler Blvd.), a major artery through the city, Port
Everglades is about five minutes from the airport and easily found
by way of I-95 or I-595. Public transportation—taxis, trolleys, and
buses—connect the airport to the ships, but the cruise lines usually
provide a transfer service for incoming and outgoing passengers.
PORT PARKING: Passengers driving to the port may use one of
two garages, the Northport or Midport Parking Garage. Garages
are security-patrolled and can accommodate RVs and buses. Both
garages charge $8 per day, $1 per half hour, and $1 every hour after
that up to the daily maximum.
LOCAL SITES: Within Fort Lauderdale, the beach area has an
art deco style with a relaxed ambience. Those looking for remnants
of old Fort Lauderdale—the ones made famous when Connie Fran-

cis starred in *Where the Boys Are*—find little remaining. At the south end of the beach, however, is the International Swimming Hall of Fame Museum & Aquatic Complex (954-462-6536) with over 10,000 square feet of Olympic memorabilia and artwork related to water sports. (Families $5, adults $3, students/seniors/military $1.)

For a very touristy but informative tour, consider the Jungle Queen Riverboat Cruise (A1A, Bahia Mar Yacht Center, 954-462-5696.) The *Jungle Queen* sails three times per day, and the 10:00 A.M. departure will feed you and return in plenty of time for the cruise. Daylight prices are $11.50 for adults and $7.75 for those under ten. At night, adults cost $24.50 and children under ten run $11.50. Shoppers should consider Sawgrass Mills, a 270-store discount/factory outlet mall (W. Sunrise Blvd at Flamingo Rd, Sunrise, 954-846-2350). To use up a couple of hours, look for a water taxi that connects by way of Fort Lauderdale's famous canals, and stop at Riverwalk, a mile-long city park that meanders along the New River (954-468-1541).

PORT INFORMATION:

Port Everglades
1850 Eller Dr
Fort Lauderdale, FL
954-523-3404
http://www.porteverglades.com

CITY INFORMATION: (same address as Port Everglades)

Fort Lauderdale Convention & Visitors Bureau
1850 Eller Drive
Fort Lauderdale, FL 33316
954-765-4466
http://www.broward.org/sunny.htm

Port Canaveral

Serving central Florida, Port Canaveral feels like a small town, mainly because it is. Cocoa Beach's edge abuts the port, but unlike its sisters in Miami and Fort Lauderdale, it's a hub of transportation but not civilization. Disney World, Universal Studios, and Sea

World are about fifty miles away. Within a short distance of the ships, however, there's not a lot of shopping except for Ron Jon's Surf Shop, a local landmark.

All cruise lines sailing from Port Canaveral offer some kind of pre- or post-cruise package that includes an Orlando hotel, theme park tickets, and other amenities. Located about an hour away, these packages include transfers to and from the pier or, many times, a car rental that is used in Orlando and then parked at the pier while at sea.

GETTING THERE: The Beeline Expressway (528) connects Orlando to the port, though expect to pay tolls along the way. Exit onto the same road if coming by way of I-95. The Beeline eventually becomes A1A. Look for left turn signs after crossing the causeway, and once inside the port, ship locations are posted. Fenced parking lots exist across from each terminal and cost about $7 per day. If flying, you'll probably land in Orlando and commute by bus. (You may fly into Melbourne, instead.) The Cocoa Beach Shuttle (800-633-0427) also offers transfers for a cost of about $20 each way.

LOCAL SITES: Jetty Park, a small beach and breakwater where the sea meets port access, is not far and a good place to lay around and soak up sun before departure. There are also a few restaurants with local flavor within the port. I recommend Frankie's for wings and garlic shrimp, but don't expect elegance or sophistication. Dress down—way down.

Kennedy Space Center (407-452-2121) is close as the crow flies, but about a half hour away as the car crawls. The tallest buildings can be seen from the port. While you can't do justice to the Center by visiting for two hours before embarkation, it's still worth a trip. A $24 adult admission and $15 child admission (ages 3–11) gains access to Kennedy Space Center's three IMAX movies, space museum, bus tours, exhibits, and launch pad. The U.S. Astronaut Hall of Fame (407-269-6100) is also located nearby but unaffiliated with the "official" space center itself. The area bills itself as the "only quadra-modal transportation hub in the world," meaning it moves freight between sea, land, air, and space.

PORT INFORMATION:

Canaveral Port Authority
P.O. Box 267
Cape Canaveral, FL 32920
888-PORTCAN (767-8226) or 1-407-783-7831
E-mail:*portcan@aol.com*
http://www.portcanaveral.org

CITY INFORMATION:

City of Cocoa Beach
P.O. Box 322430
2 South Orlando Avenue (SR A1A)
Cocoa Beach, FL 32932-2430
http://www.ci.cocoa-beach.fl.us(tourism)

Tampa

Compared to Miami, Fort Lauderdale, and Port Canaveral, Tampa comes in a distant fourth in number of cruise ships — but that number continues to grow. Tampa has aggressive redevelopment plans for its waterfront, and the Garrison Seaport Center's Cruise Terminal sits in the heart of it all.

GETTING THERE: Tampa International Airport is about fifteen minutes from the port. If your cruise does not provide transfers, except to spend up to $15 on a taxi. If traveling by car, all major interstates connect to I-4, which is well marked. Look for port signs. The port itself sits between the Tampa Convention Center and the Florida Aquarium. Nearby security parking costs about $8 per day.

LOCAL SITES: With a few hours before cruise-time, the Florida Aquarium (813-224-9583) provides a great get away, and displays the different types of aquatic life — from swamp to ocean — found throughout Florida. If you have more time, consider Busch Gardens (813-987-5171), about a twenty-minute taxi ride to the north. While billboards promote the park's Africa-themed killer roller coasters, the young crowd tends to be drawn to the action, leaving the zoo and quieter rides less crowded. They also offer a number of shows. Consider a stroll through Ybor City, a once-small town that is now just a suburb of the big city, but brought back to its former glory with a set of unique shops, restaurants, and bars. At night, it's party central for twenty-somethings, but a good place to relax during the day. Other semi-local attractions include the Henry B. Plant Museum (813-254-1891), the Tampa Museum of Art (813-274-8130), and, a bit farther away, the Salvador Dali Museum (813-823-3767) in St. Petersburg.

PORT INFORMATION:

Tampa Port Authority
1333 McKay Street
Tampa, Florida 33602
813-905-PORT (7678) or 800-741-2297
http://www.tampaport.com

CITY INFORMATION:

Tampa/Hillsborough Convention and Visitors Association
400 North Tampa St., Suite 1010
Tampa, FL 33602
800-36-TAMPA (368-2672)
http://www.gotampa.com

New Orleans

New Orleans uniquely serves America's heartland and, as such, welcomes many ships laden with supplies—but only a few cruise ships, notably Delta Queen's riverboats, Commodore Cruise Lines, and an occasional mainstream line. Thanks to extensive docking facilities and access to middle America, the port of New Orleans can expand as cruise line competition forces other carriers to seek new markets.

GETTING THERE: New Orleans International Airport is ten miles from the port and about twenty minutes and $20 by taxi. An airport shuttle service connects to the port and other areas (504-592-0555) and costs about $11 per person. By car, the port is only a short distance from the famous French Quarter. Look for signs. Port parking is limited, however, and arrangements should be confirmed through the cruise line before arrival. Cost: about $7 per day.

LOCAL SITES: The French Quarter, arguably, *is* New Orleans—at least the New Orleans of commercials, advertising, and legend.

Good food, hearty liquor, and party people—all there. The Garden District and other parts of the old city remain unchanged from early times and have a unique French-inspired influence. Consider visiting Old Absinthe House/Tony Moran's Restaurant, the oldest bar in America (504-523-3181) at 240 Bourbon St.; the Beauregard-Keyes House at 1113 Chartres St. (504-523-7257), one of the city's most famous mansions; The Historic New Orleans Collection at 533 Royal St. (504-523-4662), seven buildings indicative of New Orleans circa 1800; and for those with a penchant for the unusual, the New Orleans Historic Voodoo Museum (504-523-7685) at 724 Dumaine St. also offers a guided voodoo walking tour.

PORT INFORMATION:

Port of New Orleans
P.O. Box 60046
New Orleans, LA 70160
Phone: 504-522-2551
http://www.portno.com

CITY INFORMATION:

New Orleans Metropolitan Convention and Visitors Bureau
1520 Sugar Bowl Dr.
New Orleans, LA 70112
504-566-5003 or 800-672-6124
http://www.nawlins.com

HOME PORTS TO ALASKA

Most cruise ships depart from Vancouver, though some depart from Anchorage by way of Seward. Some smaller lines, however, depart from almost every small town fronting the water including Juneau, Ketchikan, Nome, Sitka, Whittier, and even U.S. cities such as Seattle and San Francisco.

Vancouver

More than 1,000,000 passengers now travel through Vancouver's two terminals en route to Alaska. A beautiful city of thick trees and verdant gardens, Vancouver has a European feel. Gastown and other historic districts are within walking distance of the Canada Place pier. A second pier, Ballantyne cruise terminal, may also be used by some cruise ships.

GETTING THERE: From Vancouver International Airport, either pier can be reached in about twenty-five minutes, with an average taxi fare of $17 (fluctuating based on exchange rates). Buses also make the trip for about $7 per person (602-244-9888).

LOCAL SITES: Many Northwest cities started as logging towns that, as might be expected, drew lumberjacks to town by offering hard liquor and houses of ill repute. Gastown and Chinatown are two remnants of early Vancouver life now stocked with good restaurants, shopping, and a bit of history. Granville Island, about twenty minutes from the port, draws most serious shoppers. Stanley Park (604-682-1118) offers beautiful gardens as well as the Vancouver Aquarium; the Vancouver Art Gallery (604-682-5621) displays a large collection of Canadian art; and the Vancouver Museum (604-736-4431) showcases the area's history.

PORT INFORMATION:

Vancouver Port Authority
1900-200 Granville Street
Vancouver, BC V6C 2P9
604-665-9000 or 888-PORTVAN
(1-888-767-8826)
http://www.portvancouver.com

CITY INFORMATION:

Vancouver Travel Info Centre
200 Burrard Street
Vancouver, BC V6C 3L6
604-683-2000
http://city.vancouver.bc.ca

Anchorage and Seward

It's geographically unfair to lump Anchorage in with Seward since 125 miles separate the two. But people fly into Anchorage (best airport), hop on a bus for the three-hour commute, and cruise out of Seward. A peninsula separates the two cities and cruise ships would have to add a full day of sailing to their itinerary just to sail around it.

GETTING THERE: Don't plan on driving unless you live in either city's suburbs—and they don't really have suburbs. If arriving by air, Anchorage International Airport provides easy connections to the city's downtown. Taxis cost about $15 depending on final destination. If on your own for a full day, most major car rental companies also operate there. The three-hour trip to Seward costs about $30 unless included with your cruise (it should be) and provides a pleasant first taste of Alaska's wilderness.

LOCAL SITES: Alaska's beauty—mountains, wilderness, and glaciers—requires space and walking around Anchorage or Seward does not provide much of a feel for the expansive state. Anchorage's downtown has the traditional souvenir shops; Seward's has the same but on a smaller scale. If ready for a small physical challenge, Anchorage's Tony Knowles Coastal Trail covers about twelve miles and can be accessed or exited at various points along the way; bikes may also be rented. In Seward, several hiking trails do the same thing; for info, visit the Kenai Fjords National Park Visitor Center (907-224-3175) on Fourth Avenue. While in Anchorage, also consider the Anchorage Museum of History and Art (907-343-4326) for a background on state history or a walking tour of the downtown hosted by Alaska Historic Properties (907-274-3600) during summer months only ($5 adult, $4 over fifty-five, $1 children). In Seward, consider touring Resurrection Bay by boat through one of several local companies, or travel a short distance outside the city to Iditarod Dogsled Tours (800-478-3139) to enjoy a dogsled demonstration, albeit by a wheeled dogsled in deference to the summer months.

PORT INFORMATION:

Alaska's Regional Port, The Port of Anchorage
2000 Anchorage Port Road
Anchorage, AK 99501-1024
907-343-6200

CITY INFORMATION:

Anchorage Convention and Visitors Bureau
524 West Fourth Avenue
Anchorage Alaska 99501
907-276-4118
http://www.anchorage.net
Seward also has a limited information Web site at
http://www.seward-alaska.com.

PORTS OF CALL—THE CARIBBEAN AND MEXICO

A huge underwater mountain system towers from the ocean floor in the Caribbean, and when the tallest peaks break the waterline, you find an island. From the arid deserts of Aruba in the south to the Florida-like humidity of the Bahamas, the islands differ subtly in climate and dramatically in culture. Many islands are miniature versions of European countries. The first settlers replicated their homeland's style and then adapted it to the demands of a tropical climate.

A short description of each island attempts to encapsulate a total visit—the local geography, culture, and "feel." Since similar itineraries can visit different islands, they're listed alphabetically rather than geographically. For extensive information, visit Web sites at *http://www.caribbean.com* or *http://caribbean-on-line.com.*

Consider the following:

• What you choose to do on one island may be affected by what you choose to do on the other islands. When planning, look first at the cruise's complete itinerary and pick and choose across the board. For example, visit just one volcano.

• Each island's shore excursions look similar. While each has historical and cultural variations, most have some kind of island tour, a snorkel trip, a beach excursion, and some kind of cruise around the island that usually includes drinks, snacks, and sometimes dancing. Many also offer a glass-bottom boat ride or a four-wheel tour of local natural areas. (A bit of irony since four-wheel driving can destroy a natural area.) Most also have a gambling option if legal on the island.

- Most islands accept U.S. money—but not all.
- A walking tour on any island requires more physical exertion than most people realize. A hike from their cabin just to the end of the pier leaves some people winded. Also, most near-the-dock areas are tourist friendly. To see the "real" city, you must keep walking . . . and walking. Wear comfortable shoes regardless of fashion or weather, and keep in shape—good for the heart, good for the vacation.
- For passengers with disabilities, islands rarely have the high accessibility standards demanded by law in the U.S. Roads may be cobblestone and sidewalks curbed. A shore excursion that accommodates people with disabilities may be the best option.

Antigua

ON YOUR OWN: Ships dock at St. John's, the island's capital, though all but the smaller ships use a tender to transfer passengers to land. St. John's cobblestone streets and Caribbean architecture would be idyllic with a coat of paint and a hammer and nails. On the south side of town, a market bustles on Saturday. A handful of history-laden exhibits can be reached on foot including the Museum of Antigua and Barbuda at the 250-year-old courthouse on Long and Market Streets ($2 admission charge), and St. John's Cathedral, an Anglican church dating from 1683.

SHORE EXCURSIONS: Laden with history, Antigua's Nelson Dockyard National Park is one of the Caribbean's better-known sights and, along with the Clarence House at English Harbour, generally the anchor of "see the island" Antigua tours. Because Antigua is relatively small with scattered historical sites, consider a planned tour on a first visit. The cruise line may also offer an eco-tour of the island's natural sites, as well as a boat tour that circles the island. For themed dancing, swimming, and partying consider the *Jolly Roger*, a "real" pirate ship. All tours cost between $45 and $60. Antigua also has great beaches if sun and sand appeal to you.

Aruba

ON YOUR OWN: Crime can be a concern on some islands but less so on Aruba. Shopping, parks, and water can all be explored on foot—all pleasant. Local casinos also offer gambling. Ships dock in Oranjestad, the nation's capital, and while not European-beautiful, it's a pleasant, functional city. Aruba, at the southern tip of the Caribbean, rarely receives rain and sits outside the path of hurricanes.
SHORE EXCURSIONS: The generic "see the island" tour has less to offer than on some islands, with Aruba's beaches and snorkeling the main attractions. The usual mix of diversions—four-wheel drive tours, etc.—is also offered.

Bahamas—Nassau and Freeport/Lucaya

ON YOUR OWN: Nassau, especially, is a well-traveled tourist destination with the requisite T-shirt and souvenir shops. Taxi, bus, or horse-drawn carriage options explore Nassau, though most sites can be found on foot. An information booth sits between the dock and the city. The straw market, famous mainly for its size, draws most tourists. Vendors push their handmade wares and want to haggle on a sale price. Freeport and Lucaya host fewer ships than Nassau, in part because there's nothing to see nearby. Both islands have a distinct Caribbean flavor under a thin veneer of tackiness and a tourist economy.
SHORE EXCURSIONS: Casino gambling is offered in larger resorts, and most cruise ships offer some kind of gambling/dinner/show excursion, though many people simply take a taxi. Other tour options in Nassau include glass-bottom boat tours, trips to Crystal Cay marine park for underwater viewing of coral reefs, and the traditional "see it all" bus tour. Freeport has its own straw market, as well as a handful of shopping areas, gardens, and live music at night.

Barbados

ON YOUR OWN: Shop. A walk into Bridgetown can take thirty minutes (each way), however, taking the thrill out of any exploration on foot. If not in the mood for a hike, do some shopping by the pier and then return to the ship. Consider, however, a shore excursion or taxi ride to at least one famous attraction. Barbados is, arguably, one of the more interesting Caribbean islands, thanks in part to its hold on British tradition—the United Kingdom meets the tropics. The beaches are also great.

SHORE EXCURSIONS: Consider one of the generic island tours, a good choice since Barbados has many things to see, most of which can't easily be reached on foot. A good tour includes historical buildings, plantations, gardens, and Harrison's Cave, an underground world explored by tram.

British Virgin Islands (Tortola and Virgin Gorda)

ON YOUR OWN: These islands—Tortola, Virgin Gorda, Jose Van Dyke, and other small pieces of land—are perfect Caribbean islands, down to and including the area's pirates who once called them home. Actually a series of small islands, most unvisited, the British Virgin Islands have less for tourists to do, yet in that smallness they also seem more natural. Expect to hoist anchor offshore and rely on tenders to transfer guests to the island. On Tortola, the main city of Road Town is a short walk from the pier and a pleasant spot to kill a few hours below towering mountains that border a tropical beach. Expect only a small amount of shopping, however. In Virgin Gorda, the Baths, a series of massive boulders along the ocean, draw the most sightseers. Ships again tender guests to the island, sometimes from their home spot near Tortola. Virgin Gorda has pleasant and relatively short walks through the wilderness.

SHORE EXCURSIONS: Almost all shore excursions to Virgin Gorda include the baths. Otherwise, the main tours are more ecological than historical. They're advised for those who want to get a good feel for island life in the Caribbean, but a bad choice for those who prefer man-made diversions to natural ones.

Caymans (Grand Cayman)

ON YOUR OWN: The "Switzerland of the Caribbean," the Caymans are a great place to hide ill-gotten gains thanks to liberal banking laws. They also have astounding underwater activities—scuba, snorkeling, and swimming—but only so-so beauty on land.

Ships mainly dock offshore and tender guests to the George Town pier, where a tourist information booth fronts a line of waiting taxis. In addition to shopping, the Cayman Islands National Museum on Harbour Drive serves up the area's historical background for a requested $5 donation. Swimming is also an option on the island's famous Seven Mile Beach.

SHORE EXCURSIONS: Anyone with a penchant for diving or snorkeling should consider a tour to Stingray City, a unique undersea attraction where velvet-skinned stingrays swim around, eat out of your hand, and allow you to touch them. Eerie and exciting at the same time, it's also safer than it sounds. A generic island tour includes a stop here, as well as the Cayman Turtle Farm and an ugly rock formation called "Hell," with appropriate "Hell" T-shirts sold to show the folks back home that you've "been to Hell and back."

Cozumel/Playa del Carmen (Mexico)

ON YOUR OWN: Chances are, your ship stays in Playa del Carmen just long enough to drop off passengers who wish to visit the Mayan ruins. Once disembarked, the ship then sails on to spend the day in Cozumel. (Some ships, however, go directly to Cozumel, an island part of, and close to, the Mexico mainland.) You can't walk to the Mayan ruins from Cozumel—it would include a lengthy ocean swim—and a shore excursion is the only option. Cozumel's main city of San Miguel de Cozumel looks traditionally Mexican yet suspiciously American thanks to familiar fast-food joints and a Hard Rock Café. For shoppers, diners, and crowd-watchers, the day will be interesting.

SHORE EXCURSIONS: Besides standard scooter, beach, and horseback riding tours, the two main draws here are shore excursions to one of two Mayan ruins, Chichén Itzá or Tulum. Tulum is the favored tour, mainly because it's accessible by bus, has a prettier setting, and costs less—around $70. Located on top of a cliff overlooking the Caribbean, the tour also includes Xel-Ha Lagoon, a natural (minus the 2,000 cruise passengers) setting for swimming. The world's largest existing Mayan ruins, however, can be found inland at Chichén Itzá. (The Mayans apparently did not think ahead—they did not build their cities close to cruise ship ports.) A trip to Chichén Itzá can cost up to $200 per person, and includes a forty-five-minute flight to and from the ancient city. While hot, muggy, and not physically easy with walking required, Chichén Itzá also has the biggest wow-factor. The size of the ancient city astounds you. You can't see it all in one day.

Curaçao

ON YOUR OWN: From the pier, the town of Willemstad can be reached in about ten minutes, though taxis make the trek easier. (Settle on a fare before accepting a ride.) Most of the island's natural wonders are not within easy walking distance of the ship, but the town does have enough local sites to fill a standard port of call. The Jewish Cultural Historical Museum can be found beside Mikve Israel-Emanuel Synagogue, the oldest Jewish congregation in the Americas. The Curaçao Museum showcases artistic works and local information. Other interesting diversions include the Floating Market, a group of boat vendors who sell their wares seaside, and Fort Amsterdam that dates from before the Revolutionary War. While it's not the kind of thing you explore, also check out the Queen Emma pontoon bridge near the cruise terminal — it floats.
SHORE EXCURSIONS: The general see-it-all tour covers a lot of things, though tours to individual sites give you more time to explore. Of specific interest: the Hato Caves, a walking tour, and the Curaçao Liqueur Tour, where the specialty alcohol is made. (One tour visits both.) Also consider Christoffel National Park if hiking appeals to you. The lofty mountain peak hosts everything from cacti to palms, iguanas to goats. Curaçao also has a moderately sized Seaquarium.

Grenada

ON YOUR OWN: The Spice Island, Grenada has a perfect blend of weather and fertile soil, and a real Tarzan feel. The city of St. George's where ships dock (or tender into) can be explored on foot, but expect steep hills as the city rises from the sea. While St. George's has no major museums or historical attractions, it's pleasant and a good place to have a drink or lunch. The Grenada National Museum has a limited amount of information and artifacts related to island history. A water taxi, about $4 round trip, transfers passengers from the pier to nearby Grand Anse Beach for a day of sun worshiping.

SHORE EXCURSIONS: An eco-tour, without a killer amount of walking, provides a great overview of the island, winding its way through rain forests to Grand Etang Lake and an extinct volcano that towers high over the Caribbean. A separate general tour includes a bit of the rain forest plus spice production plants; some may include small museums, forts, and other historical footnotes.

Guadeloupe

ON YOUR OWN: Two almost separate (but not) islands make up Guadeloupe, Grande-Terre and Base-Terre. Formed by volcanoes, the islands join in an hourglass shape. Grande-Terre to the east has more plantations; Base-Terre to the west has more jungles, mountains, and an active volcano. The port of Pointe-à-Pitre, right in the middle of the two land masses, welcomes ships. While shops love cruise passengers, they may close for a long lunch; at night, the city goes to sleep. Note: While English is spoken in areas close to the docks, French or Creole is spoken elsewhere. Also, U.S. dollars are accepted in tourist-oriented shops, but the French franc is the only currency accepted elsewhere.

SHORE EXCURSIONS: Check out the volcano. Most island tours cover both islands and include both man-made and natural attractions.

Jamaica

ON YOUR OWN: Cruise ships call at either Ocho Rios or Montego Bay — most of the time in Ocho Rios. In both, a shopping market can be reached within a mile of the ship. Expect very aggressive vendors, many of whom compete with each other for virtually identical merchandise, mainly local crafts. You may also be offered marijuana, which is just as illegal in Jamaica as it is in the U.S. Finally, Jamaica has a lot of poverty and, at times, crime. If on your own, stick to the beaten path. Most elegant Jamaican resorts — they have many — are virtual compounds that natives cannot visit. The island is a mixture of vast beauty and widespread poverty.

SHORE EXCURSIONS: A number of tours visit different sites, but almost all include Jamaica's most popular cruise passenger pastime, Dunn's River Falls. Dunn's River Falls cascade gently down the hillside and can be explored by the boardwalk running alongside it or in the water itself (wear your bathing suit) with a guide to help find the best footing if you prefer. (Tip him when you're done.) Other excursion options include plantation tours to working farms growing bananas and other crops, as well as general tours that point out famous sites, such as the home of Ian Fleming. Other sightseeing options include the Rose Hall Great House, a historic and notorious mansion; Greenwood Great House, another historic structure; and Rocklands Wildlife Station.

Martinique

ON YOUR OWN: In realtor jargon, Martinique has no "curb appeal," mainly because little at the pier suggests tropical beauty, civilization, or long sandy beaches. They're there; you just haven't seen them yet. The town of Fort-de-France, the home port, has a French, somewhat New Orleans flavor—once you get there. A pure walking tour takes you almost nowhere. Most people opt for a taxi ride, about $10. Cabdrivers have a monopoly and they know it. (One local store that is within walking distance also has a monopoly and knows it.) The taxi ride is short, however, and the city's style and offerings worth the trip. Once in Fort-de-France, visit La Savane, a palms and mango garden; Bibliothèque Schoelcher, a library; St. Louis Roman Catholic Cathedral, circa 1875; and Musée Departemental de la Martinique, a small museum showcasing early island history ($3.50 for adults, $2.50 for kids).

SHORE EXCURSIONS: A number of attractions exist outside Fort-de-France and are best explored on a generic island tour. Martinique's intriguing history lends itself to a guided excursion, though exact sites vary by tour operator. A 1902 volcanic explosion, for example, killed 30,000 people in 1902. The trip includes the surrounding lush forests, the ruins of nineteenth-century towns, and existing structures that still exist from that era but fell outside the destructive path of Mount Pelée's eruption. If choosing only one island tour, consider this one.

Puerto Rico (San Juan)

ON YOUR OWN: Cruise ships dock within walking distance of Old San Juan, the original Spanish heart of the city that dates back fifty years earlier than the American Revolution. A tourist information center can also be found near Pier 1, and it's fairly easy to see the sights on your own. (Your ship's location may vary, however. San Juan has eight convenient piers, but less convenient ones are sometimes used in high season.) San Juan's Old Town section not only sits near the cruise docks, but a free trolley service allows visitors to explore more on their own. It's also the best place to shop. Most major historic sites may be visited on foot, and attractions outside the historic district mirror urban activities in other cities across the U.S.—expect traffic, congestion, and a flurry of people.

Parts of Old Town date back 500 years, and many sites once performed necessary functions—and were perhaps their earliest versions in the New World. Any tour should include the local convent (El Convento), prison (La Princesa), governor's mansion (La Fortaleza and Mansion Ejecutiva), insane asylum (Antiguo Manicomio Insular), and poor house (Asilo de Beneficencia). San Juan's Old Town also has two forts protecting its ancient northern boundaries, Castillo de San Felipe del Morro (or "El Morro") and Fort San Cristóbal. A wall that doubles as a building—hospitals and homes—connects the two structures.

Old San Juan also has a number of open park areas, called plazas, including its most formal one, Plaza del Quinto Centenario, a reflection of the island's European heritage. Also look for Plaza de San José, a tribute to explorer Ponce de León; Plaza de Armas, home to the U.S. State Department (Intendencia) and City Hall (Alcaldía); and Plaza de Colón, famous for its statue of Christopher Columbus. In addition to ancient churches, museums can also be found. Look for the Museum of the Americas in Cuartel de Ballajá, a military barracks. La Casa Blanca, literally meaning "White House," also houses a small museum within a house designed for, but never used by, Ponce de León.

Gambling draws many a cruise passenger into San Juan. Located within resort hotels, the two largest casinos are found at the Ritz-Carlton and the San Juan Grand Beach Hotel & Casino, though a number of other properties would be more than happy to offer a slot for your quarters.

SHORE EXCURSIONS: One shore excursion will include many of the Old Town sites. The advantage: You don't have to plan; just go with the program. A separate tour will go elsewhere on the island, taking in some of the natural beauty, though similar natural wonders could be seen on other islands that have fewer historic diversions. The tour, however, will include a stop at the Bacardi rum plant where guests can sample the local spirits.

More information:

Puerto Rico Tourism Company
575 Fifth Ave.
New York, NY 10017
800-223-6350.
http://welcome.topuertorico.org

St. Barthélemy (St. Barts)

ON YOUR OWN: Only smaller cruise ships visit St. Barts, and even then, they anchor offshore and tender guests to the mainland. Gustavia—island capital, port city, and only city—can be explored in a few hours, and many passengers simply take to the beaches. While short on history and museums, St. Barts has a true European flavor, full of fine dining, elegant shops, and a cultured atmosphere—all to the backdrop of towering mountains and white sand beaches. While some islands expand the mind, St. Barts does more for the attitude.

SHORE EXCURSIONS: One generic island tour will be short, enjoyable, and see very little because there's very little to see beyond impressive natural beauty.

St. Kitts

ON YOUR OWN: Small and out of the way, St. Kitts welcomes ships in Basseterre, a small town with enough shops and restaurants to give visitors a feel for the local life with some shopping in the local market. While its smallness limits entertainment options, it's also its strength. A visit feels more traditional, as if stepping back in time without giving up modern conveniences.

SHORE EXCURSIONS: Brimstone Hill is a building complex adapted to the island's hilly terrain and home to early residents of St. Kitts. Dating from the late 1700s, the tour also offers visitors a panoramic view of the entire island.

St. Lucia

ON YOUR OWN: One of the best on-your-own Caribbean ports, shopping and other diversions can be found just off the docks in Castries. If strolling through Castries, visit Fort Charlotte and other historic buildings such as the Government House. If taking a taxi anywhere, confirm prices before getting in.

SHORE EXCURSIONS: As part of all see-the-whole-island tours, St. Lucia has an intriguing, if not a bit stark, volcano trip. La Soufrière, a drive-through tour, has bubbling sulfur springs, hot mud, and a landscape that looks more like the moon than the earth. Other attractions include the nearby Diamond Mineral Baths, a banana plantation, and Pigeon Island National Park's small museum.

St. Martin/Sint Maarten

ON YOUR OWN: Half French (St. Martin) and half Dutch (Sint Maarten), this single island offers the best of both worlds. All larger cruise ships dock almost a mile from Philipsburg on the Dutch side. From there, the hearty may walk; the smart may take taxis. (Taxis may charge different fares, so check first.) Once in the city, shopping, restaurants, and even gambling cater to the tourist crowd and look a bit less Caribbean than other islands.

SHORE EXCURSIONS: Consider the generic island tour since both sides of the island have different cultures and it's difficult to get a feel for the diversity if staying on only one side. A few unique excursions may be offered or included as part of larger trips, including a faux race on one of the ships that competed in the America's Cup and a trip to the Butterfly Farm. St. Martin also has its own fort (don't they all?) — Fort St. Louis.

U.S. Virgin Islands (St. Thomas/St. John/St. Croix)

ON YOUR OWN: All three islands, along with smaller relatives, form the U.S. Virgin Islands. St. Thomas is, hands down, the primary cruise ship destination in deference to the shopping it offers. Unless exceptionally busy, St. Thomas cruise ships dock next to Havensight Mall, a shopping area offering most cruise passenger basics such as a post office and duty-free goods. Downtown Charlotte Amalie is about 1.5 miles away and can be reached by foot for the strong-of-leg—but pay about $3 and take a cab for both health and security reasons. The walk does not take you through the best part of town. If exploring Charlotte Amalie, check out Fort Christian that lords over the harbor and protects citizens from wayward pirates. Two small museums, the Virgin Islands Museum and Seven Arches Museum preserve a bit of history; and a number of older buildings remain from the earliest days when Europeans discovered the Caribbean, including the Grand Hotel, Hotel 182, and St. Thomas Synagogue.

Unlike ultra-developed St. Thomas, St. John concentrates on its natural beauty and primarily consists of the Virgin Islands National Park. If exploring St. John on foot, plan to gaze at the forests as you lie on the beaches.

St. Croix, arguably, is somewhere between its siblings, with both civilization and natural areas. Ships dock at Christiansted if small, at Frederiksted if medium to large. To explore a single city, pick Christiansted, about seventeen miles from Frederiksted but easily accessible by taxi (negotiable $20) or bus (about $1). While Frederiksted has a fort worthy of exploration, Christiansted's harbor area continues to upgrade itself, restoring once-grand facilities to their original splendor.

SHORE EXCURSIONS: On St. Thomas, most excursions involve some kind of general tour but through different modes of transportation—mountain bikes, submarines, seaplanes, kayaks, and, of course, buses. St. John tours mainly cover scenery beautiful enough to be worth any price of admission, though they'll also include local plantations and, usually, a beach. In St. Croix, the generic tour is offered along with a snorkel adventure to Buck Island National Park.

AFTERWORD

That about covers the Caribbean—and Alaska, U.S. mainland ports, and everything else related to cruising. It's a lot of information, a lot to think about, and a lot of details to take care of before departure.

But the cruise itself—the part only touched on during the course of this guide—is the real adventure. There's a magical feeling to being surrounded by vast oceans; to wear a tux or gown and worry little about the wind in your hair; to move while you dine with a port waiting for your arrival the next day. There's a sense of adventure in not knowing whom you might meet at dinner, at the lounge, or by the pool.

Have a great trip. When you get back, drop me a line to let me know how it was. And if you discovered anything of value to other mature travelers, let me know that, too. Bon voyage. Send comments to:

Kerry Smith
P.O. Box 622616
Oviedo, FL 32762
http://www.maturetravelers.com

INDEX

Abercrombie & Kent, 201
Accommodations, cost and, 12–13
Achille Lauro episode, 19
Activities on board, 82, 125–126
Add-ons, 47–8
Adventure lines, 27, 28, 33, 35, 111
Air conditioning, 144
Air travel
    booking, 48–52
    departures and arrivals, 115–118
    deviations, 100, 146
    rules, 100
Alaska
    cruises to, 9, 29, 35, 94, 208
    home ports to, 215–218
Alaska's Glacier Bay Tours and
    Cruises/Voyager Cruise Line,
    186–187
Alaska Yacht Safaris, 188–189
American Canadian Caribbean Line,
    30, 35, 187–188
American Hawaii Cruises, 9, 22, 27,
    31, 32, 86, 167–168
American Safari Cruises, 35,
    188–189
American Society of Travel Agents
    (ASTA), 41
American Yacht Safaris, 28
Anchorage, 216–218
Antigua, 219
Art auctions on board, 137–138

Aruba, 220
Asian cruises, 9

Baby-sitting, 4, 82, 123
Back office systems, 75–76
Back-to-back cruises, 74
Baggage
    liability, 102
    protection, 90
    See also Lost luggage
Bahamas, 137, 209, 220
Balconies on board, 96
Barbados, 220–221
Beauty services, 82, 135
Bed configurations, 46–47
Bergen Line, 201–202
Bermuda, marriage in, 37
Birth certificates, 22, 109–110
Boarding the ship, 118–121
Booking strategies, 60–67
Boredom, 4
British Virgin Islands, 221
Brochures, 44–48
Budget cruise lines vs. luxury liners,
    12–14, 27–28, 95, 151–152.
    See also Cost of cruising
"Bumping," 117

Cabins
    amenities of, 123–124
    booking, 63–64

Cabins (*continued*)
    choosing, 93–97
    location of and seasickness, 6
    upgrades, 74
Cable and Wireless Caribbean
    Cellular, 140
Cancellation penalties, 100
Cancelled flights, 117
Cape Canaveral Cruise Line, 27,
    168–169
Caribbean cruises, 8–9, 52, 208
    cell phone use on, 140
    home ports to, 209–215
    ports of call, 218–229
    private islands on, 131–133
    shopping on, 129
Carnival Corp., 43–44
Carnival Cruise Lines, 153–155
    children on, 31
    cost on, 27
    cruise guarantee of, 105
    discounts on, 70
    insurance by, 86
    Internet information on, 42
    mature travelers on, 27
    party cruise on, 34
    points of departure, 208
    policy statements on, 100
    price guarantees by, 80
    reputation of, 43
    resort experience on, 34
    sexual assaults on, 20
Carry-on luggage, 114
Cars, renting on shore, 130
Casinos, 82, 134–135, 144
Casual wear, 112
Category guarantee, 74–75
Caymans, 221–222
Celebrity Cruises, 26, 28, 33, 34,
    155–156
Cell phones, 140
Checking in at the pier, 118–121
Children
    avoiding, 7, 15, 28–30
    baby-sitting services for, 4, 82, 123

    cabin location and, 94
    documentation for, 24, 110
    traveling with, 30–31
Classical Cruises/Travel Dynamics,
    202
Clipper Cruise Line, 33, 189–190
Club Med, 30, 33, 34, 190–191
Commissions, travel agencies and,
    61–62, 65–66
Commodore Cruise Line, 169–170
    cost on, 27
    hosts on, 54
    party cruise on, 34
    points of departure, 208
    resort experience on, 34
    theme cruises on, 32
Communications on board, 139–140
Connections, missing, 118
Cost of cruising, 3–4, 11–15, 27, 54,
    60–84
Costa Cruise Lines, 32, 34, 170–172
Cozumel, 222–223
Credit cards, 114–115
Credit payment systems, 68, 103,
    114–115, 120
Crew
    cost and, 13
    who's who, 142–143
Crime. *See* Security issues
Crown Cruise Line, 34, 54, 172–173
Cruise Line International Association
    (CLIA), 41–42
Cruise lines
    choosing among, 25–38
    insurance, 86–87
    profiles of, 151–207
    shore excursions, 128–129
    size of, 7
Cruise ships, size of, 6, 26
Cruise West/Alaska Sightseeing, 27,
    35, 192–193
Cruise-only travel agencies, 40–41
Cruising
    cost of, 3–4, 11–16, 27, 54, 60–84
    life on board, 125–126

pros and cons of, 1–6
resorts and, 34
types of, 8–12, 25–38
Crystal Cruises, 173–174
    children on, 29
    deposits on, 67
    food on, 33
    gourmet and wine themes on, 32
    hosts on, 54
    luxury on, 28
    mature travelers on, 26
    romance on, 54
    suites on, 95
Cunard Lines, 175–176
    children on, 29
    food on, 33
    health issues on, 17
    hosts on, 54
    luxury on, 28
    mature travelers on, 26
    relaxation on, 35
    reputation of, 43
    round-the-world cruises on, 15
    See also Queen Elizabeth 2 (QE2)
Curaçao, 223
Customs, 116, 148–149

Daily cruise life, 125–126
Dance hosts, 53–54
Death at sea, 18–19
Debarkation. See Disembarking
Delta Queen Steamboat Company, 9,
    176–177
    discounts on, 70
    documentation for, 21–22
    lack of seasickness on, 6
    mature travelers on, 26
    relaxation on, 35
    singles on, 54
    theme cruises on, 32
Deposit, making a, 67–68, 100,
    103–104
Destinations, 8–11, 52–53. See also
    Ports of call
Diets, special, 98–99. See also Food

Disabled access, 56–59, 102–103
    private islands and, 132
    shore excursions and, 128
    See also Cruise lines, profiles of
Disasters, 21
Disclaimers, 101–102
Discounts, 68–80
Diseases, 18
Disembarking, 99, 127, 147–150
Disney Cruise Line, 30, 32, 34, 132,
    134, 156–158
Documentation, 21–24, 102, 109–110,
    119
Double beds, 96
Dressing for dinner, 4, 11. See also
    Formal wear; Packing for a cruise

Elderhostel, 55
E-mail, 139
Embarkation, 99, 118–121
Emergency evacuation, 91
Enchanted Isle, hosts on, 54
Entertainment, 133–134
Eurocruises, 202–203
European cruises, 9. See also
    Mediterranean cruises
Excursions, 82, 115, 128–131, 145,
    218–229
Exercise, 136. See also Walking

Family cruises, 55–56
Fax services, 139
"Fine print," 99–103
Fire, 21
First aid, 18
First European Cruises, 32, 193–194
Floating Formals, 112
Food
    cost and, 13–14
    dining, 97–99, 125
    extras, 81
    meal times, 124–125
    problems with, 145
    See also Gourmet cruising
Formal wear, 111–112

Fort Lauderdale, 210–211
Full-service travel agencies, 40–41

Gay and lesbian cruises, 37–38
General information, 99–103
Getting around on board, 127–128
Glacier Bay Tours and Cruises, 35
Golf shore excursions, 82
Gourmet cruising, 7, 13–14, 33. See also Luxury liners
Grand Cayman, 221–222
Grand Princess, marriage on, 36
Grandchildren. See Children
Grenada, 223–224
Group rates, 55–56, 72–74
Guadeloupe, 224

Hawaii, 9
Health insurance, 17, 90–91
Health issues, 16–19, 131. See also Seasickness
Hearing impaired, 58
Hijacking, 19
Holland America Line-Westours, 158–160
    Cancellation Protection Plan by, 91
    children on, 30–31
    food on, 33
    health issues on, 17
    Holland America, tipping on, 141
    hosts on, 54
    mature travelers on, 26–27
    private island, 132
    reputation of, 43
    resort experience on, 34
    romance on, 54
    round-the-world cruises on, 15
Home ports
    to Alaska, 215–218
    to the Caribbean, 209–215
Honeymoons, 36
Hurricanes, 101–102

Icebergs, 21
Illness. See Health issues

Inaugural cruises, 10–11
In-room movies, 82
Insurance, 82–83, 85–93, 99–100
    baggage protection, 90
    emergency evacuation, 91
    medical coverage, 17, 90–91
    trip cancellation, 87–89
    trip delay protection, 89–90
    trip interruption, 89
International Association Travel Agent Network (IATAN), 40
Internet
    getting deals on, 77–79
    shopping for a cruise via, 42, 44
Itineraries, changes in, 101–102, 146. See also Destinations

Jamaica, 129, 224–225
Jet lag, 144

Kosher meals, 98

Last-minute discounts, 75
Laws, 104–105
Length of cruises, 14–16
Letters of permission, 110
Lindblad Expeditions, 27, 28, 33, 35, 194–195
Liquor, cost of, 81–82
Longer cruises, 15
Lost and found, 144–145
Lost luggage, 102, 118, 145
Luxury liners
    definition of, 151
    dressing on, 4, 11–12
    mature travelers and, 26
    packing for, 111
    ship size and, 8
    suites on, 95
    tipping on, 141
    vs. budget cruise lines, 12–14, 27–28
    See also Gourmet cruising

Maiden voyages. See Inaugural cruises
Mail, 139–140

Mandatory extra costs, 80–81
Marine Expeditions, 203
Marriages, 36–37
Martinique, 225
Mass market ships, 151
Massage, 135–136
Mature adult discounts, 72
Medical certificates, 110
Medical facilities. *See* Health issues
Medical insurance, 17, 90–91
Medicare, coverage by, 17, 90–91
Medications
  buying, on ship, 18
  for seasickness, 5–6
Mediterranean cruises, 2, 9
Mediterranean Shipping Cruises, 27, 177–178
Mega-cruise lines, 43–44
Mexico, 222–223
Miami, 209–210
Money, 114–115
Movies, in-room, 82

Napping, 127
National Association of Cruise Only Agencies (NACOA), 41
Nautical expressions, 105–107
Negotiating a cruise deal, 60–67
New Orleans, 214–215
Noise, cabin and, 95–96, 120, 145
North American cruises, 9
Norwegian Cruise Line (NCL), 160–162
  mature travelers on, 27
  party cruise on, 34
  points of departure, 208
  private island, 132
  resort experience on, 34
  theme cruises on, 32

Obstructed views, 96
Off-season travel, 70–71
Olivia Cruises and Resorts, 38
Open seating, 97
Optional items, 81–83, 122–123
Orient Lines, 203–204

P&O Holidays, 204
Packing
  for a cruise, 110–114
  for disembarking, 147
Panama Canal cruises, 10
Party cruises, 35
Passenger/crew ratio, 13
Passports and visas, 21–24, 102, 109
Paying for a cruise, 67–68
Penalties, cancellation, 100
Per diem rates, 69–70
Personal services on board, 82, 125, 134–136
Personal trainers, 136
Personnel
  cost and, 13
  who's who, 142–143
Phone calls, 82
Photos, 141
Pied Piper Travel, 38
Playa del Carmen, 222–223
Policy statements, 100–101
Popular group activities, 125
Port Canaveral, 211–213
Port charges/taxes, 45–46, 81
Ports of call, 2–3
  Caribbean and Mexico, 218–229
  disembarking for, 127
  ship size and, 8
  See also Shore excursions
Preferred suppliers, travel agents and, 63, 64
Premier, private island, 132
Prescription drugs. *See* Medications
Princess Cruises, 162–16
  disabled access on, 56
  food on, 33
  health issues on, 17
  marriage on, 36
  mature travelers on, 27
  party cruise on, 34
  private island, 132
  resort experience on, 34
  romance on, 54
  round-the-world cruises on, 15

Privacy, 3
Private balconies, 96
Private islands, 131–133
Private shore excursions, 129
Private vs. cruise line insurance,
    86–87
Private yacht vacation, 28
Problems at sea, 144–146
Puerto Rico, 225–226

Quark Expeditions, 204
Queen Elizabeth 2 (QE2), 10, 17, 25, 28,
    29, 54, 174–176
Quick List, 107–108

Radisson Seven Seas Cruises, 26, 28,
    33, 35, 54, 178–180
Rates vs. brochure rates, 71–72
Regal Cruises, 27, 34, 180–181,
    208
Relaxation cruises, 35
Religion, 138
Renaissance Cruises, 205
Renewal of vows, 37
Renting a car, 130
Repeat passengers, 75
Repositioning cruises, 9–10, 52
Reservations, 103–104
"Resort casual," 4, 11, 112
Resorts, 34
Reunions, 55–56
River cruises, 6, 9
Roll and seasickness, 6, 96
Romance, 7, 36–37, 54
Room steward, 123–124
Round-the-world cruises, 15–16
Royal Caribbean International,
    164–166
    children on, 31
    mature travelers on, 27
    party cruise on, 34
    private island, 132
    resort experience on, 34
    romance on, 54
    sexual assaults on, 20

Royal Olympic Cruises, 32, 181–182
RSVP Cruises, 38

Safety drill, 124
Safety of Life at Sea (SOLAS)
    program, 21
Sailing ships, 26, 33
St. Barthélemy (St. Barts), 227
St. Kitts, 227–228
St. Lucia, 228
St. Martin/Sint Maarten, 228
St. Thomas/St. John/St. Croix, 229
Sandbars, 21
Sanitation, 18
Sea Cloud Cruises, 26, 28, 33, 35,
    195–196
Seabourn Cruise Line, 182–184
    children on, 30
    food on, 33
    hosts on, 54
    luxury on, 28
    mature travelers on, 26
    relaxation on, 35
    reputation of, 44
    round-the-world cruises on, 15
Seasickness, 3, 4–6, 31. *See also* Health
    issues
Seating, meals and, 97–98, 121
Security issues, 19–21
Semi-formal wear, 112
Service, cost and, 13
Services on board, 82, 125, 134–136
Seven-day cruises, 15
Seward, 216–218
Sexual assault, 20
Ship's registry, 104
Shoes, 112–113
Shopping
    on board, 136–138
    for a cruise, 39–59
    shore excursions and, 129–130, 138
Shore excursions, 82, 115, 128–131,
    145, 218–229
Short cruises, 14–15
Sight impaired, 58–59

Silversea, 184–185
    children on, 30
    food on, 33
    hosts on, 54
    luxury on, 28
    mature travelers on, 26
    relaxation on, 35
Singles, cruises and, 31–32, 53–55,
        79–80, 101. *See also* Cruise lines,
    profiles of
Single seating, 97–98
Size
    of cruise lines, 7
    of ships, 6, 7–8, 26
Skin improvement, 136
Social hosts, 53–54
Society Expeditions, Inc., 205–206
Society for the Advancement of Travel
        for the Handicapped (SATH), 59
Spa services, 82, 135–136
Special activities, 82
Special diets, 98–99
Specialty events on board, 125
Sports equipment, 113
Star Clippers, 33, 196–197
Star Cruises, 206

Tampa, 213–214
Taxis on shore, 130–131
Telephone calls, 139–140
Temptress Adventure Cruises, 206
Theft, 20–21, 102
Theme cruises, 32, 55
Tipping, 83–84, 101, 141–142
Tortola, 221
Touring vs. cruising, 2–4
Transatlantic cruises, 10, 52
Travel agents, 39–42
    bankruptcy by, 91–92
    negotiating a deal with, 60–67
Travel clubs, 75

Travel Companion Exchange, 55
Travel documents, 21–24, 102,
        109–110, 119
Travel insurance, 82–83
Travel partners, 55
Trip cancellation insurance, 87–89
Trip delay protection, 89–90
Trip interruption insurance, 89
Two seatings, 98
"Two-for-one" cruise specials, 72

U.S. Virgin Islands, 229
Upper berth cabins, 46–47, 96

Vaccination or medical certificates, 110
Valuables, 113
Vancouver, 215–216
Virgin Gorda, 221
Virgin Islands, 221, 229
Visas, 23–24,
Vocabulary of the seas, 105–107
Voyager Cruise Line, 207

Walking
    cabin choices and, 95, 127
    shore excursions and, 131,
        132–133
Weather, 101–102
Wheelchairs, 56–58, 132. *See also*
    Disabled access
Who's who on board, 142–143
Widows. *See* Singles, cruises and
Windjammer Barefoot Cruises, 33, 34,
        35, 197–199
Windstar Cruises, 26, 28, 33, 35, 43,
        199–200
Women's Travel Club, 55
Women Traveling Together, 55
Working Vacation Inc., 53–54
World Explorer Cruises, 27, 25, 54,
        200–201